D1250465

Information
Theory
and
Esthetic
Perception

Abraham Moles

ST. JOSEPH'S UNIVERSITY   STX
BH221.F84M71
Information theory and esthetic percepti

3 9353 00002 4040

89047

BH 221
.F84
M71

translated by Joel E. Cohen

University of Illinois Press
Urbana and London, 1966

This work was originally published as *Théorie de l'information et perception esthétique* by Flammarion & Cⁱᵉ, 1958.

A grant from the Ford Foundation has helped to defray the cost of publishing this work.

© 1966 by the Board of Trustees of the University of Illinois. Manufactured in the United States of America. Library of Congress Catalog Card No. 62-13213.

Translator's Preface

When the French version of this book was published in 1958, information theory — a mathematical theory of communication — had just reached its tenth birthday. Born of papers by Claude Shannon and the book, *Cybernetics,* by Norbert Wiener, information theory looked then like the young man in a very great hurry who jumped on his horse and rode off in all directions. Standard-bearers of information theory were plunging into genetics, neurophysiology, sociology, experimental psychology, linguistics, and philosophy with great enthusiasm and greater hopes. Many problems that had long resisted even adequate formulation seemed about to succumb to information theory.

Théorie de l'information et perception esthétique appeared during, and as part of, that surge of optimistic exploration. Instead of considering communication between machines via electrical channels, which concerned the founders of information theory, Dr. Moles here considers the communication to a human being from that peculiar part of the environment called art. Dr. Moles presents the analysis of esthetic perception to which information theory has inspired him. More than that, he proposes a skeleton for a body of esthetic theory, the outline of a program of research in the psychology of perception.

As this translation reaches the press, information theory is closer to its twentieth birthday than its tenth. From this mature vantage point, information theory seems to have stimulated a great deal of highly imaginative and occasionally fruitful analysis in fields other than communications engineering. Yet many standard-bearers of information theory either have retreated from their interdisciplinary forays or, sticking with difficult problems, have exchanged information theory for other weapons. Dr. Moles's body of esthetic theory, insofar as it continues to depend on information theory, remains, I believe, rather undernourished.

In reading this book, I see two dangers to be avoided. The first is thinking that because certain esthetic problems have been redescribed and relabeled here, they have been solved. Dr. Moles would agree, I believe, that there are very few data in this book; that the few that are here are oversimplified; and that the role the specific body of mathematics called information theory would play in collecting the data still needed is small. The role of information theory in this book is mainly heuristic: suggestive and exploratory.

The second and complementary danger to be avoided is overreaction against the champions of information theory. Many of the proposals and formulations of this book, though only tenuously related to information theory proper, are, I think, ingenious. The distinction between semantic and esthetic "information" developed in Chap. V seems especially helpful. It would be a mistake to deny the possible usefulness of many of the insights into esthetic perception offered here.

With these caveats, the reader should be prepared to enjoy a book with much promise yet unexploited.

The text of this English edition differs in many details from that of the French. When I first proposed translating the book in 1961, Dr. Moles wrote: "I have written this book as an introduction to an informational theory of psychology which would not require a too extensive knowledge of mathematics, and could consequently be suitable for students in psychology."

With this function in mind, I have added sentences to clarify Dr. Moles's text where necessary, and converted European units of measurement (for example, savarts) to more usual American units (cents). I have checked, corrected, and occasionally rewritten several of the mathematical proofs and calculations and the lists of musical compositions, but I cannot hope to have made the book error-free in this regard. I will appreciate further corrections. I have also renovated a revised bibliography furnished by Dr. Moles; I do not claim the result is fully up to date.

Dr. Moles kindly read early drafts of the English translation in manuscript. He added and deleted sentences and paragraphs through-out. Chap. I, Sec. 9; Chap. V, Sec. 8; Chap. VI, Sec. 5; and Chap. VII, Sec. 5, as well as quite a number of the figures, are entirely new additions by Dr. Moles.

The bracketed page numbers in this edition give the location of the passages immediately following each in the French original.

The index is a translation of the terms listed in the index to the French edition; it does not aspire to completeness. Mrs. Carolyn McConnell assisted in preparing the index.

I am grateful to Prof. L. A. Hiller of the University of Illi-nois for his assistance in finding this translation a publisher; to Dr. Moles for his care in reading the English manuscript; and to Dr. D. D. Jackson, Editor of the Press, for his assistance and his extraordinary patience.

JOEL E. COHEN

Harvard University
Cambridge, Massachusetts
June, 1965

Contents

Figures

Introduction

To human beings, human things are all important.

N. WIENER

1. GENERALITIES

Two essential aspects of the external world are treated in science. (a) The *energetic* aspect assumed a preponderant role in physics until the beginning of the twentieth century. It gave rise to the sciences of mechanics, strength of materials, thermodynamics, etc., in which man as an individual supposedly plays no role at all. For example, man goes unmentioned in a course on bridge construction. (b) The *communicational* aspect returns man to the material world. Here the *interaction* between the individual and the rest of the world is studied. Psychology, sociology, esthetics, and, more generally, *behavioral sciences* are attached to this point of view. They study the *message* from the external world to the individual and his reactions.

One of the most remarkable aspects of the recent evolution of the sciences is the insertion of psychology into applied physics as essential to the solution of problems where a receiving subject is involved (lighting, architectural acoustics, political economy). Behavioral psychology considers the individual as a *system* connected to the world whose evolution is determined by his *environment,* which acts on him through the messages that he receives from the inert world or from other individuals, who, according to the existential thesis, remain as alien to him as the external world.

Until the end of the nineteenth century, science primarily furnished man with the means and theories for constructing a technical world with energy. To make the energy of the universe serve the needs of man seemed to be the essential mission of a science bent to utilitarian ends. In 1900 the matter-energy dialectic seemed to summarize man's grasp of the world. From this conception emerged the image of *Homo faber;* it seemed to many good minds that painting, literature, music, all arts, in short, were the barren residues of a manufacturing civilization occasionally functioning [page 10]* without a purpose, residues destined to be eliminated from a properly rational universe in which they would be deprived of importance.

Only a few years ago the development of products which were not specifically energetic made two distinct planes of human activity appear: *conquest of the world* and *communication among men.* The latter was conceived as an end in itself, a social function, and was no longer solely the machinery for the former. Beside the dialectical dichotomy matter-energy emerges another dialectic, action-communication.

Practically, radio, movies, records, and spoken literature have brought attention to the autonomy of communication between individuals, reestablishing the value of a work of art as a creator of sensations, hence as a motivating force in society and not as a social epiphenomenon.

The theory presented here arose as a result of technical problems related to communication channels. But the theory of communication extends beyond the technical viewpoint and now appears to be one of the great theories of science. It is certain to take its place beside the most general physical theories dominated by the dialectical concept, matter-energy. The concepts of *information, code, redundancy, complexity, the dialectic banal-original, foreseeability,* and *background noise* must take their places beside the quantum theory, the principles of relativity and uncertainty, and the opposition between the microscopic and macroscopic universe.

It will be the goal of the present work to try to integrate in a coherent fashion the essential concepts which have issued from the science of communication and more precisely from the body of doctrine known as *information theory,* with our vision of the world, that is, our perception, particularly in the domain, hitherto neglected, of esthetics and the psychology of perception.

2. ON METHOD IN PSYCHOLOGY

Since the beginning of the twentieth century, psychology has progressively changed to an exact science and has developed im-

---

* [The passage following this point appears on page 10 of the French edition. — *Tr.*]

mensely. As a result, psychology has been promoted to the rank of a major, and even a normative, science (cf. Husserl). Deserting its etymologic meaning, as the science of the soul, which connected it with metaphysics, it has changed to the science of man's *situation* in, and his reaction to, the universe. The introduction of measurement in psychology (Wundt, Weber, Fechner) and behaviorism (Pavlov, Watson) initiated this expansion of the model of the human sciences.

[page 11] Like any new theory, in order to get established methodologically, behavioral psychology had to adopt a dogmatic and rather narrow attitude. It refused to describe anything but the external acts of the individual. Subsequently it has expanded greatly, as much in spirit as in the scope of what it can explain, and little by little it has become identified with a deterministic theory of being.

Its basic hypotheses remain fundamental to all objective psychology and seem definitely established.

(1) The individual is an open system whose behavior, down to its smallest details, is entirely determined by the sum of his heredity, history, and environment: (a) Heredity gives the general structure of his organism. (b) The events of his particular history are inscribed in his organism by conditioned reflexes and memory. These events define his personality. (c) This organism reacts to its present environment.

(2) All behavior, present or future, of the individual may be described with a degree of precision equal to that of the description of a physicochemical system, given that the three determining factors are themselves known.

(3) Since this perfect knowledge of the individual's heredity, history, and environment at a given instant is in practice an asymptotic ideal, the individual's behavior, like that of any system, is determined only statistically. Such behavior is the proper object of experimental psychology.

(4) A *theoretical psychology* ought to develop along with experimental psychology and aim, on the basis of a normalized model of the human organism furnished by statistically cumulated experiments, to determine the individual's behavioral mechanisms, expressible in mathematical terms. Psychologists will refine this normalized individual by increasing the numerical parameters which define him and by making them vary in conformity with the concepts of differential psychology. This refinement represents the ultimate stage of this science and the complete integration of man into the physicochemical universe.

None of these constructive axioms is denied henceforth by scientific psychologies, whatever their point of view may be. The theory of form (*Gestalt* psychology), in particular, subscribes to these same hypotheses, while differing freely and profoundly in its spirit and working methods, in the hope of more rapidly determining the phenomena essential in behavior.

Thus the essential fact of all deterministic psychology remains the perception-reaction [page 12] cycle; from its simplest manifestations (tropisms in unicellular beings), psychology has been moving to increasingly complex cycles in increasingly organized beings whose patterns of behavior are governed by increasingly larger systems of equations.

If what we know of the universe results from the sum of our perceptions and of our physical or intellectual reactions as a function of our experience, deterministic psychology becomes a normative science and must automatically involve a philosophic thesis concerning our knowledge of the world. More generally, any metaphysics, any reflection of the individual on the world, implies a theory of perception, and any consideration of the latter will react on the former, whether or not one accepts the *esse est percipi* of Berkeley. Thus, a closed circuit of knowing exists; our concept of the universe depends on the knowledge that we have of the process of perceiving it.

Our purpose here will be to show the role that information theory plays in the mechanisms of perception and more particularly of esthetic perception. The theory is recent, and this field of application seems to have been nearly ignored by the theory's authors, whose outlook has been rather technical. We shall try as we go along to note the simplest and most immediate philosophic consequences of the theory, but we shall limit our subject to the field of objective or experimental psychology. The extrapolation of a new theory is indeed particularly dangerous because its limits of validity are uncertain and the normal method of extrapolation, logical extension, possesses no assured value.

3. PLAN OF THE WORK

The plan of this work is as follows:

We shall first present information theory in its general form as found in recent works written by communication specialists, principally in the technical domain, and we shall state precisely its rather complex terminology (Chap. I). Any theory is essentially a tool of thought supposed to serve to apprehend facts in a logical synthesis.

Hence, we shall give numerous examples, mostly sonic messages (speech and music) and visual messages. We shall start from the very well-determined case of reading and extend toward the vaguer domains of vision and visual arts (drawing, photography, painting, motion pictures). Hence, we shall almost follow historic order: The theory of communication developed from the time of the telegraph and [page 13] telephone and was applied progressively to increasingly complex domains (television, movies, language, etc.).

The most obvious failure of the theory in its simple form, when one wants to apply it to psychology, is that it appears an *atomistic* theory which tends to explain reality by decomposing it into simple elements. Thus, first we shall develop in it the concept of *form*, which we shall consider as the element of structuring of messages; in particular we shall consider the concept of periodicity as an elementary probabilistic foreseeability (Chap. II).

We shall next examine the perturbations affecting a message, the phenomenon of noise, and we shall show the generality of this concept. By some uncertainty principles stemming from the nature of things, noise limits the individual's apprehension of the exterior world, while creating the background from which forms stand out (Chap. III).

We shall then apply the concepts acquired to the study of the sonic message, particularly of music. The phenomenologic study of music has until now been retarded by dogmatism. We shall regard music as formed of a sonic material whose elementary structure we shall study; we shall examine the repertoire of symbols, then the microstructures: "sonic objects" and over-all organization (Chap. IV). We shall consider the phonetic message as a special case which is easier to apprehend intelligibly.

We shall develop next the fundamental distinction between *semantic* and *esthetic* information. The distinction has been rather neglected by the founders of the theory, who followed the general principle of scientific methodology, that in science one begins with that which is easiest (Descartes). This extension of the theory seems to provide an answer to some philosophical difficulties.

We shall attempt to apply this distinction between the two sorts of information to general esthetics, principally in the musical domain, and we shall endeavor to establish structural laws governing the temporal dialectic, originality-intelligibility (Chap. V).

Finally, we shall summarily examine what the thus enlarged theory can teach us about *multiple messages*, that is, those which reach the individual through several channels, several dimensions of perception (opera, movies, animated cartoons), as well as about the mechanisms by which the individual apprehends the message, so that we may know how several-channel systems affect behavior (Chap. VI).

This broadened viewpoint, returning esthetic perception to the deterministic cycle of our knowledge of the world, will lead us, finally, to try to define the philosophic role of the new theory (Chap. VIII).

General Outline
of Physical
Information Theory

CHAPTER I

La Philosophie est un décryptement de l'Univers.

HUSSERL

1. DEFINITION AND CLASSIFICATION OF MESSAGES

We shall start from the point of view that the behavior of any individual — given his heredity and his history — is determined by his environment, taken in the most general sense. The individual receives *messages* from this environment through various channels: visual, aural, tactile, etc. The term "channel" is applied to any material system which conveys a message from a transmitter to a receiver.

Transmission across space, which proceeds by means of the ordinary visual, aural, and telegraphic channels, etc., is *transmission* properly speaking.

Transmission through time, or *recording*, preserves a message by means of printed signs, phonograph records, magnetic tapes, photographs, etc. In most cases, transmission takes place simultaneously across space and through time: No spatial channel has an infinite speed of propagation. Moreover, temporal channels, the function of which is to subsist through time, can be moved through space.

In what follows we shall distinguish (a) *natural* channels (vision, hearing), closely related to the sense organs, where man is the immediate receiver of the information, from (b) *artificial* or technical channels (telegraph, telephotograph, phonograph record), where the receiver is a machine. The outputs of artificial channels are eventually used by man in a superadded natural channel, but might just as well be used by another machine (Fig. I-1).

[page 18] The artificial channels will frequently serve as examples because their structure makes them rather more intelligible than natural channels, in which it is often difficult to separate the brain from the sensory receptors. But natural channels are of basic interest here. Ruyer, Cherry, and others introduce a similar distinction between a communication theory (of natural channels) and an information theory (of artificial channels).

Messages may be spatial or temporal and may be classified according to their dimensions. Thus, as a first approximation, a printed line furnishes the senses a message in a *single* spatial dimension (L): a sequence of linearly assembled symbols. The written elements of the Central American countries emerged from *quipus*, linear successions of symbols composed of knots on a string. By exploring the line, or the *quipu*, we perceive successively the *elements* of the message, which are arranged in an order imposed by the unidimensional character of the string.

A painting, a drawing, or a photograph gives us messages in two spatial dimensions (L^2). The messages of the plastic arts or of architecture, as arrangements of volumes or masses, those of a set of punched cards arranged in a card index box, are, in a first approximation, esthetic or utilitarian messages of three dimensions (L^3). Messages such as animated cartoons or movies, having two spatial dimensions and one temporal dimension, belong to the temporal arts (L^2T).

In the following, we shall grant a special place to purely temporal messages, *speech* and *music*, which are *modulations of duration*. They correspond to the "arts of time"; the others (dance, movies, animated cartoons) have some spatial characterististics. The former will give us relatively simple examples which are more accessible than the polydimensional messages (cinerama, for example). The esthetics of such complex messages, generally belated in comparison with technical achievement, is still only beginning.

We shall note, however, that spatial messages (drawing, painting) may be expanded in time by *scanning* which decomposes them into sequences of intensive elements transmitted in a given order.

This process of scanning, of which the best-known technical examples are television and telephotograph, is very important in individual perception, although its importance has had little emphasis until now. In perception, scanning complements the integral apprehension proposed by *Gestalt* theory. Examples of scanning in visual perception are easy to find: We make contact with a picture exceeding our central visual field, a page of detailed drawings, or a diagram of electrical circuits by a process of successive *scanning* [page 19] of the various parts in some kind of order; afterward, we construct an over-all conception of the form by a process of abstraction which closely resembles that of comprehension. Scanning gives the key to an unknown alphabet at the time of learning; we shall have to come back to this point later. One must consider scanning, on the one hand, and integral apprehension, on the other, as *dialectical dipoles* of the perceptual process. Scanning, which transforms a spatial message into a temporal one, establishes an equivalence between the two types of messages.

Types of Communication

Dimensions	Message
1 spatial dimension (L)	printed line, quipus
1 temporal dimension (T)	music, speech
2 spatial dimensions (L^2)	drawing, photos, painting
2 dimensions (LT)	sound track, magnetic tape
3 spatial dimensions (L^3)	sculpture, architecture
2 spatial dimensions + 1 temporal dimension (L^2T)	motion pictures, animated cartoons
3 spatial dimensions + 1 temporal dimension (L^3T)	cinerama, live theater

2. THE MESSAGE AND ITS ELEMENTS

A message is a finite, ordered set of elements of perception drawn from a repertoire and assembled in a structure. The elements of the repertoire are defined by the properties of the receiver. A specific study will reveal the nature of the elements and the repertoire of artificial channels. For messages of natural channels directed to the sense organs, the elements of the repertoire are enumerated by the various departments of psychophysiology.

Every sensory system reacts to physical excitations in the following ways: (a) Below a certain limit of physical excitation, the receptive system is insensitive. This limit is the *sensitivity threshold*. (b) Above a certain limit of physical excitation, called *saturation threshold*, the receptive system is saturated and no longer perceives variations in excitation. Hence the system must be considered to lack a specific "response" above this threshold. (c) In order for the receptive organism to perceive a gradual increase in excitation, the increase must exceed a certain percentage called the *difference threshold* or limen (D.L.).

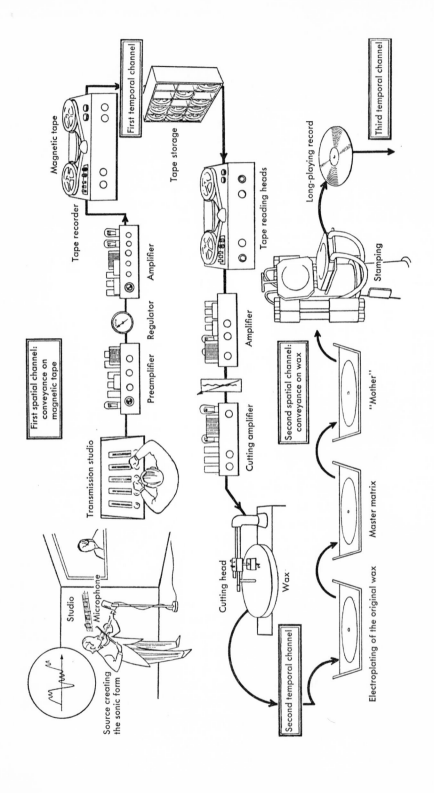

First spatial channel: conveyance on magnetic tape

First temporal channel

Magnetic tape

Tape recorder

Tape storage

Amplifier

Regulator

Preamplifier

Transmission studio

Studio

Microphone

Source creating the sonic form

Tape reading heads

Amplifier

Cutting amplifier

Cutting head

Wax

Second temporal channel

Second spatial channel: conveyance on wax

Electroplating of the original wax

Master matrix

"Mother"

Stamping

Long-playing record

Third temporal channel

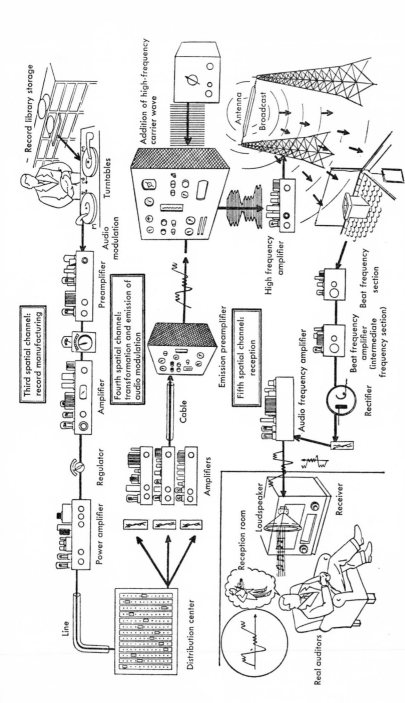

Fig. 1-1. Example of a complex sound communication channel: transmission of a commercial record by a radiobroadcasting network. The sound channel transfers a *temporal* form from one sound point to another point in space and another instant $(t + \Theta)$. The temporal form is the signal $F(t)$, which must be reproduced by $F(t + \Theta)$ as closely as possible, but in another place and at another time. The channel examined here is composed of a succession of partial channels: three temporal channels (conservation through time or recording) and five spatial channels. Considering this dizzy chain of transformations, it seems remarkable that what remains at the end has some similarity to the original signal.

Labels within figure:

Record library storage

Turntables

Audio modulation

Preamplifier

Amplifier

Regulator

Power amplifier

Line

Distribution center

Amplifiers

Addition of high-frequency carrier wave

Antenna

Broadcast

High frequency amplifier

Third spatial channel: record manufacturing

Fourth spatial channel: transformation and emission of audio modulation

Emission preamplifier

Cable

Fifth spatial channel: reception

Beat frequency section

Beat frequency amplifier (intermediate frequency section)

Rectifier

Audio frequency amplifier

Reception room

Loudspeaker

Receiver

Real auditors

Sensation may thus be quantified between the sensitivity threshold and the saturation threshold by a series of difference thresholds. [page 20] For any variable of physical excitation, there exists a finite number of elements of perception. Of these, the psychophysiologist constructs a repertoire.

The relative difference thresholds $\Delta E/E$ (where E = excitation) vary more or less around a constant value K, in certain ranges of E. The Weber-Fechner law, $\Delta E/E = K$, implies that sensation varies logarithmically as excitation: $S = K \log E$. The role of this law is fundamental, for the variations of difference thresholds are always considered as deviations from the logarithmic law. In a systematic exposition such as this, which aims explicitly at the greatest possible generality, one is bound to a certain dogmatism. In what follows, for a first approximation, we shall take the Weber-Fechner law as universally valid without restriction. The notation in decibels or in octaves of size relationships

$$N_{dB} = 20 \log_{10} p/p_0, \ p = \text{pressure},$$
$$N_{octaves} = \log_2 f/f_0, \ f = \text{frequency},$$

fulfills precisely this assumption.

The three preceding axioms delimit the *repertoire* of elements associated with a given physical sensation.

3. EXAMPLES OF REPERTOIRES

Let us apply the preceding ideas to the case of sound, which reaches us through the ear. A pure, isolated sound is a sonic entity defined by three dimensions, which may be physical: amplitude (pressure in baryes = dynes/cm²), frequency (cycles per second), and length (seconds); or they may be perceptual: loudness (decibels), pitch (octaves), and duration ($\log t$).

For loudnesses, one has (a) a lower threshold on the order of 2×10^{-4} baryes = 0 dB, the threshold of audible sensitivity; (b) an upper threshold (painful sounds) around 2×10^3 baryes $\simeq 0.01$ atmospheres = 140 dB; (c) a difference threshold $\Delta L/L$ on the order of 10 per cent (1 dB).

[page 21] As a result, there are approximately 140 linear gradations of the same pitch and duration differing only in loudness. This is no more than a first approximation, assuming that all other characteristics concerning duration and pitch remain the same.

Similarly, for pitch, one has (a) a lower threshold on the order of $f_{min} = 16$ cps; (b) an upper threshold on the order of $f_{max} = 16,000$ cps; (c) a difference threshold (which varies greatly with f) averaging 0.5 per cent or 1 comma.

As a result, there are about 1,200 distinct pitch levels.

Assuming as a first hypothesis that the difference thresholds of pitch and of loudness are independent, one may represent the sonic repertoire by a rectangle (Hartley diagram) with sides of $20 \log_{10} (f_{max}/f_{min})$ and $20 \log_{10} (p_{max}/p_{min})$, subdivided into quanta of sensation, nearly equal in number. One obtains $1,200 \times 110 = 132,000$ quanta.

In fact, this picture must be improved, because the hypotheses on

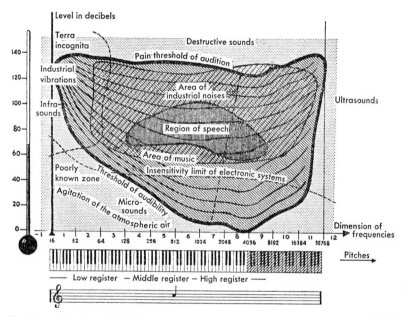

Fig. I-2. Map of the audible area. This is a section, parallel to the $L \times f$ plane, of the repertoire of sonic elements. Its limits are infrasounds and ultrasounds, and the sensibility and saturation thresholds. Stippling indicates the areas of various common periodic phenomena; terra incognita indicates zones little or not at all explored with experimental techniques.

which it is based are too simple. [page 22] (a) While the saturation threshold of loudness varies little with changing pitch, zero loudness, the sensitivity or perceptual threshold, varies enormously with pitch. Hence one must replace the lower edge determined by the points (L_{min}, f_{min}) and (L_{min}, f_{max}) by a complicated curve (Fletcher's curve for the threshold of audibility). (b) The difference thresholds of loudness and of pitch each vary with loudness and pitch. They decrease notably for average loudnesses (50 to 80 dB) and average pitches (300 to 3,000 cps); the fineness of response of the ear is greater in this region. In other words, the elementary squares representing the quanta of sensation are not equal, but decrease in size toward the middle of the "audible area." Taking account of these corrections, one is then led to draw the map of the *audible area* (Fig. I-2). The over-all repertoire of sonic elements is no longer

$$\nu = S/\Delta f \cdot \Delta L$$

but is rather

$$\nu = \sum_{f_{\min}}^{f_{\max}} \sum_{L_{\min}}^{L_{\max}} \Delta S/\Delta f(f) \cdot \Delta L(L)$$

where S is the surface area of the map, f the frequency, and L the level. The most recent findings of auditory physiology (Stevens and Davis, 1938) give $\nu = 340{,}000$ quanta (Fig. I-3).

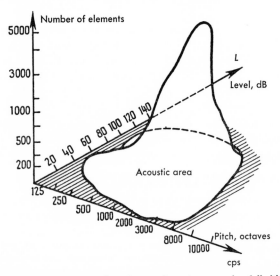

Fig. I-3. The extent of the repertoire of pure elementary sounds of limitless duration. The height N over each point in the plane L × f is proportional to the number of distinct elements per unit of area. Since the fineness of the ear is greater toward the center of the audible area, this repertoire assumes the form of a mountain circumscribed by the audible, or acoustic, area S. The volume of the mountain

$$\nu = \iint_S N \, df \, dL$$

gives the number of distinct elements.

[page 23] *The time variable:* A perceived sound is also defined by its duration. A note on a piano, or more simply, a tone from an oscillator, has a finite duration, contradicting a hypothesis implicit in early acoustics. In time we thus find: (a) a threshold of perception; (b) a saturation limit; and (c) a difference threshold.

The threshold of perception Θ could be described as the "length of the present." All phenomena which occur in a time shorter than this critical length are psychologically simultaneous. The value of Θ is not too well defined but is around 0.05 second; below this limit, moreover, pitch and loudness are no longer clearly defined.

The existence of *saturation* has been realized only in psychological works on the duration of tones. As in the other sensory dimensions, saturation appears as a psychological incapacity to appreciate duration. Beyond a certain limit, the error of estimation increases greatly. We know from studies of sustained organ tones that the listener's attention slackens notably after a duration of six to ten seconds, especially if it is solicited by another stimulus. The *presence* of the tone weakens rapidly toward the end of this interval (cf. Winckel, 1960).

Finally there exists a *difference threshold* in the perception of duration which has been well demonstrated by works of Wundt, Piéron, Fraisse, etc. This threshold varies with the duration considered. While this variability makes it more complicated to evaluate the threshold, we shall place it in the vicinity of 20 per cent (2 dB) to construct a repertoire of $1 + [\log_{10} (10/0.05)]/[\log_{10} (6/5)] \cong 30$ quanta of perception of duration. The comparatively great restriction of choice in this domain is nicely reflected by the paucity of musical time notation:

64th note	32nd	16th	8th	quarter	half	whole
1	2	3	4	5	6	7

in comparison with the relative richness of pitch notation (92 keyboard "notes") and with the loudness notation, insufficient for other reasons, used by musicians:[1]

threshold	*ppp*	*pp*	*p*	*mf*	*f*	*ff*	*fff*	saturation.
	1	2	3	4	5	6	7	

Thus, defining a pure elementary sound amounts to *selecting* a cellule L_1, f_1, t_1 from a three-dimensional *repertoire L, f, t,* analogous to the phase space of statistical physics (Fig. I-4).

[page 24] This analysis may be repeated *mutatis mutandis* for any sensory message, and we shall only hint summarily below how it may be applied to the visual message. The dimensions of the visual message characterize retinal sensation. Among them, aside

---

[1] The notation of loudness has remained very primitive because until recently music did not have available a range of loudnesses comparable to that of the ear. This was principally for instrumental reasons which we shall see later (background noise and compression of contrasts).

from time, one may distinguish position, luminous intensity, and color.

The *spatial coordinates* fixing the position of a luminous point on the retinal projection would be best expressed in polar coordinates (r, Θ) in relation to the optical axis of vision. Moreover, the parallactic coordinate of the two eyes would express the perception of relief. Here the notion of difference threshold is particularly evident. It is simply the resolving power of the eye. Its minimum value is

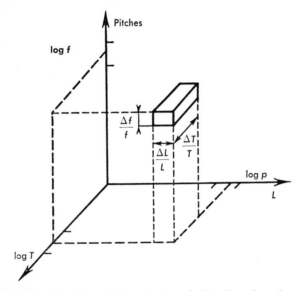

Fig. I-4. The three dimensions of the sonic channel. The dimensions shown here are (1) *level* = logarithm of amplitude; (2) *pitch* = logarithm of frequency; (3) *duration* = logarithm of time.

usually figured at one minute of angle in the vicinity of the optical axis (fovea). We know that this difference threshold varies considerably from the center to the periphery of the visible field and increases to around one degree at the edge.

The dimension of perceived luminous intensity has a theoretical sensitivity threshold on the order of several quanta of light (10^{-6} lumens) and a saturation limit on the order of 10^4 lumens. This enormous spread is only apparent, for we know that retinal sensitivity is due to two distinct mechanisms: (a) Scotopic vision is reserved for feeble illuminations where visual acuity is very reduced, color perception [page 25] is lost, and perceptual delay (latency) is very much increased. (b) Phototopic or day vision is practically the only one of interest here, because the artificial transmission of messages depends on it alone. Painting and drawing are not nocturnal arts; television is not watched without lighting the screen. In practice, the range of luminosities normally used by the individual to guide his reactions extends only between several lumens and several thousand lumens; the difference threshold, though slightly variable with illumination, is on the order of 5 to 10 per cent. Here the Weber-Fechner law is sufficiently valid for our purposes.

With these variables also goes color, corresponding to the pitch of a sound. But the extreme thresholds of color are less than an "octave" apart (0.35 to 0.7 μ). The difference threshold varies enormously with the individual; trained subjects distinguish up to 10,000 shades (timbres). Anyway, the numerous works on color vision have shown that it is always possible to reduce all colored sensation to the combination of three monochromatic sensations. This amounts simply to tripling the extent of the visual repertoire defined by the dimensions of position and intensity (cf. Woodworth and Schlosberg, 1954).

These two examples show how information theory synthesizes the varied viewpoints and results from psychophysiology in the concept of *repertoire*.

4. THE CAPACITY OF TRANSMISSION CHANNELS

From the *sensory channels* that man uses in his communicative nexus with the immediate environment, we must distinguish *transmission channels* created by technology. Spatial channels (radio, telephone, television) convey the message from a place X to a place Y, with a negligible time lag. Temporal channels (records, photography, movies, etc.) transport it from a time t to a time $t + T$.

Many of these channels have "dimensions," or independent variables, different from those of the message that they are supposed to transmit. In order to transmit and receive the message, they require a *translation* or adaptation. Thus the telephone as an artificial channel has two dimensions (frequency, intensity) which permit it to transmit, theoretically without translation, any sonic message having the same dimensions in the acoustical field. But it is unable to transmit *without preparation* a message, such as a picture, having a greater number of dimensions.

We know, however, that tricks such as interruption (clipping) or scanning a picture (transforming it into temporal sequences) permit [page 26] artificial translation of spatial dimensions, on the conditions (a) that it is possible to retranslate them inversely on reception, and (b) that the *capacity* of the channel in one of the available dimensions is substantially superior to that necessary for a normal transmission. In other words, one can *transpose* some dimensions of of a message into others (for example, the height or width of a picture into temporal signals) if the channel can transmit them *quickly enough*, that is, if it has a sufficient "frequency width" (bandwidth).

In the limit, any message whatever, no matter how complex, can be transmitted by any type of channel if the channel has a sufficient *capacity*. For example, one may record a photograph, or a series of photographs constituting a televised sequence, on magnetic tape.

Here we encounter the existence of a sort of *invariant* in the transmission of messages which hints at a conception of information as a measurable quantity. If a signal has two intrinsic dimensions, for example, loudness and pitch, and one corresponds to a range of 100 quanta and the other of 1,000 quanta per 0.1 second (these figures roughly describe the sonic message), the necessary channel must have a capacity of 100,000 quanta. But if such a channel is available, it can transmit any kind of signal delivering less than 100,000 quanta of perception in the same interval of 0.1 second, regardless of the nature of these quanta. For example, this same sonic might be *translated* by a telegraphic channel, which has a repertoire of only two elements (Yes or No, 0 or 1), on the condition that the telegraph be able to distinguish these orders (0 or 1) at the rate of 100,000 per 0.1 second. One might conceive of an apparatus retranslating the sonic message on reception (delta modulation) theoretically without loss.

This invariant quantity is what we shall call the *maximum information*. The interesting point here is that this is a *measurable quantity;* we thus introduce a measure in a domain which seemed removed from the algorithm of measurement.

A corollary of this quantitative concept of maximum information capacity of a channel is the estimation of the theoretical efficiency or output of a "translation," measured by the relative loss of information occasioned by this translation:

$$\eta_{inf} = \frac{\text{transmitted information} - \text{received information}}{\text{transmitted information}}.$$

From this it follows that: (a) It would be illusory to want to transmit a message through a channel whose maximum capacity is significantly lower than that of the message within the interval during which the message is generated. [page 27] (b) Any study of the value or quality of a message must be based on the capacity of the *ultimate* receptor, which, in the problems which interest us here, is always the human individual. This brings to the fore the role of the properties of the individual in constructing communication systems.

5. INFORMATION AND ORIGINALITY

The essential fact here is that *information* must be considered as a *quantity*. One cannot emphasize this idea too much; it appears at the origin of communication theory. We know intuitively that a book contains in general more "information" in the common sense of the word than a thin brochure or a newspaper article, that an encyclopedia contains more than a book, a long telegram more than a single word, a picture reproduced through a screen with 825 cross-rulings to the inch more than one reproduced through a screen with 40 cross-rulings to the inch. This quantitative concept is used in human activity, particularly in political economy, in jurisprudence, and in commerce. But it has been realized that this sense of the word "information" leads to paradoxes and that the quantity of information could not be directly tied to the length of the message without a relative *weighting* on the intrinsic value of the message. The search for this weighting has been laborious, due to a chronic confusion between *information* and *signification,* two concepts which must be carefully separated.

In fact, the concept of value is in itself too vague and too anthropomorphic to be directly usable. But a detour through technology permits us a sufficient abstraction of the problem to render it soluble: We separate *significance* and *value* and attribute to value an objective sense near to that given it by political economy. Value is the property of that which, by a *consensus omnium,* is *usable.* Now, if a message modifies the behavior of the receiver, the message will be more valuable — it can bring about more modifications in behavior — not just if it is longer, but if it is *newer.* (What is already known is presumably integrated by the receptor and belongs to his internal system.) Thus we shall be in agreement with the definition Mackay gives in his glossary of the terms of information theory: In the most general sense of the word, information is that which adds to a representation (cf. Cherry, 1957).

Thus, value is bound up with the *unexpected,* the *unforeseeable,* the *original.* The measure of the quantity of information then boils down to the measure of unforeseeability, that is, to a problem in probability theory, [page 28] for what is improbable is unforeseeable, what is certain is foreseeable, within the limits, naturally, of the receptor's use of his knowledge to determine conduct. But this does not remove difficulties in the case of "technological" receptors, ordinary material systems. As far as the human receptor is concerned, we shall accept this postulate on a provisional basis, leaving aside the individual who behaves *as if* he did not know some of the message that he knows with certainty.

In view of the extreme importance of a measure of information, we shall try to present it intuitively, regardless of the loss of rigor. Here we differ from most previously published studies, which appeal either to reasoning from thermodynamics which is too general to carry conviction or to abstract algebra. The arguments at the basis of the idea of information have too general a value for them to depend on a special mental algorithm.

Hence, let us examine a message composed of a sequence of elements drawn from a repertoire. The information transmitted by this sequence coincides with the *originality* of this sequence. It must be stressed that it is not directly a function of its length: If, finding myself on guard duty, I know *by heart* the text of a page about orders in case of fire, I receive less information from rereading it than from hearing the simple word "fire." This word determines the entire sequence of my conduct in conformity with a mechanism prepared in advance, a mechanism described precisely by the long text. An outside observer acquainted with the text knows that, 30 seconds after the original signal, I will run down the stairs to telephone, one minute later I will unroll the fire hoses, etc.

The given hypothesis, that I knew by heart the sheet of instructions in case of fire, is evidently arbitrary. Hence the argument is valid only for individuals of whom this hypothesis is true. If it is rather easy to define the knowledge possessed by the receptor in the case of an artificial channel, it is much more difficult to do the same when the receptor is a human being. Nevertheless, one of the goals of the sociology of culture is to try to define the set of factors common to all individual receptors. This set constitutes the sociocultural pattern, used, for example, by Silbermann (1954) in studying radio, a cultural institution. Underlying this attitude is the "structuralist" theory, which assumes that the world of representations can be divided into small pieces, elements of structure, which are put together in a definite way. The assembly of the elements is itself the structure. Some elements of this cultural repertoire can be approached in a largely objective way, for example, language. Accordingly, it must be possible to establish a measure of the information transmitted by a given sampling of the language. Here, [page 29] for example, is a collection of texts* with progressively increasing rates of originality:

(1) *No information:*
BABABABABABABABABA...
(2) *Very little information:*
"Winston tastes good like a cigarette should."
"Look both ways."
"You never outgrow your need for milk."
"Void after 90 days."
"Nontransferable."
(3) *Minimum information in everyday English:*
"Hello."
"Hello."
"How are you?"
"Fine. And you?"
"Fine. How's it been going?"
"Very well, thanks. And with you?"
"Oh, all right. . . ."

(4) *Rate of repetition close to (3) — cyclic permutations in mathematics:*

$$\frac{dF_z}{dy} - \frac{dF_y}{dz} = -\mu \frac{dH_x}{dt}$$

$$\frac{dF_x}{dz} - \frac{dF_z}{dy} = -\mu \frac{dH_y}{dt}$$

$$\frac{dF_y}{dx} - \frac{dF_x}{dy} = -\mu \frac{dH_z}{dt}$$

whence:

$$\frac{d^2F}{dx^2} + \frac{d^2F}{dy^2} + \frac{d^2F}{dz^2} = \mu k \frac{d^2H}{dt^2}$$

(5) *Partially foreseeable texts (logical connections):*
"The melting of ice necessarily involves the breaking of some of the hydrogen bonds; since this requires the expenditure of energy, ice melts only at a much higher temperature and with the absorption of a considerably greater amount of heat than would otherwise be expected. The continued breaking of hydrogen bonds as liquid water is heated accounts for the high specific heat of this substance. Furthermore, when water is changed from the liquid to the vapor state, all of the remaining hydrogen bonds are broken; hence, the boiling point and heat of vaporization are high also."

[page 30] (6) *Information in the ordinary sense:*
"From South Vietnam: Two young U.S. Army sergeants were released by guerrillas after 22 days of captivity today. The men looked tired but otherwise healthy and unharmed when they stepped from the plane that brought them to Saigon."

---

* [English texts with rates of originality analogous to the French have been selected. — *Tr.*]

"In Washington, Senate leaders announced they will move next Monday to force a showdown on the administration's literacy test bill."

(7) *Texts retaining only grammatical structure:*

"Being quite full of lucifer-matches, the pumpkin exploded surreptitiously into a thousand bits; whereon the rocks instantly took fire, and the odious little boy became unpleasantly hotter and hotter and hotter, til his knickerbockers were turned quite green. . . . Having placed the latter on the lettuce, and the other objects in a circular arrangement at their base, they danced a hornpipe round" (Edward Lear).

(8) *Text composed according to the digram probabilities of words (selections from a text):*

"The head and in frontal attack on an English writer that the character of this point is therefore another method for the letters that the time of who ever told the problem for an unexpected" (C. E. Shannon).

(9) *Maximum word information (random choice of words):*

"Income oblique forced seamanlike weakly bleeder dog rutile place canst empty stationary promiscuously gossoon bridge cutty seedling gag offend saturation."

Examination of these texts immediately reveals their increasing originality. In the last one, we have no idea of what is going to follow; in the first, on the other hand, we have a very clear idea. The intermediate cases, closest to everyday English, show that originality and signification are clearly distinct and that "intelligibility" varies inversely as originality. The collection of texts thus ordered gives us a first *reference scale* for comparison of the information of language. It suggests that the measure of information must be based on originality and not on signification. Certain [page 31] examples below will give us matter for thought later.

We have established an analogous scale of comparison for the musical message.

6. THE MEASURE OF ORIGINALITY

To measure the a priori originality of a situation, the only procedure offered us by logic is to reckon its improbability. If a given message or event is certain, it teaches the receptor nothing and cannot modify his behavior. An unexpected event has by definition a zero probability; hence it substantially modifies the behavior of the receptor. This is the essential, well-established point of every study of behavior. On it one may build.

Hence we shall say that information or originality is a function of the improbability of the received message. Considering this improbability as the received physical excitation, we are led to connect information H to improbability I by Fechner's relation. The sensation, here information or originality, is proportional to the logarithm of the excitation, here the improbability.

$$H = K \log I.$$

The improbability I is the reciprocal of the probability ω of occurrence:

$$H = -K \log \omega.$$

It appears then that the formula defining information H is closely analogous to the classic Boltzmann formula which defines *entropy S* in statistical thermodynamics,

$$S = K \log \omega,$$

as the *proportion of disorder* of a phenomena. ω is the "probability of a given state" of a system, whether it be matter or message.

We are then led to look for the probability of occurrence of a message. Let us recall that the probability ω is the ratio

$$\frac{\text{number of favorable cases}}{\text{number of possible cases}}$$

which is

$$\frac{\text{number of states identical to the one considered}}{\text{total number of possible states}}.$$

It is interesting to specify the system of logarithms adopted. We know that, since all systems of logarithms are proportional, [page 32] only the value of the constant K of the measure of information will be changed. It appears legitimate to let the unit of information correspond to the choice between two mutually exclusive choices which are a priori equiprobable for the receptor, that is, to a dilemma (Yes or No, 0 or 1, etc.). Let there be a message answering a dilemma: Did or did not Miss X wear a hat when you met her? There are two possible cases, and there is only one message. Its a priori probability is evidently one-half. We shall write:

$$H = -K \log \tfrac{1}{2} = K \log 2.$$

We have a *unit of information* (a *bit* in communications terminology) if we take logarithms to the base 2:

$$H = -\log_2 \omega. \tag{1}$$

It is advisable to emphasize that the dilemma must be a choice between two a priori equiprobable hypotheses in order to represent a unit of information. Obviously, if I ask a waiter in a restaurant, "Are your eggs fresh or not?" the probability of "Yes" is much greater than that of "No." Therefore, a negative response, because of its unexpectedness, would give me much greater information than an affirmative response, which scarcely tells me anything more than I knew before about the freshness of the eggs.

Most messages represent a choice among a multiplicity of possible cases, but they may always be resolved into a sufficient number of successive dilemmas by successive dichotomies of the possible cases.

We shall say that *the quantity of information transmitted by a message is the binary logarithm of the number of choices necessary to define the message without ambiguity.*

This form of the definition has the advantage of being extremely general and of including all the more explicit forms. It includes notably those, based on the idea of combinations of elements of the repertoire, which are expressed in the now classic formula whose integral form is given by Wiener and whose usable form is given by Shannon:

$$H = -Nt\sum_{i=1}^{n} p_i \log_2 p_i. \tag{2}$$

Here p_i are the probabilities of occurrence of the symbols drawn from the repertoire of n symbols and assembled in a sequence of length Nt.

To make the sense of Eq. (2) clearer, we shall try to derive it from Eq. (1). We shall take, as an example, the case of a typographical message whose elements are printed characters.

The typographer making a message, considered here as the transmitter, constructs a sequence of elements by assembling [page 33] in the lines of a "form" one element (character) after another from a repertoire of symbols (the typecase). In the most simplified Latin alphabet of small letters, without punctuation, there are, for example, 27 symbols (26 letters plus a space which may be considered as a 27th). In practice, the repertoire of linotypes includes around 200 symbols.

In the typecase, the symbols are distributed in different trays, and the number of characters in each tray varies greatly because some letters are used much more often than others. In English the order of decreasing frequency E - T O A N I R S H D L ("-" = space) is well known to cryptologists. Hence the typecase is representative of the statistical structure of the language in which the typographer is composing.

We shall assume first, and this does not restrict the question, that the typecase has an infinite capacity, that is, that each of the trays has an unlimited quantity of characters, although the relative percentages of each of the symbols remain constant. In fact, this is really the case with a very long message such as a book. When the case is nearly empty, we may assume that it will be renewed by the purchase of other characters, always in the same proportion (for example, 18 times more e's than v's). More simply, it suffices to let the capacity of the case be much greater than the length of the message which is composed from it. The number of characters in each tray is then proportional to the probability of p_i of occurrence of each symbol i in the repertoire.

We shall next assume that each message (if, at least, it is long enough) is representative of all messages, that is, of the language in which it is expressed and therefore of the typecase. The typecase is also representative of the language since it was constructed (definition of p_i) by statistics based on the language. This is the ergodic hypothesis assumed by Boltzmann in establishing the well-known expression of entropy $H = K \log \omega$.

To study the message then is tantamount to considering the probabilities of occurrence (expressed by the distributions p_i in the source of symbols) or the numbers of occurrences of the symbols in the message. The latter differ from the probabilities only by a factor constant for all symbols and proportional to the length of the message: If per 100 letters there are probably 18 *e*'s and 10 *a*'s, in 200 there are probably 18×2 *e*'s and 10×2 *a*'s.

Let us suppose then that the typographer or linotypist composes the message at the constant rate of N elements per second. At the end of time t the sequence has Nt elements, $Np_i t$ of which are of the type of symbol i. We know (from a theorem in permutations) that there are $(Nt)!$ ways of arranging the Nt symbols, but not all of these arrangements are distinct. If there are several i's, switching two of them does not change the appearance of the message since the two are indistinguishable. Now, if there are $Np_i t$ symbols i in the message, there are $(Np_i t)!$ ways of arranging them without changing the message. Hence only

$$\frac{(Nt)!}{\Pi (Np_i t)!}$$

messages are really distinct. The probability of obtaining one of these messages is then:

$$\omega = \frac{1}{\dfrac{(Nt)!}{\Pi (Np_i t)!}} = \frac{\displaystyle\prod_{i=1}^{n} (Np_i t)!}{(Nt)!}.$$

[page 34] The information furnished by one of these messages, that is, its degree of originality, is, from Eq. (1),

$$H = -\log_2 \omega = -\log_2 \frac{\displaystyle\prod_{i=1}^{n} (Np_i t)!}{(Nt)!}.$$

By Sterling's approximation:

$$p! = e^{-p} p^p \sqrt{2\pi p}$$

or

$$\log_2 p! = p \log_2 p - p \log_2 e + \tfrac{1}{2} \log 2\pi p. \tag{3}$$

Hence:

$$
\begin{aligned}
H &= -\log_2 \omega \\
&= -\Big(\sum_i Np_i t \log_2 Np_i t - \sum_i Np_i t \log_2 e \\
&\quad + \sum_i \tfrac{1}{2} \log_2 2\pi Np_i t - Nt \log_2 Nt \\
&\quad + Nt \log_2 e - \tfrac{1}{2} \log_2 2\pi Nt \Big) \\
&= -\Big(\sum_i Np_i t \log_2 Np_i t - Nt \log_2 Nt \Big), \tag{4}
\end{aligned}
$$

since

$$\sum_i p_i = 1 \text{ and } \sum_i Np_i t = Nt.$$

We now expand $\sum_i Np_i t \log_2 Np_i t$. Since Nt is a constant, we can remove it from the summation.

$$\sum_i Np_i t \log_2 Np_i t = Nt \sum_i p_i \log_2 Np_i t$$

$$= Nt \left(\sum_i p_i \log_2 p_i + \log_2 Nt \left[\sum_i p_i \right] \right)$$

$$= Nt \sum_i p_i \log_2 p_i + Nt \log_2 Nt. \qquad (5)$$

Substituting in Eq. (4), the term $Nt \log Nt$ is eliminated, and we have:

$$H = - Nt \sum_i p_i \log p_i. \qquad (2) = (6)$$

Thus, information H is proportional to time t. Common sense takes this for granted when it assumes a priori that two successive pages of a text, read at constant speed, contain, or at least can contain, twice as much information as one. Information is also proportional to the number N representing "density" of elements; the smaller each piece of type is, the more can be put in a line, on a page, or, in reading, in a second. But information is also a function of the extent of the repertoire of elements (n) and of the way in which the repertoire is used (p_i).

The measure of information may be extended without difficulty to an infinite repertoire (one with an infinite number of symbols) provided that (a) the elements are denumerable, (b) it is possible to arrange them in order of decreasing probability of occurrence, so that $p_{j+1} \le p_j$, and (c) this probability of occurrence decreases fast enough. We get:

Rank: 1   2 ... $j-1$ j $j+1$
Probability: p_1 p_2 ... p_{j-1} p_j p_{j+1}.

[page 35] Then the sum $\Sigma p_i \log_2 p_i$ has a meaning.

This remark has great practical importance. It justifies limiting calculations involving repertoires as extensive and ill defined as, for example, the dictionary of words, once the contribution to the summation of each term becomes small enough.

A correspondence is established here between output in space (number of elements per line) and output in time (number of transmitted, received, or apprehended elements per second) by means of the process of scanning already mentioned. Examples are the typographer's filling up of successive lines of the "form," an operation which, it is not absurd to suppose, may be performed at a constant speed, or a glance along a printed line, or any other analogous process. This process of scanning is subject to several criticisms and extensions in the theory of form perception; we shall consider them later (cf. Chap. II).

The rate R of information, which it is convenient to distinguish from the quantity of information carried by the Nt elements, is then

$$R = H/t = -N\sum_{i=1}^{n} p_i \log_2 p_i \text{ bits/sec.} \qquad (7)$$

If $N = 1$, that is, one symbol is delivered per unit of time,

$$R = -\sum_{i=1}^{n} p_i \log_2 p_i \text{ bits/symbol.} \qquad (8)$$

This represents the weighting that we must attach to the symbols to express their greater or less originality. More succinctly, neglecting the temporal extension of the message due to exploration or to the successive output of the elements, we shall say that the information is

$$H = -M\sum_{i=1}^{n} p_i \log_2 p_i, \qquad (9)$$

where M is the total number of elements of the sequence.

The two formulas (6) and (9) are fundamental and will constantly be referred to in what follows. That is why it was necessary to derive them in detail in a perfectly accessible manner.

7. FIRST EXAMPLE: THE SOCIOCULTURAL ORIGINALITY OF MUSICAL PROGRAMS

Here is an application of this formula (Eq. (9)) to a problem in the sociology of music, which will make clear how to use it.

For practical reasons, symphonic concerts are all about the same length. It is well known to musicologists that the programs of [page 36] these concerts follow perfectly defined rules, which are the fruit of experience and which constitute one of the branches of musical sociology.

In view of the average duration of symphonic works (overtures, concerti, symphonies), most concerts include between four and six pieces. The pieces are ordered to afford a defined optimum. A brilliant, well-known, and relatively short piece at the beginning creates atmosphere; overtures or classical symphonies follow; more serious or more difficult works belong in the body of the concert; a final work of variable length but generally ending in a brilliant *crescendo* brings off a final feeling of unity.

To simplify, let us assume an average of five pieces per program and per "classical concert," *mutatis mutandis* for the others. Let us also assume that the difficulty of performing the works does not enter into the reckoning, either because rehearsals *ad libitum* are possible or because the concert is of recorded music. These restrictions scarcely decrease the scope of the argument, which still extends to 80 per cent of ordinary symphonic concerts.

[page 37] The problem of "programming" then appears as follows: "What are the ways of choosing the five titles which define the program of a concert from the repertoire of classical symphonic works?" The information H yielded by the grouping of these works — whatever sense one

gives H here — will measure the concert's "originality coefficient"; the originality of the program thus becomes objectively defined.

To measure this information, it is necessary to know the probabilities p_i of each of the symbols (titles of the works) of the classical repertoire. A priori one would tend to believe this repertoire to be limitless or at least very large. This is not the case. The two Tables I and II give some indications in this regard. In the first, composers are listed in order of decreasingly effective roles as measured by a coefficient p_c proportional to the product: hours × listeners.

TABLE I: RELATIVE FREQUENCIES OF OCCURRENCE OF COMPOSER'S WORKS IN MUSIC PERFORMANCES

No.	Composer	p_c	No.	Composer	p_c
		per cent			per cent
1	Mozart	6.1	40	Couperin	0.65
2	Beethoven	5.9	41	Mahler	0.6
3	Bach	5.9	42	Rameau	0.6
4	Wagner	4.2	43	St. Saens	0.6
5	Brahms	4.1	44	Massenet	0.6
6	Schubert	3.6	45	Donizetti	0.55
7	Handel	2.8	46	De Falla	0.45
8	Tchaikovsky	2.8	47	Scriabin	0.45
9	Verdi	2.5	48	Meyerbeer	0.45
10	Haydn	2.3	49	Gluck	0.45
11	Schumann	2.1	50	Paganini	0.45
12	Chopin	2.1	51	Milhaud	0.45
13	Liszt	1.75	52	Bartok	0.4
14	Mendelssohn	1.75	53	Borodin	0.4
15	Debussy	1.7	54	Bruckner	0.4
16	Wolf	1.65	55	Vivaldi	0.4
17	Sibelius	1.6	56	Elgar	0.4
18	R. Strauss	1.4	57	Mascagni	0.4
19	Moussorgsky	1.3	58	Offenbach	0.35
20	Dvořak	1.3	59	Palestrina	0.35
21	Stravinsky	1.3	60	Monteverdi	0.35
22	Fauré	1.2	61	Shostakovitch	0.35
23	J. Strauss	1.2	62	Schönberg	0.35
24	Smetana	1.1	63	Walton	0.35
25	Rachmaninoff	1.0	64	Honegger	0.35
26	Purcell	1.0	65	Albéniz	0.3
27	Puccini	1.0	66	Buxtehude	0.3
28	Grieg	0.95	67	Chabrier	0.3
29	Weber	0.95	68	Delius	0.3
30	Prokofiev	0.95	69	Gershwin	0.3
31	Berlioz	0.95	70	Lully	0.3
32	Rossini	0.95	71	Suppe	0.3
33	Ravel	0.95	72	A. Thomas	0.3
34	Rimski-Korsakov	0.85	73	Bloch	0.25
35	D. Scarlatti	0.85	74	Delibes	0.25
36	Franck	0.7	75	Glazounov	0.25
37	Gounod	0.7	76	Glinka	0.25
38	Vaughan Williams	0.7	77	Granados	0.25
39	Bizet	0.65	78	Gretchaninoff	0.25
			79	Khatchaturian	0.25

No.	Composer	p_c	No.	Composer	p_c
		per cent			per cent
80	Hindemith	0.25	91	J. C. Bach	0.2
81	Lalo	0.25	92	P. E. Bach	0.2
82	Leoncavallo	0.25	93	A. Berg	0.2
83	Josquin des Pres	0.25	94	Bruch	0.2
84	Poulenc	0.25	95	Britten	0.2
85	Orlandus Lassus	0.25	96	Corelli	0.2
86	Boccherini	0.25	97	Busoni	0.2
87	Bellini	0.25	98	Dukas	0.2
88	Telemann	0.2	99	Ponchielli	0.2
89	Pergolesi	0.2	100	Tartini	0.2
90	Enesco	0.2	150	Others (1 work each)	6.0

——————— One-half of the musical works performed
.... Three-quarters of the musical works performed

Table I is in good agreement with Folgman's (1939) results obtained from professional musicians. From year to year this table evolves according to the "musical fashion" which it reveals rather precisely, especially in the order of the composers in the last two-thirds of the table.

Table II completes Table I by giving approximately, for some of the great composers, the product (hours × listeners) for some of their best-known works.

TABLE II. APPROXIMATE PROBABILITIES OF OCCURRENCE FOR VARIOUS WORKS OF SOME GREAT COMPOSERS

BEETHOVEN

Works	p_w	Works	p_w
	per cent		per cent
Symphony No. 5	4.2	Symphony No. 2	1.5
Symphony No. 7	3.1	Coriolan Overture	1.5
Sonata No. 14 ("Moonlight")	3.0	Piano Concerto No. 3	1.5
Symphony No. 8	2.7	Piano Concerto No. 4	1.4
Piano Concerto No. 5		Leonore Overture No. 3	1.4
("Emperor")	2.7	Quartet No. 11	1.4
Violin Concerto	2.7	Quartet No. 15	1.4
Appassionata Sonata	2.3	Sonata Opus 21	1.4
Symphony No. 9	2.3	Fidelio Overture	1.2
Symphony No. 3	2.3	Quartet No. 8	1.2
Egmont Overture	2.3	Quartet No. 9	1.2
Symphony No. 6	2.3	Quartet No. 12	1.1
Prometheus Overture	2.0	Sonata Opus 29	1.1
Waldstein Sonata	2.0	Sonata Opus 30	1
Symphony No. 4	1.6	Kreutzer Sonata	1
Symphony No. 1	1.6		

BACH

Works	p_w	Works	p_w
	per cent		per cent
Brandenburg Concerto No. 5	3.6	Brandenburg Concerto No. 2	2.5

Works	p_w	Works	p_w
	per cent		per cent
Cantata No. 147	2.5	Chromatic Fantasy	1.4
Mass in B Minor	2.5	Toccata and Fugue in D Minor	1.4
Brandenburg Concerto No. 1	2.2	Partita No. 2 for Solo Violin	1.4
Brandenburg Concerto No. 3	2.2	Sonata No. 1 for Solo Violin	1.4
Brandenburg Concerto No. 4	2.2	Sonata No. 2 for Solo Violin	1.4
Brandenburg Concerto No. 6	2.2	The Musical Offering	1.4
Christmas Oratorio	2.2	Passacaglia and Fugue in	
Concerto for Two Violins		C Minor	1.4
in D Minor	2.1	St. John Passion	1.4
St. Matthew Passion	2.0	Concerto No. 2 for Two	
Chaconne (from Sonata No. 4		Claviers and Orchestra	1.1
for Solo Violin)	1.8	Concerto No. 4 for Clavier	
Concerto No. 2 for Violin		and Orchestra in A Minor	1.1
and Orchestra in E Major	1.8	Concerto No. 8 in A Minor	1.1
Concerto No. 2 for		Concerto for Three Claviers	
Three Claviers	1.8	and Orchestra in C Major	1.1
Concerto for Four Claviers	1.8	Fantasy for Clavier in C Minor	1.1
Third Suite for Orchestra	1.8	Fantasy and Fugue for	
Clavier Concerto in F Minor	1.4	Organ in G Minor	1.1
Concerto No. 1 for Violin		Fugue for Organ in G Minor	1.1
and Orchestra in A Minor	1.4	Toccata in D Major	1.1
Italian Concerto	1.4	Pastorale for Organ in F Major	1.1

MOZART

Works	p_w	Works	p_w
	per cent		per cent
Don Giovanni	7	Overture: La Festa Giardiniera	1
The Marriage of Figaro	7	Bastien et Bastienne	1
The Magic Flute	4	La Clemenza di Tito	1
The Abduction from the Seraglio	3	Concerto K.314	1
Symphony No. 36	2.5	Divertimento No. 15, K.287	1
Symphony No. 39	2	Divertimento No. 17, K.334	1
Symphony No. 41	2	Mass No. 10	1
Concerto for Clarinet K.622	2	Mass No. 16	1
Exultate K.165	2	Mauermusik	1
Flute Quartet K.285	2	Quartet No. 15	1
Les Petits Riens	2	Quintet K.406	1
Symphony No. 40	1.6	Quintet K.516	1
Symphony No. 33	1.5	Quintet K.593	1
Symphony No. 35	1.5	Symphony No. 31	1
Symphony No. 25	1.5	Symphony No. 34	1
Quartet No. 17	1.5	Symphony No. 29	1
Divertimento No. 10, K.458	1.5	Zaide	1
Idomeneo	1.5	Concerto K.260	1
Motet K.618	1.5		

A very rough approximation suffices for this example. Hence the method of establishing these two tables by statistical samplings permits us to write that the probability p_i of the occurrence of the work w of composer c is always given by the product:

$$p_i = p_w \times p_c$$

where p_c and p_w are the coefficients in Table I and Table II, one for composers and the other for their works.

[page 38] The combination of titles on a program gives a measure of information, and thus an originality coefficient for a proposed program. For example, the coefficient would be very low for a program of the type:

1 Beethoven   Coriolan Overture
2 Haydn   Military Symphony
3 Mozart   Jupiter Symphony
4 Beethoven   Piano Concerto No. 3
5 Beethoven   Symphony No. 5

On the other hand, it would be much higher for a program such as:

1 Weber   Overture to Oberon
2 Ravel   Nuits dans les jardins d'Espagne
3 Debussy   Reflects dans l'eau
4 Fauré   Nocturne de Shylock
5 Bizet   First Symphony in C

and very high for this program:

1 A. Berg   Concerto for Violin and Orchestra (1935)
2 Schönberg   Survivor from Warsaw
3 Vivaldi   Quintet in F Major
4 Busoni   Concerto for Violin, Op. 35
5 Britten   Variations on a Theme of Frank Bridge

[page 39] To be sure, many practical restrictions must be added to this idea of "the originality coefficient" of a program. For example, the sociological structure on which these probability tables rest is arbitrarily schematized in a way that leaves out, in particular, the public of professional musicians and neglects the fact that the probabilities express an average opinion, which is not set but changes significantly. Thus in reconstructing Table I several times at intervals of four years we found notable differences which reflected the evolution of the musical taste of the masses, of what is called the *sociocultural background* (cf. Silbermann, 1954).

However, this coefficient of originality does express an objective social phenomenon and is valid within the limits of statistical sociology, which is interested only in quantities likely to obey the law of large numbers.

It is known that the size of the public interested by a concert varies inversely with the originality of the concert. The preceding formula establishes a weighting law which ought to make it possible to learn the a priori interest of any given program. This law becomes increasingly valid as the hypotheses circumscribing it are better fulfilled, as, for example, in radio music. It is particularly valid in the case of recorded music, where assembling a musical program in radio, for example, is simply the timed collocation of a number of records in an order.

Assuming, as we shall show later, that the "public" may be standardized as a mass of individuals, each possessing a personal coefficient of musical culture, that is, a certain capacity for apprehending the originality of musical forms, we may then relate the degrees of originality H of programs,

$$H = -5\sum p_i \log_2 p_i$$

with these personal coefficients of apprehension. In this way we schematize numerically one of the essential problems of musical sociology: that of recruiting the public and defining a program's "appeal" to the public. This formulation of the problem is valuable — even and especially if it is schematic — because sociomusical problems are so delicate.

This example brings out one of the most remarkable characteristics of applications of information theory. The theory offers not only properly new results, but a new method of presentation, a synthesis of known facts in a new structure, making evident the gaps, destined to be filled, in our knowledge. It may be classed, with the great scientific theories, among the *heuristic methods,* and more particularly among those which we term methods of *presentation* and of *phenomenologic variation* (cf. Moles, 1957b). From the philosophic point of view, this aspect will be apparent throughout this book.

8. SECOND EXAMPLE: THE COMPLEXITY OF SOCIAL GROUPS

To show the universality of the preceding formula, we apply it to an entirely different type of structure: a social structure of individuals.

[page 40] Any closed social group (an administration, company, secret society) is composed at a given time of N individuals who belong to n different categories i. The categories may be social classes or aptitude classes, for example, laborers, employees, engineers, administrators, etc. The number of places within each category may legitimately be considered to be proportional to the size N of the group: There are normally more places for doctors in a city of 100,000 inhabitants than in a city of 10,000, and as a first approximation we may assume that there are ten times more. Hence we shall write that the number of places in the class i is p_iN.

The group includes $\sum_1^n p_iN = N$ individuals $\left(\sum p_i = 1 \right)$; p_i is then roughly the probability of encountering an individual in category i.

One fundamental hypothesis, affirmed by the praxis of the labor market, is that individuals may be permuted, after a short training, within the same class i without modifying the structure of the whole.

There are then $(Np_i)!$ possible permutations within a given class i which do not change the social structure. Altogether, there are $\Pi(Np_i)!$ such permutations in the group. We shall assume here that the complexity C of a social group is measured by the logarithm of the number of permutations that one may effect among individuals without changing functional relations, compared to the total number $N!$ of permutations which could be effected on an amorphous mass having the same number N of individuals.

$$C = + \log \Pi \, (Np_i)!/N!.$$

By a legitimate simplification of Sterling's formula, we have

$$\log \, (Np_i)! = Np_i \log Np_i - Np_i.$$

Hence

$$\sum Np_i \log Np_i - \sum Np_i = \sum Np_i \log N + \sum Np_i \log p_i - N$$
$$= N \log N - N + N \sum p_i \log p_i$$

since

$$\sum p_i = 1.$$

Moreover, the log of the denominator $N!$ is $-N \log N + N$; hence

$$C = + N \sum p_i \log p_i.$$

The analogy between this expression for the complexity of a social group and that for *information H* is immediately apparent.

We may demonstrate the same result more neatly, but at the same time cast doubt on our hypotheses, by noticing that the structural complexity of a group is characterized by the multiplicity of possible *situations* of an individual in the group, and thus by the information that we obtain in knowing that an individual is found in one situation rather than another. Hence

$$H \equiv C \text{ (up to a constant factor).}$$

The measurement of the complexity of a structured group is of great interest in applied sociology, notably in the theories of mathematical sociology by K. Lewin and Moreno.

One may interpret the measure in several ways. For example, in bits (that is, binary logarithms), it gives an idea of the number of "Yes — No" questions which must be asked and answered to know the complexity of an enterprise or human group.

In every message, "information" is nothing other than a *measure of the complexity* of the temporal *Gestalten* presented: *H* measures complexity, which is very important in [page 41] all theories of form, that until now have lacked an instrument with which to compare forms. The concept of redundancy then measures the intelligibility of forms.

9. COMPLEXITY AS A MEASURE OF THE STRUCTURE OF ORGANISMS

Any organism, including any machine, is a structure; to understand a machine is to perceive that structure. The only universal dimension of a structure independent of its elements is its *complexity*. It would appear then that a measure of complexity furnishes a universal measure applicable to all structures; hence, it allows us to create a *ranking,* an ordering of mechanisms.

If the machine is itself a message from the external world, the measure of complexity C must merge with the measure of information H. Suppose the message is composed of a set of N elements drawn from a repertoire of n symbols with a relative frequency of occurrence p_i for the ith symbol. We then have available an objective measure of the complexity of machines as forms:

$C = +\log_2 N$ for a number of organs all different and equiprobable (complicated system);

$C = -N\Sigma p_i \log p_i$ for a series of organs belonging to different classes.

Such a measure of the structural complexity of organisms has several properties:

(1) It automatically fits the problem of the hierarchy of material structures and their construction. Most systems are constructed from *elements* which are not simple, but are multiterminaled components composed of elements; each component has a complexity C_i, and the over-all organism has a complexity C. The complexity of the over-all system thus depends on the nature of the elements considered as symbols or signs. The complexity is additive where the combinations of elements are multiplicative, as Shannon (1949) has demonstrated with switching relays. (See Fig. I-5.)

(2) Complexity does not change when two identical elements are permuted; in a telephone exchange one can permute identical relays. That is one of the important aspects of the standardized construction of modern machines. It is not unreasonable to maintain that old machines aimed implicitly, even if they did not succeed in fact, toward standardization.

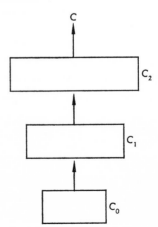

Fig. I-5.

(3) The structural complexity of a machine also depends on the way in which the repertoire of elements is defined. Thus, as a first approximation to the repertoire of a hardware store, one may say: i screws, j nuts, k rivets, l cotters. . . . One may refine the representation into: i_1 screws of size a, i_2 screws of size b, i_3 screws . . . j_1 nuts of size m, j_2 nuts of size n, j_3 nuts . . . k_1 rivets of size x . . . l_1 . . . .

We may examine two different types of complexity. One is related to the *structural* description of the organism: "a machine is *composed* of . . ."; it interests the builder or the draftsman. The other relates to the *functional* description of the modes of action (degrees of freedom) of the organism: "a machine is made to . . ."; the functional description is for children and inventors. We thus define two dimensions in the world of organisms: structural complexity and functional complexity.

This measure of complexity has immediate applications. Complexity is connected with assembly time, at least statistically; machines on the same level of complexity have a certain number of similar properties. Maintenance time is a direct function of complexity; the number of parts used or stored in a shop or service station is a function of complexity. The measure of complexity is connected with the intellectual level of the individuals charged with maintenance; they must perceive the "message" of the configuration of the mechanism in order to see what is wrong with it. Finally, the map of machines onto the coordinates (C_s, C_f) (that is, structural complexity, functional complexity) is one indication of technological evolution.

10. APPLICATION OF INFORMATION THEORY TO THE SCORE: THE INFORMATION OF MELODIC PATTERNS

Let us suppose that a simple melodic pattern of classical music, such as might occur in a Beethoven symphony, consists of 20 notes and that it takes about 20 seconds to play the melody.

Let the durations of these 20 notes be taken from the following repertoire:

64th note	32nd	16th	8th	quarter	half	whole
1	2	3	4	5	6	7

We assume that a dotted quarter note is equivalent to a quarter plus an eighth; we also assume a uniform probability distribution. Then the information given by the rhythmic pattern of 20 notes is $H = -20 \log_2 1/7 = -66.4 \log_{10} 1/7 = 56$ bits. Thus there are $56/20 =$

2.8 bits per symbol, and if we assume that the theme lasts 20 seconds, the rate of information is 2.8 bits per second.

Now let us calculate the information of the melodic theme, ignoring the duration of the notes. We do not suppose that the intervals are equiprobable. We could use the note frequencies found by Fucks (1960) and others. Instead, we adopt the simpler hypothesis that the frequency of a musical interval varies inversely as its size, that is, the bigger it is, the less its probability of occurrence.

Making this assumption is simpler than studying the actual probabilities, and it is supported by Zipf's (1949) study of a bassoon concerto by Mozart. (We ignore the difference between intervals that move up and those that move down.) Thus,

1 unison
2 second
3 major or minor third
4 fourth
5 fifth
6 sixth
7 seventh
8 octave

[page 42] gives a very rough weighting, but one sufficient for the other hypotheses. The probabilities of the intervals are $p_i = k/i$ with $\sum_{i=1}^{8} k/i = 1$; hence $k = 0.37$ approximately. A melody of 20 notes, or 19 intervals, then has an information of

$$H = -N \sum_{i=1}^{8} \frac{k}{i} \log_2 \frac{k}{i} = -19(0.37) \sum_{i=1}^{8} \frac{1}{i} \log_2 \frac{k}{i}$$

$$= -19(0.37)(3.32) \left(\sum_{1}^{8} \frac{1}{i} \log_{10} k - \sum_{1}^{8} \frac{1}{i} \log_{10} i \right)$$

$$= -23.4(2.7)(\log_{10} 0.37) + 23.4 \sum_{1}^{8} \frac{1}{i} \log_{10} i.$$

But $\log_{10} 0.37 = 0.57 - 1.00 = -0.43$ and $\sum_{1}^{8} \frac{1}{i} \log_{10} i = 1.025$.
Thus $H = 23.4((0.43)(2.7) + 1.025) = 51$ bits approximately. There are then 2.55 bits per interval. Actually, the information will be lower because many notes will be repeated.

Let us now determine the information that would be yielded if all the intervals occurred equiprobably, that is, the maximum information. $H_{max} = \log_2 8 = 3$ bits per interval. Because intervals do not occur randomly, the intervals in the melody have a redundancy of

$(3.0 - 2.55)/3.0 = 15$ per cent. The constraints on musical language due to the inequality of frequencies of occurrence are slight.

[page 43] The total information furnished by the melodic pattern (isolated from its accompaniment and its counterpoint) includes the information from the intervals and that from the time structure. We assume these two kinds of information are additive as a first approximation. Then $H = H_{intervals} + H_{durations} = 51 + 56 = 107$ bits approximately. The rate of information is 5.35 bits per second.

This rate is not very far from that calculated for words in language (5 bits per second); the semantic aspects of language and of music thus come together.

The patterns of pitches and of durations present approximately the same quantities of information or originality. These values of information are very close to those which would be obtained in playing a game of chance, because here the two types of patterns are considered independent, which is obviously not true. One goal of the study of musical structures will be to determine the constraints connecting durations and pitches.

11. CONSEQUENCES OF THE MEASURE OF INFORMATION

We now explore the consequences of adopting the formula

$$H = -M \sum_{i=1}^{n} p_i \log_2 p_i$$

[page 44] to measure the originality of a sequence of M elements. The measure is here expressed independently of the time t during which the message lasts. The sequence yields uniformly M/t elements per second.

In accord with intuition, information increases, all other things being equal, with the length M of the message. The *Encyclopaedia Britannica* probably contains more information than a page extracted from it; more precisely, it is probable that 20 of its pages contain twice as much information as 10.

But this is true only if all other things *are* equal, that is, if

$$-\sum_{i=1}^{n} p_i \log_2 p_i$$

is perceptibly the same from one part of the message to another (the ergodic hypothesis). This quantity represents a *measure of the originality* of the form which the message constitutes. Let us turn our attention to it.

This quantity increases a priori with the extent n of the summation, that is, with the extent of the repertoire of symbols. Indeed, the greater the repertoire, the greater the number of symbols among which one has to choose, hence the greater the number of p_i's, and the greater the a priori variety of possible choices.

In Sec. 2 of this chapter, on difference thresholds, we saw that the receptor's structure and particularly his difference thresholds determine the elements of the sensory message. The extent and the nature of the repertoire depend uniquely on the discriminative properties of this receptor. For example, in a visual message, the difference thresholds of the eye determine the extent of the repertoire of symbols. A symbol of the visual message is any element defined by the set of difference thresholds relative to each of the parameters [page 45] and dimensions which characterize the symbol. Thus, for the eye, these are the respective difference thresholds of position (angular and radial), of luminous intensity, of time, and of color; the repertoire of symbols for the visual message appears very large. A page placed in our visual field at reading distance or a movie screen of the same angular dimensions is capable of bringing us extraordinarily large quantities of information, if we assume that they are perceived as a mosaic of elements of all imaginable luminous values.

We know, however, that this excessively psychophysiological schematization corresponds to reality only under exceptional circumstances. It is very unusual for an eye to act as a scanning machine; we rarely exploit all the discriminative capacities of our sense organs. In fact, this physiologically conceivable situation practically never occurs, because the individual is incapable of using the information which he would thus obtain. We are led to conclude that the receptor considered here is not the isolated eye, but rather the whole individual, including a brain behind the sense organ, and this system is capable of using only a much more restricted repertoire.

We know that we can discern two distant stars because we fix our attention on two defined points by neglecting *ipso facto* the rest. On the other hand, when we read a page of text, the little defects of the paper on which the text is printed do not interest us at all, though they may be right in the middle of our visual field and even though we have only a diffuse and latent perception of the style of typographical characters used. At an even higher level, we know from psychological studies of the reading of printed texts (Zeitler, Shen; see Woodworth and Schlosberg, 1954) that in cursive reading the number of fixation points of the eye does not exceed two to three per line and that it is materially impossible for the eye to apprehend the form of each letter. We know that numerous "typographical illusions" exist. These considerations support the theory of form rather than the simpler idea of scanning.

How will information theory take account of these essential facts? We must distinguish several levels of perception in the same sensory channel, each corresponding to a distinct message and each possessing symbolic repertoires which differ widely in extent and structure.

Visual messages may be differentiated according to the symbolic elements to which each has recourse. For example,

[page 46]

Types of possible variations			Number of symbols of the repertoire
Reduction of contrasts, distortion (optical illusions)	Raw visual message	Image, pattern, film	Elements of retinal difference thresholds
Set of all characters, of all type styles, of all alphabets	Alphabetical message	Typographical letters	Set of a typographical alphabet
Set of manuscript texts	Messages of letters	Letters conceived as topological forms	Normalized reduction of typographical symbols to simple forms
Set of languages formed of words, including ideograms	Messages of words	Words considered as over-all forms	The vocabulary

The succession of levels of perception reflects the concept of *Gestalt*, of form perceived as a whole. Though built up of the same basic visual elements, the levels are distinct; their repertoires grow smaller as they appeal to higher functions. Thus the printed page may be considered as a set of luminous spots in two dimensions (for example, by a monkey), as a one-dimensional alignment of letters (for example, by a proofreader), as an alignment of words in one dimension (by a reader), and as an expressive block in two dimensions (by a typographical artist or a page compositor).

Each of the visual receptors just mentioned is different; each receives a *different* message composed of symbols drawn from repertoires of differing extent n. Each message obeys different syntactic rules, introducing different codes of conventions between receptor and transmitter.

Thus n is of the order of 1,000,000,000 for the raw visual message, of 200 (approximately) for the message composed of letters, of the order of up to 50,000 for the message composed of English words. In each of these repertoires the probabilities of occurrence will vary tremendously.

Although we are trying, above all, to apply [page 47] information theory to esthetics, the psychology of perception, etc., where the receptor is an *individual*, the final link of the channel, we must recall that the general theory may be applied to any channel whatsoever. This generality is the goal of such a theory, because the artificial communication channels constructed by man can enlighten us on the processes of communication between individuals.

For example, in the modulation transmission system of music by coded impulses, called the delta system, the signal is decomposed into quanta, all of the same size. Sent through the channel at sufficient speed, impulses are either a positive quantum or a negative quantum. Here, the "vocabulary," the repertoire of symbols, is reduced to its minimum. The reality of this system shows that one can transmit any musical signal, of any complexity, by sending a series of "Yes" or "No" signals at a sufficient rate to drive the process of reconstruction at the receptor.

The repertoire and the over-all structure of the channel will depend on the receptor at which we stop our analysis. If we stop at the discriminating system inside the "technical receptor" (for example, nerve fiber impulses), the vocabulary is reduced to two terms of a priori probability one-half. If we push our analysis to include the ear of the hearer, we must consider a repertoire containing roughly 340,000 different elements. Finally, if we try, by penetrating a musical structure, to know what the individual has perceived of the piece of music, we shall find a notably smaller repertoire. This repertoire corresponds to the symbols effectively differentiated by the individual's musical sensitivity. One of the goals of the psychophysical study of music is precisely to denumerate this repertoire, a point which we shall take up again later (see Chaps. IV and V).

12. MAXIMUM INFORMATION, RELATIVE INFORMATION, AND REDUNDANCY

The terms over which the summation $\Sigma p_i \log_2 p_i$ extends are a *weighting* function of the symbol probabilities. They represent an evaluation of the quality of the symbols used. Guilbaud (1959) points out that $\Sigma p_i \log_2 p_i$ may be considered as an average of the logarithms of the probabilities; the total information is the average of the partial information furnished, according to the most general expression from which we started, that is, the logarithm of the reciprocal of each symbol's probability.

What is most remarkable is that this formula, in conformity with elementary intuition, implies that maximum originality or information is transported by messages in which all [page 48] n symbols have equal probabilities $p_i = p = 1/n$. The equal distribution of probabilities furnishes in effect the maximum of choice. The letter w has a relatively small probability p_w of occurrence in French and hence informs us much by its presence exactly because there are much more frequent letters, for example, the letter e. The presence of e gives us, on the contrary, very little information about any peculiarity of the message. Cryptographers know this well: While the presence of w in a coded French message (without transposition of letters or after the elimination of this transposition) indicates almost surely the presence of a foreign word, and hence greatly restricts the field of research, this is true of only a single symbol. The advantage is destroyed by the presence of a great number of letters such as e, s, a, . . . for which it is necessary to find a much greater number in a known situation before learning something positive about the message. The preceding formula shows us that the banality of these frequent letters compensates, and overcompensates, for the originality of the rare w.

Thus, all other things being equal, the most original message is that composed in a system such that all the symbols are equiprobable and where

$$\sum_{1}^{n} p_i \log_2 p_i = np \log p,$$

in which case p is precisely equal to $1/n$; up to a constant, then,

$$H = -\log_2 (1/n).$$

The fundamental measure of information theory hence presents an upper limit to information output with a limited number of symbols. This ideal occurs when a uniform distribution of the occurrence of symbols (equiprobability) gives the maximum possible choice in constructing the message.

Shannon, following remarks of Boltzmann and Szilard, has given the name *maximum entropy* to this maximum information. Shannon thus specifies an *ideal* for communication with a group of symbols. Later we shall examine to what extent this ideal, valid for artificial channels, is valid for the human receptor.

In practice, or at least in written, spoken, televised, telephoned, etc. messages, the symbols are not equiprobable. Thus the letter w is 40 times less probable in French than the letter e or the space. If H_1 is the information content of some message, one [page 49] can compare it with the information

$$H_m = -\log_2 (1/n)$$

which would be transmitted if all the symbols were equiprobable. Following Shannon, we shall call the ratio H_1/H_m the *relative information* of the message. This ratio is evidently independent of the length of the message, since the number N of elements disappears. It is a measure of the relative originality of the message and varies between zero and one.

The complementary magnitude

$$1 - H_1/H_m,$$

which we shall call *redundancy*, is very interesting. It is a measure of the relative "wastage" of symbols in transmitting a given message. Zero when $H_1 = H_m$, that is, when the symbols have been "well" (equiprobably) chosen, redundancy tends toward 100 per cent when the output is low, that is, when the efficacy of transmission, characterized by the frequencies of the vocables of *the language used*, is low. Here we have a *coefficient of efficacy* of the language used in the transmission channel. If each channel is characterized by a repertoire of symbols, a typecase, or a given vocabulary, redundancy estimates the *efficiency* of the language *for transmitting information*.

In the applications of interest here, where the human receptor is always the last link in the chain, the redundancy is never zero. Redundancy plays almost as important a role as the concept of information itself.

13. INFORMATION OF THE TYPOGRAPHICAL MESSAGE

To show how information, maximum information, and redundancy are measured, here are two examples. We will reflect later on the meaning of the results.

First example:

The Hebrew Bible (Torah) contains 647,390 letters (M) belonging to an alphabet of 22 letters $(i = 1, \ldots, 22)$ for which we have determined the probabilities p_i from a sample text of 1,000 letters.

symbols:	aleph	bayz	gimel	daled	hay	vov
p_i per cent:	6.5	10.5	0.6	3.4	6.8	12.5
symbols:	zion	chess	tess	yod	cof	lamed
p_i per cent:	0.6	0.3	1.2	9	10	8.2
symbols:	mem	nun	samech	ayen	pay	
p_i per cent:	8.2	3.4	0.5	3.4	1	
symbols:	tsadek	koof	raysh	shin	tof	
p_i per cent:	0.9	0.8	3	4.5	6	

From this, we have the order of decreasing frequency: vov, bayz, cof, yod, lamed, mem, hay, aleph, tof, shin, daled, nun, ayen, raysh, tess....

Considering the normal error involved in determinations of letter frequencies, it is legitimate to simplify the calculations by dividing the p_i into five groups as follows:
[page 50]

I: vov, bayz, cof, yod each have

$$p_I \cong 10 \text{ per cent}$$
$$4p_I = 40 \text{ per cent}$$

Very frequent letters, diacritical marks, and grammatical signs

II: lamed, mem, hay, aleph, tof each have

$$p_{II} \cong 7 \text{ per cent}$$
$$5p_{II} = 35 \text{ per cent}$$

Very frequent letters

III: shin, daled, nun, ayen, raysh each have

$$p_{III} \cong 3.5 \text{ per cent}$$
$$5p_{III} = 18 \text{ per cent}$$

Bulk of the alphabet

IV: tess, samech, tsadek, zion, koof each have

$$p_{IV} \cong 1 \text{ per cent}$$
$$5p_{IV} = 5 \text{ per cent}$$

V: gimel, chess, pay each have

$$p_V \cong \tfrac{2}{3} \text{ per cent}$$
$$3p_V = 2 \text{ per cent}$$

Rare letters

The information is then:

$$H = - \, 647{,}390 \sum_{i=I}^{i=V} n_i p_i \log_2 p_i$$

where n_i = number of letters in group i;

$$H = 2{,}586{,}000 \text{ bits.}$$

If all of the 22 symbols of the Hebrew alphabet had been used equally ($p_i = 1/22$), the maximum information that these 647,390 letters would have been able to transmit is $H_m = -\, 647{,}390 \log_2 1/22 = 2{,}890{,}000$ bits. The ratio H/H_m is 0.896, and the redundancy is 10.4 per cent.

Second example:

Take a French text of any length. Let us find the *rate of information* of the French language, that is, the information H per unit of length ($N = 1$ unit of message length).

From Eq. (8):

$$H = - \sum_{i=1}^{26} p_i \log_2 p_i.$$

Following cryptographic practice, let us neglect the spaces between the words. Cryptographic works give the probabilities in percentages (here rounded off) of letters in French:

E	SANI	RT	UOL	D	CMP	Q BFGHV	X
17	8 8 8 8	7 7	6 6 6	4	3 3 3	1.5 1 1 1 1 1	0.6

J Z	K W Y
0.2 0.2	0.1 0.1 0.1

Condensing into groups of nearly equiprobable letters, we have:

$$1 \ p_\mathrm{I} = \qquad\qquad\quad = 17 \text{ per cent}$$
$$6 \ p_\mathrm{II} = 6 \times 8 \text{ per cent} \cong 47 \text{ per cent}$$
$$3 \ p_\mathrm{III} = 3 \times 6 \text{ per cent} \cong 17 \text{ per cent}$$
$$4 \ p_\mathrm{IV} = 4 \times 3 \text{ per cent} \cong 12 \text{ per cent}$$
$$6 \ p_\mathrm{V} = 6 \times 1 \text{ per cent} \cong 6 \text{ per cent}$$
$$6 \ p_\mathrm{VI} = 6 \times 0.2 \text{ per cent} \cong 1 \text{ per cent}$$

[page 51] The *information content* in written French *considered as a sequence of letters* is

$$H = -\sum_{i=a}^{i=z} p_i \log_2 p_i = -3.32 \sum_{i=\mathrm{I}}^{i=\mathrm{VI}} n_i p_i \log_2 p_i$$

$$= 3.32 \times 1.16 = 3.86 \text{ bits/symbol.}$$

Relative information might be called the coefficient of "quality in the literal expression of thought." The maximum information output for the letters which would have been attained if all the letters had been equiprobable, $p = 1/26 \cong 0.04$, is

$$H_m = 3.32 \log_{10} 26 = 4.8 \text{ bits.}$$

Hence the relative redundancy of French letters is $(4.8 - 3.86)/4.8 = 19$ per cent. Obviously, these calculations are approximate.

This figure is clearly larger than that for Hebrew. This is due to the plethora of useless vowels in French. In Hebrew, exclusive use of consonants (excepting the two *matres lectionis* waw and jod) creates a more nearly equal distribution of written symbols and, in return, a majority of words composed of three root letters.

The redundancy determined here, based on Shannon's fundamental formula, is for a language in which letters are assembled according to their respective probabilities of occurrence (monogram probabilities). But this mere first approximation to real language does not express the total influence of our a priori knowledge about the message, which introduces a supplementary redundancy due to the connections between successive symbols (a stochastic Markoff process). In any kind of language, the words determine each other successively just as the successive letters within a word determine each other. These n-gram probabilities are difficult to assess: To determine them is one of the objectives of a scientific study of languages. But more direct experimental methods permit approximate measurement of the *gross* effective redundancy of a language.

We have attempted to determine this over-all redundancy for French by suppressing, at random, increasing percentages of letters in French texts. After we suppressed 10, 20, 30, 35, 40, 45, and 50 per cent, we investigated the delay necessary for individuals to reconstruct the texts. The delay increases very quickly as more letters are suppressed. It tends toward infinity for a certain proportion.

This proportion indicates the "excess" percentage of symbols which permitted the subject to reconstruct the others by their presence alone plus his intuitive statistical knowledge of the language. We give below three samples of these texts. [These are English equivalents of the French originals. — *Tr.*] The space between words is here considered as a 27th letter.
[pages 52, 53]

THE BABOON OF COURSE IS NO WIT OUT RESOURCE. HE
IS FAIRLY POWERFUL. IK ALL RIMATES HE LACK
CLAWS BUT HIS NAILS ARE FORMIDABLE. HE HAS CANINES
LIKE AGGERS. AND HE H S WITS. IF WHILE HE I
PL NDERING A MA COMES OUT OF A FARM H USE HE
WILL LEE. IF A WOMA CO ES OUT HE WILL I NORE HER.
BUT I DETERM ED MALE H MAN E MY DRE SES IN
WO ANS CLOTHES THE BOON W LL IN TANT Y TAKE TO
 HE WOODS.

IN GE ER L I PO TANT ECONOMIES IN SA ES ROM ON
  H N ASES O S ALE UP T THAT OF A S NGL
OPTI AL PLAN SEEM L KELY TO E P NT IN T E
AUTOM BI YPE RIT R T AC R AND PE R LE M
RE NI G I DUSTRIE . REASO S THAT C CONOMIES
A E STRO GL USPE T N HESE USTRIES ARE (1 N AL
OF HE EIT ER EX NSIV D A ER E ER-SE I E OR
FI LD- R CE ORGA I ATIONS ARE E S N IAL T
 FFECTIVE S PROMO ON.

F M HI D SCRIP MIGH E S D THA
  E E I I OF E SEVEN E C UR
D NOT MA ER L Y D ER F O TIC M R
O L HOU PE OF R I . ER E H W V
S ME I ORT T OF IS A CTER I O BE
 OT D H CH L GRE I Y THIS S MA
U LE D A H S AND U LI D E AS STI L
I O E T IMPO T NT P I S A GE L MAN.

[page 54] From the experiments we have performed with these texts, it appears that the gross redundancy of the French language on the letter level lies around 45 per cent — a figure very comparable to the results of Shannon and Oliver for English. This proximity would seem to indicate a neighboring linguistic structure.

As Shannon points out, the fact that the redundancy of English is 50 per cent means that half of what we write in English is determined by the structure of the language and half is freely chosen. The interesting point is that this redundancy is an over-all measure of what we know intuitively about the structure of the language, but it is not a property of any isolated element.

Several experiments have been performed with texts of various contents. With rates of suppression on the order of 40 per cent, which became rather critical, these experiments showed that an average audience's ability to reconstruct varies significantly with the difficulty of the text. This suggests a method of measuring the "apperceptibility" of written texts (in essence very much like the "Cloze index" test of Taylor [see Woodworth and Schlosberg, 1954], of which we learned only after writing this). We have also performed, by making a series of magnetic tapes, analogous experiments on spoken language by random suppression of speech elements having the average length of a phoneme.[2]

A remarkable consequence of redundancy nicely illustrates the over-all character of our intuitive knowledge of language. It is the possibility of making crosswords, that is, of attaching each letter to systems of different n-gram probabilities. If the redundancy were zero, any collection of letters would be a possible and meaningful message, as is the case with certain secret telegraphic codes used in commerce. If the redundancy is too high, the structure of the language imposes too rigorous internal constraints. In order for two-dimensional crosswords to be possible, redundancy must be at most 50 per cent; three-dimensional crosswords are possible if the redundancy does not exceed 33 per cent. Thus from the above example, it should be possible to make three-dimensional crosswords in classical Hebrew. Such crosswords have been realized by H. Bluhme in Munich.

How then do we relate to each other the experimental results on gross redundancy, for example, of the French language (45 per cent) and on the redundancy based on letters (19 per cent) which is clearly smaller? The difference is due to the over-all structure of the language, the effect of which is added to the simple inequality of probabilities.

As we have seen, the impact of thought on language takes place in this interstice:

---

[2] To perform these experiments we used an experimental device which may be of interest. Instead of using a clumsy mechanical rotating switch or a complicated electronic switch, we used three tape recorders M_1, M_2, M_3. The first M_1 carries the text to be cut rhythmically. Its output enters the recording input of a good professional tape recorder with several (for example, three) speeds. On this recorder is placed a loop of tape made up of an assembly of short pieces (for example, three inches long) of magnetic tape and of splicing tape (of the same length). The speed and the ratio of magnetic tape to splicing tape of this interruption loop determine the ratio of live to suppressed signal. The output of this second tape recorder goes into the third machine, which records the result. This device allows very complicated patterns of interruption on any kind of material without any transients.

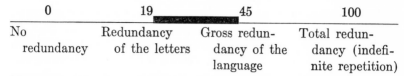

0	19	45	100
No redundancy	Redundancy of the letters	Gross redundancy of the language	Total redundancy (indefinite repetition)

Thought organizes, structures, and [page 55] codifies language by binding the symbols to each other in a Markoff process; the probability of each letter j is no longer independent (p_j) but depends on the letter i which precedes it.

In short, our conception of the production of the linguistic message has been too simple. To revive an example of E. Borel, in our original model one could have supposed that the transmitter was a chimpanzee. Upsetting a typecase into a bag, he mixes up the char-

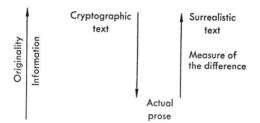

Fig. I-6.

acters, then, by drawing them out one by one, lines them up in a form. He would thus respect the probabilities p_i but would obtain a message having an originality, an information output, clearly greater than that of the language. The monkey, lacking intelligence and the ability to read what he writes, would choose successive letters independently. By the ingenious myth of magnetized words which attract each other, Plato has already suggested the concept of linking n-grams.

The n-gram probabilities take account of the difference between the redundancy calculated from the elementary letter probabilities by the basic formula for information and the redundancy experimentally determined by random destruction of message elements.

This difference is easy to express numerically. It represents the margin which separates the real message of language from the technical message composed of collections of letters, such as telegraphic codes.

But at the same time, from the operator's viewpoint, this difference represents the results of the mental difference between the typesetting monkey and the intelligent individual. Assembling characters from an overturned typecase scarcely exceeds the training capacities of superior monkeys. Hence, this difference is ultimately the result of the impact of intelligence on the structure of the message; this is a very important point. Often, n-gram probabilities are unknown and in any case are nearly impossible to introduce in the calculation of information. By expressing their effect, this difference expresses the difference in intelligence of the [page 56] authors of the language: the difference between man and our typographer-chimpanzee.

This point may also be made more profitably without recourse to typing monkeys. Some human beings perform mental operations designed precisely to return language from its organized level to a level *apparently* very close to that furnished by our monkey. Coders using the transposition method, without changing the original letters, simply modify their position according to a known key unknown to the uninitiated.

Here is an example of such a cryptogram:

A S U R U L T R E A E E U E T N Q H T N M A R N C T T R L Y N U E E E I Q E T O E A E N O M T E C.

This does not differ in appearance from what a typographical monkey could give us. But we *know* that it has a sense, that is, that it represents real words. (See Fig. I-6 and its inverse Fig. I-7.)

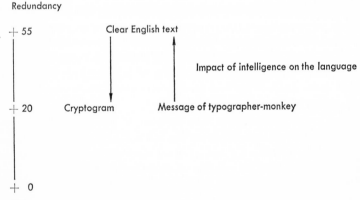

Fig. I-7.

Thus, the coder reverses the work which separates the creation of the monkey from that of the writing human. Now, we know the series of mental operations the cryptographer performs to destroy meaning. But we do not know explicitly the linguistic laws which fill in the gap between randomly assembled letters and language conforming with the set of n-gram probabilities. In principle, a statistical understanding of the operations of the coder, of the proportion of additional disorder that he introduces, can furnish a quantitative method of estimating the n-gram probabilities which are so hard to get directly.

14. DIFFERENT MEANINGS OF THE WORD "CODE"

We call the set of coding operations, which the receptor is supposed to know, the *code* of the message. We are now going to examine the code.

[page 57] When information is transmitted by an artificial channel, it becomes *expensive* to transmit each symbol. To carry information, we want to use all of the channel's capacity. Hence we adopt, for transmission only, a language perfectly adapted to this channel. That is, after having defined the discriminative properties of the intermediate mechanical receptor placed at the end of the channel, we choose a language with this property: All of the symbols defined by the effective difference thresholds, taking account of the varied inherent perturbations in the functioning of the channel, are *equiprobable,* or at least are as close as possible to this ideal. We are especially interested in finding this language if we are restricted to a particular translation.

Translating the message into a special language adapted to the channel in order to increase the channel's information rate is called *coding.* It is accompanied at the receptor by a decoding following the same rules intended to readapt the message to individual perception. Thus the distant transmission of messages may be schematized:

Composing a message in telegraphic style is an obvious example. The individual deletes the common words such as articles, polite formulas, verbs, etc. in order to concentrate on the meaningful, more improbable words, which are therefore more original and more economical. When the telegraphed message is delivered, the person for whom it was intended reestablishes, at least mentally, the intelligibility — and the articles — in order, for example, to communicate the news to someone else.

Probability considerations determine the choice of an efficacious code. Coding aims to adapt, first, man to the channel and, second, the channel to man at the other end. But this coding is not always practiced. In the telephone or in normal radio broadcasting, the adopted code purely and simply transcribes into another field of variables (frequencies and electrical intensities as a function of time) the corresponding variables (sonic frequencies and sonic intensity) of the initial message; the code does not try to reduce them. Thus the radiotelephone channel has been adjusted to the signals furnished by man at the price of an extraordinary loss of efficiency. Gabor has indicated that, *with an efficacious coding*, a band of 2.5 cycles and of several decibels would suffice to transmit all the information of the sonic channel that normally exists in speech. Experiments we have performed (Moles, 1952a) show that, even without recourse to coding, [page 58] the sonic channel may be reduced extraordinarily (to $\frac{1}{3}$ octave $\times$ 1 dB) as a result of redundancy.

When man wanted to surpass natural communication by the direct sonic channel to which he was adapted, he had to have recourse to a technological channel whose properties had no a priori reason to correspond to the natural. Only then did man become interested in these problems. His attitude at first, at the stage of technical improvement, was to try to match the properties of the technological channel to what he wanted to transmit. In the sonic domain, for example, he nearly succeeded, but not without a considerable expenditure of effort, energy, and *means*. Only recently has he reexamined the problem from the viewpoint of the quantity of information to be transmitted. One goal of this book is to examine to what extent this viewpoint is justified. Assuming that communication between individuals aims effectively at transmitting information, the question then becomes one of determining the exact nature of information, the repertoire, and the repertoire's elements.

Our sketch of the transmitter is inadequate. While it is rather well fitted to a transmitting system such as a telephotograph, a teletype, etc., it is too rudimentary for the study of language. It supposes that the transmitter chooses symbols from an infinite case.

We have just seen that most messages cannot be characterized by probabilities of *mutually independent* symbols. Rather, the probability of a symbol depends on the preceding symbols in the sequence. In French the probability that the letter q will be followed by the letter u is very close to unity, $(30{,}000 - 3)/30{,}000 \cong 1$; that is, it is nearly certain, since words in which the letter q is followed by a letter other than u are extremely rare (*coq, cinq, Iraq*). Similarly, in a painted picture, if we choose randomly a point of angular dimensions approximating the retinal element, the odds are very high that the shade of the immediately adjacent element is extremely close to the shade of the first element. Viewed on this scale, a picture is composed of a great number of colored surfaces of flat shades. On a higher scale, these appear to us as the elementary touches of the paintbrush.

The choice of successive elements of the message is a Markoff chain process. In successive approximations, we follow the probabilities of the different symbols p_i, p_j, . . . , with the digram probabilities p_{ij}, p_{jk}, . . . , then the trigram probabilities p_{ijk}, p_{jkl}, ... On the whole, these probabilities become smaller and smaller for messages composed of finite numbers of symbols, as soon as the n-grams attain several elements, even if there are occasional exceptions.

A collection of five letters corresponding to a very frequent word (for example, -yes-, -the-, -are-, -when) may have a very high probability, but the average p_{ijklm} [page 59] remains very small, because one must consider not only this particular 5-gram but also 5-grams composed of the four characters "the-" (counting the space) and a fifth letter coming from the following word, and that word is nearly arbitrary.

In the simple case of two successive symbols i and j, it is easy to see that the uncertainty of the combined event ij is the uncertainty of i plus the uncertainty of j when i is known. Thus,

$$H(ij) = H(i) + H_i(j) = -\sum_{i}^{n} p_i \log_2 p_i - \sum_{i,j=1}^{n,m} p_i(j) \log p_i(j).$$

Since the digram probabilities $p(ij)$ and the monogram probabilities p_i may be found, one can determine the variation of information due to the digram liaisons between symbols. Introducing combined probabilities permits us to estimate the redundancy due to liaisons.

A particular redundancy is connected with each level of coding used. According to the viewpoint that we pick, we can consider a printed page as a drawing in black and white (artist's viewpoint); as a collection of letters (typographer's viewpoint); as a collection of words (reader's viewpoint); as a collection of printed blocks (page compositor's viewpoint). In each case its repertoire of symbols is different. In the first case it is reduced to two: a white spot or a black spot. In the second, it extends to the some 200 typographical signs; in the third, to some 30,000 words; in the last, to the usual dimensions of typographical columns which form a "repertoire" well known to professional printers. For each of these messages, redundancy is a function of the statistical laws governing the collection of symbols and hence governing each of the "languages" considered.

The extent of the interaction between elements of the repertoire (as reflected by n-gram probabilities) characterizes the receptor's knowledge of the language. It determines the redundancy for him. [page 60] Excluding technological channels where the receptor and transmitter are perfectly and objectively defined, there is no a priori unique information output in communications between individuals. The real information depends on the common knowledge of the transmitter and receptor. Here again we have the notion of a sociocultural matrix A_{mn} between two individuals m and n which determines the real information that they exchange in a message.

The concept of a social-communication matrix is an important

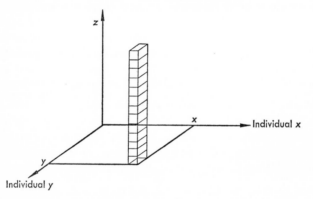

Fig. I-8.

extension to the concept of communication. The basis of the communication concept, as established by Wiener, Shannon, and others, was the existence of a "common" repertoire for an ensemble of senders and receivers, each sharing the same a priori knowledge of their language. Now the same scheme of communication is applied to an ensemble of just two individuals, the sender and the receiver, who share a restricted repertoire taken out of a larger one.

We could define this repertoire in a three-dimensional representation: At the point (x, y) representing the pair of individuals, the repertoire is given as a set of elements ordered along dimension z according to decreasing probabilities of occurrence in the entire set of past messages exchanged between x and y. The focus of attention for communication studies shifts from the process of communication to repertoires. One could distinguish in the ensemble of repertoires, corresponding to the ensemble of pairs, $(x, y) =$ (transmitter, receiver), a part (that situated near the (x, y) plane, if the elements are ordered in decreasing frequency) which is nearly the same for every (x, y) inside definite bounds for (x, y), that is, the ensemble of English-speaking people, the ensemble of people having a high-school education, etc. One could then distinguish the sort of repertoire which could be called the "personal repertoire" and base on it a "personal information." (See Fig. I-8.)

We have rediscovered here what could be predicted from the sociology of culture, that the measure of information varies with the course the message must travel. Assuming "high-fidelity" and complete transmission, information is a variable quantity depending on the point of departure m and of arrival n of the message in the sociocultural field, and on the intermediate subjects which transmit it.

If x informs y of an "interesting" sentence via intermediaries, the original interest of this sentence depends only on x and y. It does not depend on the personal knowledge of the intermediaries, who may find the message banal or original as they please, provided that they do not change it.

In practice, the study of messages deals principally with the probabilities p_i of the symbols, and less frequently with the digram probabilities p_{ij}. The latter represent a statistical *base* for "all analogous messages"; arguments based on them are valid a fortiori for a more differentiated, more subtle study of the "language" used in the channel considered — whether it be musical, phonetic, literary, or pictorial. The precise search for the supplementary redundancy resulting from each receptor's individual knowledge about messages of a given category will arise only *in fine* in a "differential theory" of information, in the sense of a sociological differential psychology. (Cf. K. Lewin's theory of the social field.)

The main idea of this chapter is that information is a *measurable* quantity, independent of the particular message considered, susceptible to statistical treatment. In the following chapters we shall adopt the basic viewpoint of a standardized human receptor. This assumption will permit us to draw conclusions by analogy with technological receptors and still leave us free to revise these conclusions in a differential theory.

15. CONCLUSIONS

[page 61] In this chapter we have tried to present the foundations of information theory as it stands currently, in its most dogmatic form.

1. The behavior of individuals is determined by messages from

their environment. Messages are complex forms arising from a sequence of elements chosen from a *repertoire*.

2. In elementary psychology we recognize only the immediate messages coming from the immediate *Umwelt* (von Uexküll, 1934). Besides them, we must distinguish distant messages in time or space which come into the environment by means of spatial channels (for example, transmission) or temporal channels (for example, recording).

3. The psychophysiological properties of the receptor define the elementary structure of a message, as far as the individual's ulterior reactions are concerned.

4. One may create a correspondence between spatial and temporal messages by scanning, that is, by going through a spatial structure in a given order.

5. *Messages* are measured by a *quantity of information* which is the originality, that is, the quantity of unpredictability (unforeseeability) that they present.

6. This originality of information is expressed by the logarithm of the number of possible messages having the same apparent structure among which the transmitter has had to *choose*.

7. A message of N elements chosen from a repertoire of n symbols with probabilities p_i of occurrence has an information H in bits:

$$H = -N \sum_{i=1}^{n} p_i \log_2 p_i.$$

8. The output of information is maximal $H_{\max}$ for a given number of symbols if in the "language" defined by the repertoire and by the usage of the channel's transmitter — ultimately the individual — each symbol is equiprobable.

9. Information is hence a *quantity* essentially different from *meaning* or *signification* and independent of the latter. A message of maximum information may appear senseless if the individual cannot *decode* it in order to make it intelligible. Generally speaking, intelligibility varies inversely as information.

[page 62] 10. Information appears to be a measure of the *complexity* of the patterns of perception. Complexity of structure, and information of a form or of a message, may be taken as synonymous.

11. Redundancy is the quantity $1 - (H/H_{\max})$. It expresses what is *superfluous* in the message, the waste of symbols caused by defective coding, at least from the viewpoint of transmission efficiency. Redundancy furnishes a guarantee against errors in transmission, since it permits the receptor to reconstruct the message even if some

of its elements are lacking on the basis of his a priori knowledge of the structure of the language.

12. The redundancy and information furnished by a given type of message are, by definition, independent of the particular extract of the message chosen. They do depend on the common knowledge shared by the receptor and transmitter. This introduces the idea of a *differential information*, at least in the case of human receptors.

13. It is always possible to define an average receptor by the same method used in psychology to define the normal characters of the individual. Here we could use the method more validly, because the theory considers more elementary aptitudes: basic knowledge of a language, of a system of thought.

14. In short, to construct an "information theory" of a given system of communication, one must fulfill the following requisites, which delineate a *method:*

(a) Define a "situation of communication," that is, a channel and a level of observation adopted by the experimenter toward the pair: transmitter, receiver. This is a problem of situational psychology.

(b) Find the nature and state the repertoire (sign-set) corresponding to this situation. This is a problem of behavioral psychology.

(c) Through statistical study, find the probabilities of occurrence (expectancy) of each element of the repertoire.

(d) Through experimental modification of the message, compute its redundancy and try to account for redundancy in terms of constraints upon the transmitter's freedom of choice.

(e) Sum up these various rules constituting the code as the whole of the laws of assemblage known a priori to receiver and transmitter.

The exposition of doctrine in this chapter may arouse various criticisms, which fall into two categories:

(1) Criticisms of the roughness and lack of rigor of the numerous hypotheses of the theory and of the examples chosen to establish the arguments. We shall consider them minor and shall neglect them. The very essence of information theory consists in cutting through the complexity of reality to find an intelligible conception, hence, to schematize reality; like any new theory, information theory is presented as a *thesis* and does not claim universal validity.

(2) Criticisms of the very concepts invoked: code, originality and signification, redundancy.

The latter are very important. To them we shall devote the following chapters.

The Concept of Form in Information Theory: Periodicity and Elementary Structures

Remember that a picture, before it is a battle horse, a nude, or some anecdote, is essentially a plane surface covered with colors assembled in a certain order.

MAURICE DENIS

The objective of this chapter is to develop information theory by enlarging it to fit more closely to the complexity of reality. Developed as a physicomathematical theory for application to material systems, information theory is often presented with a dogmatic rigidity which makes it obviously inadequate when we want to apply it to the human receptor, that is, to problems of perception.

In its elementary form, it is atomistic. It considers the individual receptor as a scanning apparatus. While this is very practical and generally justified for the psychophysiologist, it deliberately rejects just those aspects of perceptual reality which are considered by theories of the whole or aggregate (*Gestalt* theories). It would be presumptuous to assume that all psychology can be reduced to psychophysiology, even as a working hypothesis, and we find in this conflict one of the dialectical oppositions which divide experimental psychology. Can information theory go beyond this opposition?

1. THEORIES OF FORM AND THEORIES OF SCANNING

The two theories, one of *scanning* and one of *form*, claim to give two conceptions of our perception of the external world. They are what recent philosophy calls "structuralist" and "dialectical" points of view. Superficially, they are contradictory. The first describes perception as an integrated *scanning*. It finds analogies to vision in the scanning apparatus of television cameras combined with memory systems. [page 64] Developed by the psychophysiologists, the theory continually finds new experimental confirmation. For example, recent results of electroencephalography strongly support the hypothesis of a cerebral scanning of the visual field (Walter, 1953); they verify that while the diffuse visual field is very extended, the *efficacious* visual field on which our attention concentrates is very restricted. Otherwise we would not have to move our eyes to read a page.

Integral theories, derived from theories of form, have the advantage of one piece of evidence: It is impossible to deny that we perceive a letter or an ideogram in its totality. But we know that, even in the cases most favorable to these theories (vision of a picture or movie screen), the process of scanning intervenes very rapidly when we want to perceive exhaustively and to memorize. Besides, while the terms *Gestalt* and form are based on fact, they tell us very little about the details of the phenomena subjacent to perception. By *form* (*Gestalt*) we mean here a group of elements perceived as a whole and *not* as the product of a random collection. More precisely, a form is a message which appears to the observer as *not* being the result of random events. One should notice that this negative definition implies (a) reference to an observer, that is, a subjective aspect of forms, and (b) the hypothesis that the concept of random event is known a priori, which fits with the psychology of probability (Borel, Cournot).

Both theories are supported by incontestable facts. However they may evolve, it seems that, in one way or another, a synthesis must occur between them. Even if this synthesis is not achieved, the concept of quantity of information introduced in the preceding chapter suggests a border to the reciprocal fields of validity of these two theories. Indeed, it is conceivable that the scope of application of the *Gestalt* in vision may be measured exactly, neither by an angular field of vision nor by the minimum temporal interval for achieving exhaustive perception, but rather by the *quantity of visual information* received per unit of time.

Further, the preceding theory gives us, among other things, the means of calculating the channel capacity using the number N of effectively apprehended elements in the visual field. N is obtained from an expression of the type:

$$N = \int_0^{\Omega_m} \frac{L}{L_0} \, (\Omega) \; d\left(\frac{\Omega}{\Omega_0}\right),$$

where Ω is the solid-angular dimension of the element, Ω_0 is the angular resolving power, Ω_m is the maximum solid angle of vision, L is the contrast, and L_0 is the contrast discrimination power. For the sake of simplicity, this expression ignores depth and color.

The length of the present represents the temporal limit Θ_0 on "simultaneous" apprehension of elements of perception. We may say hypothetically that the theory of form is valid when apprehension of a form occurs within the interval Θ_0. In other words, [page 65] we will say that, even if there is a retinal or cerebral scanning mechanism, our perception of forms gives us no conscious knowledge of it.

Another hypothesis will be of frequent use, and it has found repeated experimental justification (Hick, Bruner, Miller, Frank). We assume that within the interval Θ_0, which the individual considers infinitesimal, and which is in any case irreducible, the individual can apprehend only a *limited* number N_0 of elements. If the picture presented to him contains a clearly larger number, he will no longer apprehend it *in toto* but rather by scanning. Thus for $N < N_0$ the theory of form is at first sight valid, at least as a hypothesis, that is, without in any way prejudicing the real psychophysiological mechanism in action. For $N > N_0$ the theory of scanning, more or less elaborated, is at first sight the most valid. In the analysis of perception one finds some kind of scanning mechanism, and the perception of the visual field requires an interval Θ which is a multiple of Θ_0.

The overly simple hypothesis presented here does not permit us to predict this interval Θ, because we still do not know the instantaneous extent of the perceiving subject's interest, and we need that in order to have an idea of the manner in which he scans the image presented to him. Estimating Θ is particularly complicated since his interest depends precisely on what he finds in the image. One can simply remark that there are numerous special cases.

In one special case, the subject has a limited time to look. In experimental psychophysiology, tachistoscope pictures may be suddenly lighted; in everyday life, a glance may have to determine a rapid reaction (for example, in driving an automobile or flying an airplane).

At the other extreme, there are cases where the subject must scan a visual field thoroughly, as in, for example, certain attention tests or descriptions of pictures. In these cases the subject tries methodically to assimilate the whole field. The variable of interest is thus eliminated, since everything is a priori equally interesting.

In the last case, a major simplification is introduced when the scale of discriminated contrasts $L(\Omega)$ reduces to two values through infinite clipping or because the signal is binary. The expression for N then reduces simply to the number of instantaneously appreciated elements, as in the case of reading a manuscript or printed text. Works on the reading of ideograms and on the speed of apprehending typographical characters as a function of their size (see Woodworth and Schlosberg, 1954) show the existence of a proportionality relation between the scanning time and the exhaustion of the perceived field. This indirectly confirms on one hand the preceding remark and on the other [page 66] the application of information theory to the visual field and to reading. The works mentioned reveal the superiority of ideographic systems of writing, which make better use than alphabetic systems of our capacities for total apprehension of the form of ideograms. They convey more meaning in a single symbol — whatever their other disadvantages may be.

2. LIMITS ON THE FLOW OF PERCEPTIBLE INFORMATION

Limiting the receptor's channel capacity simply interprets precisely the banal fact that we spend more time getting to know a complicated drawing than a caricature of three strokes; we take longer to explore a painting of Hieronymus Bosch than to perceive a portrait of Philippe de Champaigne. The interest of the preceding description is that it makes this fact accessible to measurement and connects it with a collection of experiments in very diverse fields.

By considering the individual as a receptor of information and by limiting the flow of signals that he can receive, one can limit the flow of *quantities of originality* to the receptor.

Practically, this remark is axiomatic; it acts as one of the fundamental laws of perception. If one assumes that psychology is an objective science, obeying general laws as enunciated in the Introduction, it would be a priori absurd to suppose that the individual — a psychophysiological mechanism — could instantaneously absorb an unlimited quantity of information. Such an assumption would immediately lead to numerous paradoxes. The individual would then be omniscient, since the only limit on the information he could absorb from the external world would be the information that it could furnish him. Such an individual would instantaneously perceive the entirety of a geographic map in its tiniest details. He would be able to apprehend a page of an encyclopedia in a single glance, etc. To avoid these paradoxes, one is led to assume axiomatically that the individual possesses an *upper limit to the apprehension of information* per "elementary instant" [page 67] (length of the present). If this "length of the present" may be considered constant, one supposes that a *maximum flow of perceptible information* per unit of time exists.

In most cases, this maximum flow of perceptible information is very much lower than the output of the surrounding sources (visual, aural, or tactile). In other words, we make use of only an infinitesimal fraction of the information which reaches us from the external world — a trivial fact in psychology. The most recent works on the human operator seem to show that this limit of apprehensibility is on the order of 10 to 20 bits per second (Quastler, 1955). H. Frank has made a thorough collection of various figures available on this subject; he showed that in most cases where one would appear to find higher raw figures, one could, on closer examination, find standard mechanisms to account for a seemingly higher output of information.

Adaptation to the environment, learning from the environment, consists precisely in being able to *select* from the complex and redundant messages of the environment a few elements assembled so as to provide for constant control over the external world. We shall try to determine (Chap. III) how this selection proceeds and what rules it obeys. *To perceive is to select;* to apprehend the world is to learn the rules of perceptual selection.

3. FORM AS DESTRUCTIVE OF INFORMATION: THE MESSAGE MOST DIFFICULT TO TRANSMIT

In the operation of choice arises the concept of form: abstraction from the complexity of reality. To progress in studying the selection performed by the individual, we must take advantage of the explication offered by *Gestalt* theories.

Any form, *Gestalt*, is the first element of a structure and as such expresses the ascendancy of the intelligible over the perceptible. To make this fact clear, we shall first state precisely the need for elementary structuring of the perceptual field. In the theoretical interpretation followed here, we shall do this by examining, as a consequence of the notion of maximum information, the correlative concept of the *message most difficult to transmit.*

The above theory tells us that the message carrying the most information and hence the most difficult to transmit is one which reduces its symbols to the elements just perceptible by the receptor, that is, it adapts to the channel. For example, if the receptor is a human being and the message affects the visual channel, the message will be a cross-ruled halftone screen of elements whose areas, at the normal angle of vision, approximate those of the separable spatial elements (Chap. I). The values of these elements will cover the whole scale of contrasts that human photosensitive elements can discriminate. The message most difficult to transmit is also that which, from the receptor's viewpoint, has no a priori foreseeable order in [page 68] the values of the successive elements. The probabilities of the elements will all be equal ($H = H_{max}$).

Such is the (visual) message most difficult to transmit, which makes the most extensive use of the capacities of our ocular channel. (We leave aside, for the sake of simplicity, the extension to colored messages.)

We know well what this message will look like (for example, on a television screen). It will appear to us like a gray, perpetually agitated, foggy undulation with little, capricious, constantly changing outlines. In over-all appearance, it will be *indistinguishable* from *background noise*, with a uniform probability distribution for its elements. It loses all interest because it lacks intelligible meaning.

We have here a paradox analogous to the ninth example (Chap. I, Sec. 5) whose unit symbols, words, are composed in no apparent order. This paradox arises because the message contains too much information, because it exceeds our capacity for understanding and creates boredom.

To explain this paradox, we shall try first to view the question differently. We note that such a message appears indistinguishable from background noise, that is, from a senseless, anarchic phenomenon, because the receptor is unaware of the intentions of the transmitter. This apparent noise is *here* a *special* message to be transmitted. It cannot be replaced by an approximation or by an analog; its authenticity (integrity) must be respected. While it is very easy to make up a message having perceptibly the same appearance as this special one, it is very difficult — most difficult — to reproduce this particular one *exactly,* with each black and white spot at the proper place at the proper instant; if the message happens to be degraded or destroyed in the course of the transmission, it is irremediably lost. The reason is that the receptor has no a priori knowledge about its perpetually evanescent structure; the message has no redundancy. Thus, this special message, most difficult to transmit, although the easiest to render approximately, is at the same time *the most fragile*. It contains no n-gram liaisons which permit the receptor to guess, practically, what will follow on the basis of what has preceded.

Though this message is totally uninteresting for the indifferent eye, it is no longer so if the receptor knows a priori that the arrangement of the points and lines of each square centimeter in it carries a secret message, decipherable by some known process. Similarly, a cryptogram often appears as a disordered collection of letters, the most uninteresting message for the uninitiated, but for utilitarian reasons it carries a considerable rate of information, mixed up by a complicated process; for the forewarned cryptographer, [page 69] it is more interesting than any sentence in clear language. (In statistical psychology, one finds an analogy: The perfectly average individual, that is, one having the set of most probable characteristics, is the *rarest* of individuals.)

This particular message, taken among all other possible analogs, is "interesting" only if it is declared a priori interesting and if we *know how to organize it*. In no way does it capture our attention spontaneously; it lacks esthetic value completely, because it does not appeal at all to the natural capacities of the receiving *individual*. It interests only translating or decoding machines. In the theoretical sense, this absence of natural meaning is connected with an overly large flow of information; in the current psycho-esthetic sense, with the absence of *structure*, that is, of internal organization. Hence, absence of structure or internal organization is connected with too large a flow of information. In fact, the absence of structure, of apparent organization, is equivalent to too large a rate of original information; in the same way, a postcard of a wide view, no matter how clear it may be, affects us less than a prominent foreground and a characteristic view taken by a talented photographer.

Corroborating the preceding results, we see that all intelligent perception is opposed to scanning pure and simple. Such perception may even eliminate scanning in favor of the organized human mode of perception, which uses a priori knowledge about the message. We have seen that *redundancy* measures this knowledge, expressing statistically how much excess is transmitted.

The *maximum information capacity* of a channel is a limit attained only for a receptor who is totally ignorant of what might be transmitted to him, for whom all symbols are equiprobable — the case in general of technical channels. The real information transmitted to any particular receptor A is always lower. The receptor's a priori knowledge establishes a network of probabilities $(\Sigma\ p_i)_A$ *unique* to him. As a function of A's knowledge, the message supplies a certain residual amount of information; this particular residual amount is what A "learns" from the message.

The socio-matrix of communication $||A_{ij}||$ designates the repertoire of signs known to individuals i and j. In the practice of human communication, $||A_{ij}||$ always has a part $||A_0||$ common to an ensemble of people who are thus defined as a group. We then have:

$$||A_{ij}|| = ||A_0|| + ||A_{ij}^*||.$$

As we particularize the subject A, that is, as an observer identifies the characteristics of the receptor A, as he gets to know A's intellectual, cultural, and social structure, the information decreases from its possible maximum; the information tends progressively to zero or to a very low value (cf. Chap. V, Sec. 1).

This is expressed in the following scheme. By particularizing the considered receptor more and more, this scheme decreases the information from the theoretical value that it would have for a "receiving machine" to a real value, clearly much lower. (See p. 64.)

[page 70] The interest of this scheme is that each level in the hierarchy brings into play *new forms*, structures which may be widely different. At the beginning, the *symbol* results from the mere set of elements. Then patterns of symbols, organisms, appear as *supersymbols*. Then again these latter group together in a stereotyped way, building another set, and so on. Just as a word is a supersymbol of letters, so is a grammatical rule a supersymbol of words.

In fact, symbols and rules of organization play the same role; both contribute to defining a repertoire. A symbol is a constant mode of grouping subelements which is known a priori; a rule defines a set of collections following the rule. Each is the mark of intelligibility which opposes information in the dipoles:

Foreseeable	$\longleftrightarrow$	Unforeseeable
Intelligible	$\longleftrightarrow$	Informative
Banal	$\longleftrightarrow$	Original

Thus, the concept of symbol is intimately connected to that of form. The concept of intelligibility [page 71] or of signification becomes explicit through this connection. The study of signification

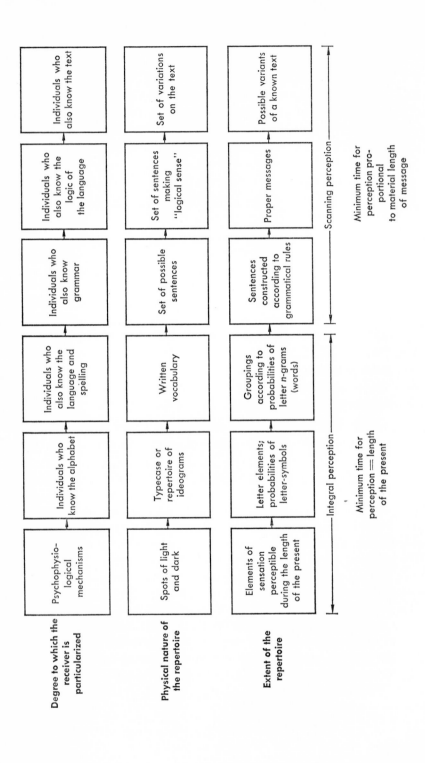

Degree to which the receiver is particularized	Psychophysio-logical mechanisms	Individuals who know the alphabet	Individuals who also know the language and spelling	Individuals who also know grammar	Individuals who also know the logic of the language	Individuals who also know the text
Physical nature of the repertoire	Spots of light and dark	Typecase or repertoire of ideograms	Written vocabulary	Set of possible sentences	Set of sentences making "logical sense"	Set of variations on the text
Extent of the repertoire	Elements of sensation perceptible during the length of the present	Letter elements; probabilities of letter-symbols	Groupings according to probabilities of letter n-grams (words)	Sentences constructed according to grammatical rules	Proper messages	Possible variants of a known text

Integral perception

Scanning perception

Minimum time for perception = length of the present

Minimum time for perception proportional to material length of message then is essentially a study of *symbolism,* an idea advanced independently of information theory by Langer (1957).

Obviously, we are dealing here with a study of tremendous scope. For centuries this field has been the domain of formal logic, yet without great profit to the search for "the meaning of meaning," in Ogden's clever formulation. Information theory is too recent to furnish substantial results here.

4. FORMS AND PREDICTIONS

Until now, form has been one of the most confused concepts in psychology. In the most elementary cases that we can imagine, it would, however, be interesting to discover how the concept of form may be conceived on the preceding basis. Very elementary perception of forms is probably expected of artificial channels.

To create an elementary form is to assure in the message a redundancy, an at least statistical foreseeability. In other words, to foresee means to see beforehand. Foreseeability is the receptor's capacity to know, as the message unfolds in time or space, what will follow on the basis of what has been transmitted; it is the capacity to extrapolate the temporal or spatial series of message elements (cf. Wiener's work), to imagine the future of a phenomenon on the basis of its past.

Since this foreseeability evidently can be only statistical, it is not absolute, but has a quantitative aspect: There is a *degree of predictability,* which is exactly the message's *degree of coherence,* the proportion of regularity. If we interrupt transmission of a message to a receiving subject, the existence of a form or structure expresses the subject's capacity to reconstruct what is to follow, at least approximately, to *extrapolate* to the succeeding part of the message. Thus, foreseeability is a statistical liaison between the past and the future. It expresses a coherence, a *correlation,* between what has happened up to time t and what will happen at time $t + \tau$.

Mathematicians (and particularly, Wiener, one of the creators of information theory) express this correlation precisely by the *autocorrelation function.* This is a function of the interval over which the considered foreseeability extends. If $f(t)$ represents the element of the message at time t, and $f(t + \tau)$ represents the message element at the future time $t + \tau$, then this function is simply the mean value of the product $f(t)f(t + \tau)$. Thus,

$$F(\tau) = \int_0^\infty f(t)\, f(t + \tau)\, dt$$

[page 72] or

$$F(\varsigma) = \int_0^\infty f(z)\, f(z + \varsigma)\, dz$$

depending on whether we examine the message developing in time t or in space z, τ and ζ being the interval or the distance between the correlated points.

Practically, correlating what occurs at time t with what occurs at the later instant $t + \tau$ requires the simultaneous existence in some place of $f(t)$ and of $f(t + \tau)$, that is, of some kind of recording device to compare $f(t + \tau)$ and $f(t)$. This is the functional definition of a *memory*.

From the viewpoint of scientific methodology, it is interesting to note that the concept of memory, a product of the sciences of man and particularly of psychology, has been able to penetrate the physicochemical sciences only with the technological progress of recording systems.

The concept of mean autocorrelation is very important in all statistical phenomena, because it expresses their internal coherence, hence their tendency to become structures. The autocorrelation function is zero for a perfectly disordered phenomenon and tends to either ± 1 for a perfectly ordered, that is, indefinitely foreseeable, phenomenon.

If the form of a phenomenon is related to its autocorrelation, reciprocally the information content of the message must be a function of autocorrelation.

This is Neidhart's (1957) formula:

$$H_{\max(\text{actual})} = H_{\max(\text{theoretical})} + \tfrac{1}{2} \log_2 (1 - k)$$

where k is the autocorrelation coefficient, that is, the mean value of the autocorrelation spectrum.

5. PERIODICITY AND PREDICTABILITY

As an example of how an ordered phenomenon tends to give rise to *forms*, let us consider periodicity, which plays a very large role in temporal messages such as music and speech. The pitch, rhythm, and every other temporal structure of a sound emerge from periodicity.

Mathematicians say that a phenomenon is periodic when it repeats itself at the end of an interval of time, called the period, or of space, called the wavelength. A considerable number of works have been based on this definition. Indeed, knowledge of a phenomenon within its period is sufficient to predict its behavior indefinitely and to know it completely. Such a definition of periodicity is suited to temporal (or spatial) interpolation or extrapolation.

This definition is not entirely satisfactory even in the natural sciences. Its fundamentally excessive dogmatism leads to numerous paradoxes. Thus, in Fourier analysis, there exist "components" and negative frequencies; in extending Fourier's integral to nonperiodic phenomena, there are harmonic "components" which precede in time the phenomenon itself. These creations of the mind [page 73] suddenly congeal to become material entities which can be measured by experiment.

Awareness that a message is periodic, plus knowledge of a single period, make the information furnished by the message tend to zero. (Cf. the first example of texts of increasing information in Chap. I: repeated letters BABABABABA.)

Historically, the natural sciences adopted this definition of periodicity because of its simplicity. Studies of musical tones, for example, were oriented by mathematical works on perfect periodicity. They assumed implicitly that musical tones had neither beginning nor end, that the sun neither rose nor set, that the waves of the sea never changed, that events remained indefinitely stable. In the case of attacks, the Fourier integral reduced a pizzicato note to a sum of periodic phenomena by the introduction of transients. In this case and in the modulation process, the simple theory decidedly did not furnish correct numerical results, but it was assumed that while some corrections might be necessary, they were secondary to the essential affirmation: "Let us consider the phenomenon as a periodic function of time. . . ."

Psychological experience of the external world teaches us exactly the opposite. What characterizes a musical tone and what differentiates it from an oscillator tone of the same pitch is precisely the fact that it has a beginning and an end.

The intelligible substance of speech is the modulation of nearly periodic phenomena which constitute it, "filling out" its form. The temporal form of the fluctuations conveys the message through consonants and vowels: Our ear grasps the microscopic periodicity of sound no more directly than does our eye directly perceive the wave nature of light. The scale itself creates the phenomenon; the vibrations of a musical tone are much too short (for example, 1/256 second) to be in our perceptual field. Only recording, oscillography, or mathematical theory can reveal to us the subjacent, hidden periodicity. In phenomenological experience, the "substance" of a musical tone is a "stuff" of which we grasp immediately only the beginning, the duration, the variations, and the end.

In short, periodicity appears only in phenomena on our temporal scale. It disappears when the rhythms become more rapid than 16 to 20 per second (as in the movies or in "musical" sounds), precisely at the moment where, for technological and historical reasons, the [page 74] exact sciences see it appear. We know that the essence of the moving picture for us is *continuity*, not the periodicity which concerns only the engineer or technician. The phenomenological approach here opposes the scientific approach a priori, for it suggests to us the concept of the length of the present — the perceptual threshold of duration.

We have measured the length of the present rather precisely by the following process of degrading temporal forms. We take a melody with rather simple intervals (fifths, fourths, thirds, octaves) and several rather short notes (thirty-second and sixty-fourth notes). After recording this fragment, several seconds long, on a tape loop, we repeat it to hearers at progressively increasing speeds. At some point this form is degraded. The briefest intervals of time modulation (sixty-fourth notes) dissolve and disappear; they mix with what precedes and follows. Then the thirty-second notes disappear, etc. The speed at which the form dissolves gives the perceptual threshold of sonic duration: 1/15 to 1/20 second.

Phenomena perceptible on the human scale suggest the concept of periodicity. When it is *regular* (isochronous), *repetition* leads to the concept of rhythm. Repetition opposes multiplicity to unicity; it impresses on the mind the *possibility* of multiple occurrences without suggesting the concept of periodicity. A completely irregular repetition provokes no *expectation:*

unicity	→ repetition	→ isochronism	→ periodicity
unforeseeable	possible but unforeseeable	statistically foreseeable	foreseeable

As soon as it is perceptible as such, the appearance of an isochronism, no matter how approximate, creates *expectation*, an essential condition of foreseeability. Our experiments suggest that the duration of intervals may vary by a factor of from one to two. The concept of rhythm is connected with that of expectation; the criterion of rhythm is that after an event one *expects* the following one.

However, in this psychological reconstruction of the concept of periodicity, it is essential to note that the looking forward is not certainty but expectation. More precisely, it is a *wager* based on a preceding series. At each instant, the individual subjected to the rhythm bets that at the end of nearly the same interval of the time, the event will occur again. His bet is based on a mathematical expectation, which is an increasing function of the number of elements already produced. That this expectation is not certainty implies that the looking forward will be disappointed at some time or other; there is no reason for the phenomenon — whatever it may be — to last indefinitely, but there is every reason to assume that it will stop, for in the natural sciences there is no infinity. [page 75] Even if it is progressively extinguished, the notion of rhythm is still not destroyed.

Infinite duration, the ultimate element of periodicity, is a supplementary and perfectly abstract condition, since it is never experienced. In physical experiments, it is only a limit, an asymptote, an ideal condition, as is the condition that successive events repeat themselves identically and at *equal* intervals. None of these conditions is essential to the perception of rhythm.

Thus, on the basis of phenomenological experience we view the mathematical concept of periodicity as a limit only rarely approached by perception. But historically, in rational formalism this dogmatic concept appeared in its absolute form; only after conflicts with experience did it become more tractable (for example, with the introduction of pseudo-periodic, quasi-periodic, and transient functions). This last procedure has been followed in the history of science to the detriment of *agreement between theory and perception*.

The phenomenological viewpoint presented here has emerged only recently. Instead of taking periodicity as given, it considers foreseeability as a quantitative factor, as an estimate of the mathematical expectation of forthcoming events in a series. Hence it is concerned with the extrapolation of temporal series into the future.

We are led to the notion of *degree of periodicity* to express the foreseeability, that is, temporal structuring, of a phenomenon having a fixed range of values. Periodicity, or elementary temporal form, is the mathematical expectation of knowing what will occur on the basis of what has already occurred; it is the autocorrelation between the past and the future. More precisely, we replace the classical definition of periodicity by the following: The "periodicity" of a time-limited function (or of any variable whatever) is the mathematical expectation of knowing its coming evolution on the basis of its past evolution.

The amount of periodicity is then a *degree of order* in temporal organization. Isochronism is the quantitative resemblance of the successive events which mark rhythm.

The very existence of a temporal form would then appear measurable, quantitatively apprehensible. The autocorrelation function and the degree of periodicity are each connected with the mathematical expectation, with the intensity and the certainty of the expectation expressing perception of a rhythm.

From this discussion, it appears that if we wish [page 76] our theory to adhere to the perceived, that is, to express its modalities immediately, we must approach the concept of periodicity as an ideal limit to the organization of forms; we must insist on the real cases, where periodicity is only partial, incomplete, or approximate, before developing the ideal cases.

6. PHENOMENOLOGY OF THE PERCEPTION OF PERIODICITY

When a message is received, the certainty of the wager that coming elements will be grouped like elements already transmitted increases with the number of past events; the receptor extrapolates into the future according to a law established with growing certainty. Logical theories of probability suppose that a *law* appears only when a sufficient number of previous *points* has been established. In fact, the human receptor is much less prudent; he predicts on the basis of data that the statistician would consider entirely inadequate.

Suppose we have subjects listen to series of sonic events: thuds, musical notes, etc., separated by delays, on the order of a second, which permit us to ask a simple question without interrupting the progress of the experiment. Certain series will be perfectly disordered in time: simple, repeated events, absolutely nonperiodic. We interpolate them between clearly rhythmical series with extremely variable numbers of events in order to create a priori uncertainty. We may then try to find the minimum number of rhythmical events which the subject's mind requires to establish a presumption, no matter how rough it may be, about the periodicity of the series, or more precisely, the number of events in the series for which more than 50 per cent of the subjects incline to a presumption of periodicity.

We find then that this number is extremely low, surely lower than five; actually, it is on the order of three to four events. Thus, it is sufficient for an event to be reproduced isochronously three to four times in order to give the mind of a perceiving subject an expectation of a following event, that is, to awaken to the concept of periodicity. Though the human mind catches sight of the foreseeability of events much sooner than the rigorous statistical theory of samplings considers valid, certain theories of intuitive reasoning make a wager of periodicity on a short series of events. Intuition may often be regarded as a statistical conclusion drawn from a very small sampling.

This simple experiment calls for several comments. Among the many possible sources of error in it is suggestion, which could seriously vitiate its validity if its results were not confirmed by diverse other sources. However, the minimum number of repetitions of a musical theme in a score intended to suggest repetition coincides with the number found in this experiment; again, the number of bars necessary to establish a rhythm at the beginning of a musical score agrees with the number found experimentally.

Other remarks ought to deal with the nature of the event (here sonic) used. We shall leave them aside, noting simply that the most unadorned dull thud is more evocative than a complex or evolving phenomenon, not to [page 77] mention musical structures properly called, which would require a special study because of the interference of internal rhythms.

The amplitude of successive events seems the most independent factor. Very large relative changes in amplitude (10 to 20 dB) scarcely interfere with the subject's eventual perception of a rhythm, save perhaps when there are only three or four events. The event seems to be conceived simply as marking off intervals of time; it does not attract much interest itself, if it is brusque, fully detached, and keeps its specificity (for example, a radio pip with infinite spectrum).

Thus the temporal variable is really the fundamental element of rhythm. This has been confirmed by all psychologists concerned with the question.

An essential factor in the perception of periodicity, which goes beyond the framework of the experiment cited above, is the *period* between two events. We know that below around 0.1 second, the phenomenon of repetition dissolves into continuity and the concept of periodicity vanishes. We know, moreover, that very long periodicities are not perceived as such by the human mind: Recall the difficulty of young children in grasping the concept of annual periodicity. Experiments performed with visual or sonic events seem to show that with a period longer than five to ten seconds, the perception of periodicity wanes rapidly. The mind does not fix upon the return of the events; it does not expect them anymore. These results corroborate those on the estimation of durations that we reviewed briefly in Chap. I.

The human individual's perception of periodicity is most sensitive around one second. Compare this result with the works on physiological rhythms (Cloudsley-Thompson, 1961).

The isochronism of the period between events is the essential factor in the perception of periodicity. Every rupture of isochronism weakens this perception. Variations in period by a factor of much more than one to two end up by destroying it. Without being absolute, its precision must be such that the fluctuations of period remain below the difference threshold for perception of durations, on the order of 10 per cent.

The statistical study that we have just applied to the simplest of temporal forms, periodicity, has been pursued in the temporal dimension with a view to its application to music, which is periodic in rhythm and in repetition. In the sense of the classical mathematical ideal, music is *not* a periodic phenomenon; it is a phenomenon with a high degree of periodicity. The hidden periodicity of the sounding material plays no phenomenological role, for the auditor perceives it only as a continuous substance (*Klangstoff*), as we have already noticed. Periodicity [page 78] as such here interests only the physicist, who alone, by artificial processes, can make it appear. We shall see in Chap. IV how perception is cognizant of this characteristic of the sonic material, the physically periodic characteristic called harmonicity and pitch, without consciously penetrating to the rhythmic aspect.

From the viewpoint of artificial channels of information transmission, the sonic phenomenon is perfectly periodic during a certain time interval. A tone which is constant and stable for a second may always be considered as the repetition of elementary sounds. This obvious remark, which we shall take up again later (Chap. IV), leads to an application: To transmit a continuous tone by any channel, other than a human being, all one has to do is to transmit first its initial or attack transients, then the beginning of the tone as a sample of what is going to follow, and finally the instruction to keep repeating that sample indefinitely, until a new instruction to terminate the tone arrives. An adequate receiving apparatus following these directions will reconstruct the tone originally emitted.

Though it seems a priori somewhat artificial, this process is rather simple to realize experimentally with the assistance of magnetic tape recordings, which may be cut up at will (Moles, 1956a). We have effectively applied it to speech, which is just a special type of sonic message. Cutting the magnetic tape permits us to manipulate the message easily.

The experiment showed that the attack transients of the phonemes of speech — the consonants — must be left intact, although altogether they represent scarcely 5 per cent of the total duration of speech. But a sampling of only some 10 to 15 per cent of the total length of the vowels was sufficient to leave them perfectly recognizable to the ear. Under these conditions, systematic trials permitted us to eliminate up to 80 per cent of the length of a spoken message, or in other words to accelerate it by a factor of one to five, while keeping it intelligible. This result is important to the theory of language because it furnishes a method of apprehending directly the *redundancy* of spoken language. The sense-carrying elements are hence essentially the consonants; the vowels serve only to support the consonants. Here then is a practical use of predictability: to accelerate speech.

On reception, it is possible under these conditions to perceive speech directly, but a mechanism (the Vocoder system) could return each vowel to its real length on the basis of the vowel sampling, and hence reconstruct the initial speech in apparent integrity (Moles, 1956a).

The operation performed in transmitting the message consists in "wagering," on receiving each sampling of vowel, that this vowel ought to last a certain time. The time may be known, for example, on the basis of language statistics or from orders incorporated in the transmission. This is precisely the definition of statistical periodicity that we gave above.

[page 79] An important application of predictability to the experimental esthetics of the sonic message is the possibility it offers of suppressing part of a sonic signal without altering its character, that is, modifying the length of a signal without changing its pitch, timbre, or spectral contents. Such change would be effected by subtracting or adding surreptitiously samples from its continuous parts and reincorporating them by technical artifices (for example, a tape recorder with several turning heads). The apparatus constructed under the name "Zeitregler" (time regulator) by Schiesser, Springer, and Fairbanks allows expansion or contraction of a musical or phonetic message by ± 30 per cent. This application is important for musical composition and performance since it can adjust the time of a symphony in a film background or of radiobroadcast programs.

A similar analysis would apply in the spatial dimension, where the message elements are distributed in space in a certain, actually arbitrary order. The spatial dimension is connected in any case to the temporal by scanning. Nevertheless, we may study this spatial order independently of temporal periodicity. The latter remains simply the predictability of what follows on the basis of what precedes; it is a statistical, and not absolute, concept.

An experiment analogous to the one cited above would be this: Show subjects varying numbers of parallel, equidistant bars through a frame hiding any continuation of the pattern to the right or left. Ask the subjects, as they look at three, four, five, eight, etc. bars, "How much do you wager that these bars are part of a grill?" This is a one-dimensional periodic lattice. One may predict the results of such an experiment from examining sketches or caricatures representing villages, trees, men, or houses as an element of a scene. In other words, we are asking: "How many trees are needed to make a forest? How many houses to make a city?" The numbers are unbelievably small (four to eight). Logic tells us that the value of a wager made on such a restricted sampling is extremely low; the fact that such wagers pertain to everyday life, that is, that they succeed, throws some doubts on the use of logic over mathematical probability in the psychology of situations.

In space, continuity may also be considered as the particular case of statistical periodicity where the intensity function is constant over contiguous elements. It corresponds to the gesture of the painter filling in a flat color not one dab at a time, but with a broad stroke of the brush.

Though present systems of visual transmission channels — television in particular — rather primitively use a systematic scanning of the points (dots) of a picture, from what we have just seen they might conceivably *make use* of this foreseeability. Thus, there already exist transmitting processes and devices which *predict* from line to line of a picture, [page 80] that is, wager at each instant that line $n + 1$ will on the whole be identical to line n, save for corrections; it is more economical to transmit the corrections to this assumption than the complete line itself.

7. CONCLUSIONS

This chapter is devoted to microanalysis of the structure of messages. We summarize our conclusions as follows:

(1) Psychology includes two groups of perceptual theories: (a) integral theories, derived from the concept of form; and (b) scanning theories, strongly supported by experimental psychophysiology.

(2) Information theory, considering the individual as a special type of receptor, offers a synthesis of these two views. It assumes that, within the length of the present, the human receptor can integrally apprehend only a limited, maximum number of information elements as a form. If the message has a higher number, either the receptor neglects them or proceeds to scan the field. Both processes occur in reading, where the eye fixes on only a few points per line.

(3) One of the fundamental characteristics of the human receptor is the existence of a maximum *limit* to the flow of perceptible information. When this maximum flow is exceeded, the individual selects, with the aid of criteria derived from his previous experience, forms from the message presented to him. Forms are abstractions, elementary stages of intelligibility. If these criteria fail him, the individual is overwhelmed, left behind by the originality of the message; he loses interest.

(4) The message most difficult to transmit is that without redundancy (with maximum information), hence without any a priori *form*. It is both easiest to give an approximate picture of it and most difficult to give an exact picture of it. It is the most fragile of messages. Interestingly, this message is most devoid of esthetic value — and of a priori meaning.

(5) Structures are equivalent to mental forms. The more structured a message is, the more intelligible it is, the more redundant it is, and the less originality it has.

(6) The concept of forms conceived a priori includes that of *symbols*. Symbols are collections of elements known in advance. The study of structures of the mind is thus connected with an experimental study of symbols and symbolism.

[page 81] (7) Every *form* is the expression of a statistical predictability measured by a degree of coherence, more precisely, by an autocorrelation of the sequence of elements. To be perceived, the message requires the functional existence of a *memory* in the receiver.

(8) One of the most elementary temporal forms is *periodicity*. It must be considered, not as an abstract and absolute property, but as a measurable and contingent property. It must be approached in conformity with the phenomenology of perception.

(9) In the sonic domain, periodicity is perceived only on a scale above the length of the present and below the saturation threshold of the perception of durations. Not physical periodicity, but variations in it, enter perception directly; rather, in perception sound is continuous.

(10) The perception of periodicity is the receiving organism's unconscious and immediate wager that he knows what will occur on the basis of what has happened in the past. It is a wager resting on a mathematical expectation which is precisely a phenomenon's degree of periodicity or of coherence.

(11) The human mind wagers about the future on the basis of a much smaller sampling than one should accept according to mathematical logic. In reality — that is, apparently — a degree of periodicity, no matter how weak, is perceived as soon as there is expectation of a later event analogous to those events which have already happened.

(12) Periodicity is not only the continuity which conveys a form, but is also foreseeing what comes on the basis of the past. Applications of periodicity in the sonic and visual domains are given.

The above study of the concepts of form and of periodicity constitutes a microanalysis of the most elementary structures of the message perceived under ideal conditions. The receptor's attention is supposed perfect, and his perception complete. These conditions are arbitrarily simple. The object of the following chapter will be to approximate reality more closely by introducing the concepts of perturbation and the opposition between form and background.

Uncertainties in
Perception and Memory's
Structuring of Symbols

CHAPTER III

If I give you probabilities, ask no more of me.
PLATO

Pursuing the application of the general theory presented in Chap. I to the human receptor, we now study the conditions imposed on the message by the special structure of this receptor. First, we shall try to state precisely how a message is destroyed by noise and, reciprocally, how it emerges from the backdrop of the universe, noise. Then, on the basis of a functional scheme of the receptor, we shall try to elucidate how the memory can organize the forms of the message. Indeed, it is memory which, on the basis of the set of past messages, defines symbols, and hence the actual information of messages to come.

1. FORM AND GROUND IN THE MESSAGE

Rather than to establish isolated concepts, one of the most productive procedures of philosophic thought is to make evident dialectical dipoles in the conceptual network, between which the creative activity of the mind takes its bearings.

The preceding chapters have suggested a number of dialectical oppositions, namely:

Banality	vs.	Originality
Redundancy	vs.	Information

Intelligible form	vs.	Informative output
Periodicity, order	vs.	Disorder
Foreseeability	vs.	Unforeseeability

We shall use the same heuristic process in the following, in order to state precisely the role of *intent* in transmission.

[page 83] The preceding chapter emphasized the concept of *form* (*Gestalt*) as an absolute. In particular, we stressed the interpretation of form as a correlation of the signal with itself, an autocorrelation on the basis of an internal, intrinsic coherence. We left everything outside the form indeterminate, describing the remainder simply as "different."

A difficulty then arises: By what criterion can we establish a form in the "field" of the message, for example, the spatial extent of the visual field or the tonal (L, f) extent of the perceptible sonic field? So far we have been content to say that what was not part of the form was "different," namely, that the autocorrelation function over a temporal or spatial interval larger than a certain size became perfectly erratic. But it is possible that outside the contour of the form exist other forms; though these may have a null correlation with the original form, they may have their own high, or in any case significant, autocorrelation in their own domain. In other words, we have not established a criterion of what to integrate in a perceptible form and what simply to oppose to the form, that is, the *background*.

One essential idea of the psychology of form, whose results we claim to interpret, is the opposition figure-ground. The figure (form) is defined completely only by its opposition to the background: Its organization detaches it from the disorganized ground. Experiments on optical illusions such as those with Schroeder's staircase, which are well known in *Gestalt* psychology, show the differentiation which must be established between an amorphous background and contrasting, symmetrical, negative, complementary forms.

We are thus led to turn our attention to the "amorphous" background. From it the meaningful signal must emerge, much as theatrical action stands out against a backdrop characterized by its lack of interest. This lack of interest in fact defines backgrounds against which interesting phenomena are to stand out.

Moreover, within the message are perturbations or errors, which also do not interest the receptor. We shall now study the role of these disturbances. The concept of channel used in Chap. I will aid us in this study.

2. THE CONCEPT OF NOISE

Until now, we have in effect supposed that the message from our environment, near or distant, reaches us undisturbed without distortion, as transmitted.

We call "noise" any undesirable signal in the transmission of a message through a channel, and we use this term [page 84] for all types of perturbation, whether the message is sonic or visual. Thus shocks, crackling, and atmospherics are noises in radio transmission. A white or black spot on a television screen, a gray fog, some dashes not belonging to the transmitted message, a spot of ink on a newspaper, a tear in a page of a book, a colored spot on a picture are "noises" in visual messages. A rumor without foundation is a "noise" in a sociological message. In the following, we shall talk about sonic messages, where the term "noise" sounds familiar.

At first sight, it seems that the distinction between "noise" and "signal" is easily made on the basis of the distinction between *order* and *disorder*. A signal appears to be essentially an ordered phenomenon while crackling, or atmospherics, are disordered phenomena, formless blotches on a structured picture or sound. In reality, this morphological distinction is logically inadequate. Several examples may convince us of this.

When we listen to a concert, the sounds of the tuning up before the concert certainly are musical sounds, however the latter may be defined. Nevertheless, by a *consensus omnium* and at least in French, German, and American radio broadcasting, this succession of sounds is considered annoying and is not transmitted.

On the other hand, the applause which follows the concert consists of perfectly aperiodic elementary clicks, totally deprived of harmonicity in the sense in which one generally thinks of a musical sound. At first sight these clicks would seem to be noises, whatever this category's morphological definition may be. Nevertheless, these impacts are considered meaningful and to a large extent part of the concert's brilliance of execution. Applause is transmitted and a special microphone — called an "ambiance mike" — is available to capture it. There even exist recordings of applause to use at the end of concerts of recorded music. Can it be that, though formless, these sounds are meaningful?

In theatrical broadcasts, some noises are part of the action and must be transmitted: the banging door, the ringing telephone, etc. Others, of exactly the same nature, coming from the audience, are logically considered disturbances. These are noises in the proper sense, just like the shocks and crackling which may arise in transmission and which are not morphologically distinguishable from meaningful noises.

In short, there is *no* absolute structural difference between noise and signal. They are of the same nature. The only difference which can be logically established between them is based exclusively on the concept of *intent* on the part of the transmitter: *A noise is a signal that the sender does not want to transmit.* The rattling of the sheet of paper from which the actor reads his part into the microphone, the mixture of two originally separate signals from two channels intended to be separate (as over the telephone or in conversation in adjoining rooms) are noises.

[page 85] We have assumed a transmitter capable of having objectively definable purposes. But in the case of messages from the environment to the individual, the transmitter as an individual does not exist; only the receptor remains. We generalize our definition: *A noise is a sound we do not want to hear.* It is a signal we do not want to receive, one we try to eliminate.

But we have just seen that there is no absolute morphological difference between signal and noise. The desire to eliminate takes effect through a mechanism which selectively obliterates perception of some of the message "noise" which reaches an individual. The individual then has a problem of choice: How will he be guided in selecting message elements to accept or reject?

Now we reintroduce a morphological classification based on habit. Generally, the immediate choice will be guided by difference in structure, in form, which may become extremely subtle; for example, a listener can follow at will either of two fables by La Fontaine successively recorded at the same level by the same speaker, but replayed simultaneously, so that the speaker's voice gets mixed up with itself.

This exemplifies one of the most general methods of experimental esthetics: studying forms by mixing them up. The method illustrates the well-known aphorism, "The pathological illuminates the normal." To analyze a perception by this method, we destroy progressively the message which provokes the perception, then follow the correlative degradations of the perception and of its cause in order to estimate the relative values of the various message elements. Obviously the degradation of esthetic perception is not a linear function of the destruction of message elements, but rather depends on complicated laws varying with the nature of the message, from Rorschach blots to wind-eroded sculptures of the Egyptian Sphinx. Valéry (1956) cites the example of the form in the sand, whose origin could equally well be human or marine.

Over restricted ranges of destruction, one finds that information increases as the logarithm of the number of elements; for example, the densities of an engraver's cross-hatchings of a drawing nearly follow Fechner's law.

Because we want to know the structure of the message, we shall apply the general method outlined above to the message and shall try to see, in what follows, how perturbations make a message deteriorate.

It is easy to conceive the concept of noise in artificial channels, for in these it first came to the attention of technicians, then of physicists, and finally of theoreticians. From the philosophical viewpoint, it is interesting to underline the heuristic value of what is artificial: Noise existed well before transmission channels, [page 86] and men did not await conversation by telephone for their conversation to be disturbed by traffic in the street. But the essential scientific concepts in communication were *first* made clear in communication channels and then transferred to the most natural, if not the simplest, case, and to the banal example which has given science only an analogical terminology. In reality, there has been a change in attitude toward natural and artificial phenomena. While man always feels under the sway of the former and, at least subconsciously, considers them immutable, he adopts a deliberately combative attitude toward the latter.

Although a noise is a sound which the receiver does not want to hear, we shall begin with a morphological analysis, following the above remarks. First we look for the ideal noise, the perfect perturbation. Then we shall assume that intent becomes manifest in ordering, for example, in the creation of a structure, of a form which creates *expectation* in the receptor.

In the sonic message, such ordering is essentially periodicity. The ideal perturbation is then something unexpected in period and amplitude. Its temporal form, the function $f(t)$, is analytically defined by what is called its *spectrum*, which is the distribution of its component frequencies. Because the phenomenon exists, the number of frequencies cannot be zero, and therefore will be infinite: All "frequencies" will be present simultaneously. We then have a uniform, continuous spectrum. This spectrum defines the brusque elementary impulse, the infinitely short "pip" (Dirac's needle function), the elementary shock. The clapping of hands represents this type of noise. On a screen where a visual message is to appear, noise would consist of spots, each less than or equal to the spatial perceptual element in size (depending on the discriminative power of the retina) and of any intensity whatever: Their position and value would be random.

Since each elementary perturbation lasts an infinitely short time, it comes to the receptor's attention, for example, to his ear, only during the length of the present, his perceptual quantum of time. By extension, a more or less continuous noise consists of erratic repetitions of elementary shocks, recurring with such a large average density as to become indiscernible, yet without any correlation of either amplitude or interval of succession (that is, with the auto-correlation function always zero). The noise of a shower of metallic pellets on sheet iron, of rain against a windowpane, of a jet of steam, etc. approximates such a signal. In a sufficiently long time, all possible amplitudes of the signal can occur. The superposition of all these continuous spectra produces a permanent continuous spectrum where all [page 87] the "frequencies" have the same probability of occurrence. By analogy with light, this is what we call a *white noise*, the prototype of perfect, ideal noise. It has no characteristic other than its perfect disorder; white noise is the expression of perfect disorder.

If the message repertoire has the dimensions of loudness and pitch, then in white noise any element of the repertoire can occur within any interval. This, indeed, is a perfectly *formless* message.

This message is identical to the message most difficult to transmit (described in the preceding chapter) since it uses simultaneously and randomly all the available elements of the repertoire. Attaching a *convention* — known both to transmitter and receptor — to each element gives this message the maximum possible information. This "optimum coding" makes the most extensive use of all available elements of the repertoire, eliminating redundancy.

Naturally, the receptor will have to decode this message and recast it in an intelligible form. The length of decoding varies as the efficacy of coding; its delicacy varies with the fragility of the message. Since the message has no "form," no redundancy, each element in it can be modified without the receptor being aware of it. In real noise, since no coding convention exists, the message is free of intent, both apparent (since it is formless) and conventional. Thus white noise is no longer "fragile" because we care nothing about its modification en route; one white noise looks like any other. No matter how completely different the details of evolving white noises are, their spectra are infinitely similar. The only possible difference may be in the over-all intensity, but two white noises of the same intensity are indiscernible.

White noises, which have very broad spectra, are still, however, subject to modification by the channel, because they use a very extended and hence very cumbersome repertoire. Most artificial *chan-*

nels lack the capacity for such messages, which, after all, one might want to transmit.

The applause of a large crowd in a theater constitutes a set of elementary shocks which corresponds exactly to the definition of white noise. Because artificial channels generally have shortcomings in terms of the capacities [page 88] of the human ear, it is very difficult to transmit the applause precisely; the shocks include all the frequencies of the audible range. On the other hand, nothing is easier than reconstructing applause approximately, because no radio listener is interested in the applause at 54.6 seconds past 7:45 P.M. of the spectator in seat 378, even if the listener can perceive the clapping of individual hands.

Thus, although the absence of intent more than the absence of form distinguishes a noise from a message, the limiting morphological case, perfect noise, is important.

Applying the general method described above, we may be interested, inversely, in the emergence of form in noise, in the birth of an identifiable character in noise. In the last chapter we looked for the *minimum perceptible structuring* in temporal organization (periodicity, rhythm); now we look for it in material organization. If the sonic material of white noise is formless, what is the minimum "personality" it must have to assume an identity? What is the minimum of spectral form it must have to attain individuality? This is the problem of "coloring white noises."

This problem is analogous to coloring white light by adding a colored beam of increasing intensity, until the resulting light no longer seems rigorously white to an observer (Moles, 1953c). What must be the relative level of a "band" noise which, when added to a white noise, creates the perception that the resulting noise, though totally disordered, has assumed a color, a determinate pitch, which gives it an individuality? (A band noise is a continuous spectrum noise lying within a frequency range of, for example, one octave.) We found that the loudness in excess of background (difference threshold) depended very little on the loudness of the principal noise in the normal sonic domain of speech and music (40 to 90 dB). The threshold is on the order of 6 to 8 dB *below* the level of the principal noise when the added "color" is low pitched, and 12 to 14 dB when the added octave is above 500 cps.

Beyond their intrinsic interest for sensory psychology, these results have a properly psychological interest, for they can be interpreted as a study of the masking of a morphologically defined but noisy sound (the noise one octave "wide") by a "perfect perturbation," a noise of practically infinite spectrum (white noise). What is remarkable is that, to mask the human receptor's perception of a phenomenon whose form is as ill defined as an octave-wide noise, the perturbation must be *much stronger* than the phenomenon; in fact, two to four times greater (6 to 12 dB). Thus the receptor can perceive an organized phenomenon *hidden inside* an amorphous phenomenon. This result seems a priori rather paradoxical: One would assume that a signal is masked when a more intense one is superimposed.

[page 89] We repeated these experiments with much more highly organized messages: purely periodic phenomena and speech and music (fragments of discourse in languages known or unknown to the subject, piano or orchestra pieces). We masked these with white noise to find the loudness necessary to "drown" the musical or phonetic message. In order to destroy an intelligible message, the intensity of the noise must be four to eight times (12 to 18 dB) stronger than the *fortissimi* (loudest passages) of the transmitted message.

3. LIMITS TO THE APPREHENSION OF MATERIAL PHENOMENA

We can interpret these results with information theory. Again, we look for inspiring technical analogies in order to transfer them to the human receptor.

Within a channel, every message may be expressed as a *temporal form*, a function $f(t)$ of time. Mathematical physics analyzes and defines these temporal forms (as furnished by an oscilloscope, for example) in terms of two statistical features: one, the over-all *amplitude* of the temporal form, proportional to the energy it conveys; two, the register of the instantaneous forms that the message can assume. The very general Fourier theorem indicates that all these forms may be reduced to the sum of many simple, periodic, harmonic *components*, defined uniquely by their frequency and their relative amplitude. The set of these components is represented by a diagram of amplitude as a function of frequency: the *spectrum*. The statistical variety of forms a signal assumes is represented by the extension of its instantaneous spectra over a certain *range* Δf of frequencies and by the range of its amplitudes. Every alteration of the signal's form is reflected by an alteration of its spectrum, and reciprocally.

The discovery of the principle of amplifying electrical signals provoked an upheaval in scientific philosophy around 1920 somewhat analogous to that provoked by the invention of the microscope, but here the upheaval was even clearer.

Amplification was opening an a priori limitless view of the infinitely small; it appeared that every phenomenon, no matter how small, would become measurable. If one amplifier has a gain of 100, two connected amplifiers will have a total gain of $100^2 = 10,000$, three amplifiers of $100^3 = 1,000,000$, etc. In the limit, small phenomena are no more, and there is no theoretical reason not to hear plants grow, not to hear an airplane 1,000 miles away.

It soon appeared that the situation was actually different and, just as diffraction [page 90] limits in principle the "gain" of optical microscopes, electrical amplification could not be pushed beyond a certain limit. This limit is reached when the phenomenon drowns in erratic background noise, which is perceptually a white noise, without any defined periodicity. At that point, all further amplification increases the noise and the signal simultaneously, and loses interest.

Nevertheless, the invention of the electron microscope arrived in time to evade the theoretical limit on the gain of optical microscopes, and one might wonder if some artifice would not similarly permit the reduction of background noise more efficaciously than present technological procedures. But Einstein showed that, in the last analysis, background noise is due to the agitation of electrons in conductors; he established that this noise is thus inherent in the nature of things and proportional to the absolute temperature — just like the molecular agitation causing Brownian movement — and to the frequency band considered. As a result, the only way to reduce the perturbation which drowns a signal in any channel, particularly in the receptor, is to diminish what is called the "pass band" Δf of the channel, that is, the range of frequencies that it transmits. In other words, one must reduce the channel's capacity, the extent of the repertoire of elements that it can convey. That amounts to saying that the choice of elements is reduced, that we particularize a priori the nature of the signal which we want to amplify or receive, but it is just this that is unknown.

For example, encephalography, at the limit of the technical possibilities of amplification, operates in the range of 5 to 100 cps with potentials of 2 to 50 microvolts. If, in order to double the sensitivity of the apparatus, we want to halve the background noise, we have to reduce the passing frequencies to the range 8-50 cps. It is then ordained a priori that the message which interests us will have to be within this restricted range; that is, we particularize a priori the message to be received. We decree that there are no waves with frequencies greater than 50 cps or that they are only uninteresting, erratic phenomena.

The information gained in one direction is lost in the other. What is gained in sensitivity is lost in the variety of elements. Here emerges an *uncertainty principle* which stems from the *very nature of things*.

This uncertainty principle may be stated as a generalization of the axiom about the limitation of channel capacity given in Chap. II.

Let N be the level of noise prevailing at the input of an information receptor within a given quantum of duration, the length of the present (later we shall see the importance of this condition). It is evident that the sensitivity, that is, the minimum perceptible signal σ cannot go below a certain fraction $1/K_{min}$ of the background noise N, since the sensitivity must be sufficient to separate the signal from the noise. Thus $\sigma = N/K_{min}$. Ultimately determined by N, σ constitutes the possible error in the determination of the level of a signal. If M is the saturation level [page 91] of the receptor, the number of signals of varying intensity is M/σ. Now let Δf be the band of frequencies to which this receptor is sensitive; it defines the repertoire of elementary forms of periodicity that the receptor can distinguish. The narrower it is, the more "ignorant" the receptor is of the exact form of the signal, since a greater number of possible frequencies escape him; if he has a narrow band Δf, he cannot know whether a particular harmonic of the signal exists outside his pass band. To within a constant, the error made on the form of the signal is then proportional to $1/\Delta f$.

Under these conditions, the relation

$$\frac{\sigma}{\Delta f} = \frac{N}{K_{min}\Delta f} = Q$$

is constant. One may write this equation in the form

Error in amplitude $\times$ error in frequencies $=$ constant,

directly recalling the uncertainty principle formulated by quantum physics. We have derived a principle *limiting the information which can be received from the external world.*

As a consequence, in order to increase sensitivity indefinitely, it is necessary to know more and more about the nature (frequency) of the message to be received. This remark has very concrete technological applications: In the limit, the message would have a unique frequency, and it would be a periodic signal of the frequency to which the receptor was tuned. Qualitative differentiation by frequency among the elements of the message would disappear, and the only question which could be posed would be whether or not the message was *there.* Thus in the limit we reach the binary code used as an example in Chap. I.

This analysis demonstrates the principle that a receptor or a channel has a limited information capacity. It is a demonstration based on perfectly general laws, which justify the quasi-axiomatic character we gave the principle in Chap. II.

Noise thus appears as the *backdrop of the universe,* due to the nature of things. The signal must stand out from noise. There is no signal without noise, no matter how little. Noise is the factor of disorder contingent on the intent of the message, which is characterized by some kind of order. It introduces a dialectic, figure-ground, connected with the dialectic, order-disorder, which constitutes the second law of thermodynamics. The general theorem about entropy, "disorder can only increase in an isolated system," amounts to saying that noise can only degrade the orderliness of the message; it cannot increase the particularized information; it *destroys intent*.

Noise is thus an irreducible phenomenon which limits our [page 92] knowledge of the universe in every domain. The limit in principle of electron microscopes will be reached when the spontaneous agitation of the ultimate constituents of matter enters the field. However, in the preceding analysis we have not stated accurately how the message disappears into the background noise. The experiments with acoustic noise have shown that this disappearance is not a simple deficiency, a "drowning" of the interesting, meaningful phenomenon in the uninteresting background noise; rather, for the human receptor this disappearance is an "intellectual" operation, or more exactly, the failure of this operation. For the human receptor, it depends directly on the psychology of perception. How is it explained by the theory of perturbations just sketched? Can we find in technological receptors an analogous mechanism which sheds light on it?

Let us try to state precisely how perceptual selection is performed. From our first uncertainty principle we have deduced that in order to increase the receptor's sensitivity to messages from the external world, it is necessary to diminish the band of passing frequencies, decrease the possible uncertainty about periodicity. In the praxis of artificial channels, this restriction of the operative field is done with the aid of a device called "filtering." One inserts in the channel an arrangement (filter) which selects a *sensitivity band* from the range of frequencies. As the filter is perfected, this sensitivity band gets narrower and narrower.

One would then imagine it possible to upset the uncertainty principle stated above by assembling an arbitrarily large number of these filters and restricting their pass bands as much as necessary to lower the perturbing noise as far as desired. This is fallacious. In the preceding we supposed that we wanted to know the state of the message instantaneously — within one quantum of duration. However, no filter, no matter what its mechanism, responds instantaneously to the problem set it. Rather, it requires a response time Θ proportional to the narrowness of its band, or $1/\Delta f$. The uncertainty for each element of the form, then, for each elementary periodicity, is connected with the background noise N by the equation,

$$N = Q_2 \Delta f = \frac{Q_2}{\Theta}; \text{ hence } N\Theta = \text{constant.}$$

Instead of overturning the uncertainty principle, the above theoretical artifice only provides a different formulation of it by changing the magnitudes to which it applies. This artifice "extracts" the meaningful phenomenon from the background noise. It makes explicit the meaning of the coefficient K_{min} defining the ratio of the background noise N to the minimum perceptible signal. We regarded K_{min} initially as constant within a given maximum interval (for example, the quantum of psychological duration). We see that this coefficient may become infinite; indeed, with the aid of a filter, we can go draw [page 93] a phenomenon as weak as we like from the surrounding background noise which masks it, and, with the aid of a sufficient number of these filters, redescribe its exact form, its spectral composition. Devices which do this exist and are called "analyzers."

However, we can extract the signal only on the condition that we have an *increasing amount of time*, an amount tending to infinity as the phenomenon is more deeply drowned in noise. Thus we can uncover a message from the external world buried arbitrarily deep in surrounding noise only by devoting a double *infinity of means* to the task: (a) an infinite number of arbitrarily narrow filters, and (b) an infinite interval of time to observe or to perceive the message.

If we are interested only in knowing the message's amplitude, assuming for example that we know a priori its frequency, f, the preceding relation becomes:

Error in amplitude $\times$ necessary delay for perception $=$ constant.

When the delay necessary for observation increases greatly, the chance increases that the phenomenon considered has changed before we realize it. As it happens, we know that no natural phenomenon is strictly periodic; the longest notes in music (organ notes) scarcely last longer than five seconds. In any case, the delay Θ for observation represents the error that we are susceptible of making about the duration (that is, about the temporal nature of the observed event), since within the period Θ it can change without our knowledge. We thus arrive at the *second uncertainty principle:*

Error in amplitude $\times$ error in duration $=$ constant.

The contrivances described above show, for instance, that a computer can act as a filter, if the message is transcribed through an analog-digital converter into the machine's language. The computer can be programmed to analyze the various recurring frequencies in the phenomenon and to draw out their respective amplitudes (autocorrelation analysis). Thus these contrivances are not simple mental images.

In fact, a very common apparatus behaves like a series of tuned filters on narrow bands of juxtaposed frequencies: the human ear. For a perceptual delay on the order of one quantum of psychological duration (0.1 second), its threshold of energetic sensitivity is around 5×10^{-16} ergs, very slightly above the molecular background noise of the atmosphere in the acoustic range (2×10^{-16} ergs/cm^2). This illustrates the adaptation of the human organism to the conditions in which it lives, a remark already made by physiologists with regard to the eye, since retinal sensitivity is in the neighborhood of several quanta per second.

The concept of quantum of duration or length of the present also appears in a new light. The length of the present is the delay necessary for the psychophysiological "filters" to function if their sensitivity is used as well as possible in the environment where the individual finds himself. It appears that the individual's adaptation to his environment may be taken as a heuristic law of psychophysiology; witness the fact that the range of acoustic, that is, audible, frequencies, has a limit around 16,000 to 20,000 cps precisely because the physical properties of ultrasounds prevent them from propagating in the air over a substantial distance, and hence render them useless.

[page 94] What is pertinent here is the role played by *time*, or rather the perceptual delay interval. This delay (in the case of both filters and the ear) serves to *integrate* the rhythmical impulses received and to differentiate this regularity from the background noise's total lack of rhythm. When this difference is great, sensation appears, order and predictability arise perceptibly from disorder. The signal's autocorrelation rather than noise comes to the human being's attention.

In this view, the sensation of form is the *perception of autocorrelation;* periodicity expresses the nature of the sonic material. The analysis could be repeated *mutatis mutandis* for visual perception. We again find the principal results of Chap. II with regard to a directly apprehensible periodicity, rhythm. Again, the signal's predictability, measured by its autocorrelation, is essential to the perception of a defined form, whether structural (pitch) or material (spectrum). There is redundancy when the signal lasts longer than necessary for integrative perception.

Psychologists of hearing have studied integrative perception thoroughly and have made it clear that a *minimum of around four complete periods is necessary to apprehend unambiguously* the pitch of a tone, that is, to perceive the nature of the sonic material constituting it. This figure coincides remarkably with the number of rhythmical events necessary to the perception of periodicity, namely, three or four.

Below this number, musical tones — for example, certain *pizzicati* in the low registers of stringed instruments — dissolve into noise without giving a feeling of defined pitch. The existence of the quantum of duration prevents our perceiving — in a really appreciable way — a duration much less than 1/16 to 1/20 of a second. But though the message lasts longer unchanged, as is the case generally for musical tones (for example, 40/256 second for a middle C), everything beyond 1/16 of a second *adds nothing* to the perception of pitch. If the tone is longer, the perception of length begins. This, however, does not interest us for the moment. The important fact is that, in general, musical tones and vocal phonemes last considerably longer than the minimum interval of about four periods required for recognition. A syllable lasting 1/12 second at 480 cps (middle voice) yields, for example, 40 complete oscillations; we get the same results for musical tones (if we have, say, 80 quarter notes to the minute). The sonic message given us by the external world is always *largely redundant* merely by virtue of its duration. In comparison with what is strictly needed for comprehension, it is *repeated* a considerable number of times ($40:4 = 10$ times in the preceding example). The experiments in temporal compression of speech described above strongly support this statement. The masking of a musical [page 95] message by a uniform white noise (cf. end of the preceding section) appears then as a typical illustration of the protective role of redundancy against perturbations, making up for the fragility of the message. Indeed, we can perceive a musical or phonetic message drowned in a white noise 15 to 20 dB greater just because each significant element of the message is very redundant. Because each such element is repeated, for example, ten times, within the duration of a tone, it is *protected* by integrative perception against erratic noise — it stands out from this noise because of its periodicity.

This is an application of the second uncertainty relation. The receptor has available an interval greater than that strictly necessary to perceive the elements of the message, which is conserved in time and integrated in perception. Therefore he reduces possible error about its level, here its presence. We perceive the high autocorrelation of the message by contrast with the zero autocorrelation of the noise, rather than perceiving the signal drowned in the noise.

4. EFFECTIVE USE OF SYMBOLS AND THE RISING OF THRESHOLDS (ACCOMMODATION)

The two uncertainty principles that we have just examined are limits *de jure* of perception. They determine the basic elements of sensation itself, the "texture," the "grain," of the message. For example, they determine the material grain of a cinematographic emulsion, the texture of the negative, and the texture of a televised picture. If we do not want to notice the artificiality of a channel, its physical grain must be definitely smaller than the "psychophysical" grain determined by the elements of sensation. We have just seen that, in the limit, the uncertainty principles define the latter.

However, it is rare for messages to be so weak that the attention they demand from the receptor is limited by the above uncertainty principles. On the contrary, from a more psychological than physical point of view, the human being is *well off* in this world. He does not constantly feel limitations.

The individual does come in contact with limits only in exceptional cases: The aviator's perceptual and reaction delay must be as short as possible; the laboratory subject with whom an absolute threshold of audibility or a difference threshold is determined in slow and scrupulously careful experiments must make maximum use of his sensory capacities. Like those of theoretical physics, our two uncertainty principles are important in determining the structure of our universe, but their importance in everyday life [page 96] is rather small. Most of the signals our senses receive, especially esthetic messages, have a coarse structure.

It is proper to investigate whether the enormous richness of the repertoire of perceptual elements defined by the absolute capacity of sensory channels is well used in practice. In reality, there is a sort of *schematization* of the message, which is a function primarily of the time interval that we devote to it. One of the most remarkable characteristics of sensory organs is this adaptive capacity: the ability to pass at will from the crudest sketching of form to the most detailed scanning.

The ear alone could distinguish among 340,000 sonic elements per 0.1 second, transmitting information at a rate of $H = 10 \log_2 340,000$ bits/sec. With its 100,000,000 different elements, the eye would also furnish fantastic amounts of information. But this fineness agrees poorly with the poverty of our mental images or of our memories which, in some way, must have some of the characteristics of the original perception, and it disagrees strongly with everything we have said about the capacity to apprehend information. It is evident that, to memorize, one must first perceive.

We know that a maximum rate of apprehensible information, an "apperceptual limit," dominates perception. In reality, *to perceive is to select*. We must try now to state precisely the role of the structure of the individual receptor in selection. One may consider the whole nervous system as a machine for selecting increasingly sketchy outlines of the richness of elementary stimuli. This selection is what psychophysiologists call "integrative processes"; they distinguish at least four different stages of such processes.

There are two ways to reduce the information of a message: (a) Reduce the number of elements actually used. (b) Increase the redundancy, by increasing the predictability, that is, the number of statistical liaisons between elements and groups of elements (symbols).

Let us take a typical example of information storage in an artificial channel. A geographic map is an accumulation of pieces of information to be transmitted through time. It is a temporal channel, a memorization of a region's geography. We consider a map which can be read by the naked eye. On the basis of the capacity of the visual channel, one might think that the scale of the map should be chosen in such a way that the smallest details that one wishes to transmit (a house, a water supply point) are represented by the minimum visual element, one minute of angle, and that there is room on the map for all details clearly distinct at this scale. Such considerations are indeed at the basis of the minimum dimensions of map details in France's National Geographic Institute. In the last century, with the progress of printing, there were attempts to make such maps, which would in principle be perfect information warehouses. It soon appeared that they were impractical and they have been abandoned. While they stored the maximum of information, this maximum exceeded the reader's apperceptual limit. The dimensions of details in normal maps are not directly related to the real scale of the map [page 97] which is generally much larger than what would be theoretically sufficient for the desired goal, whatever may be the advantages of this latter scale (crowding in a large amount of information). In other words, by unanimous convention, a great number of details — a great quantity of information — has been deliberately renounced. Correspondingly, the size of the symbols is augmented relative to the scale, and hence the number of symbols in the map or per unit of map surface is decreased.

The second method (of increasing redundancy) consists in stricter coding and restriction of the repertoire. The symbols found on a map are much less numerous than the variety of objects they represent: roads, houses, etc. One thus increases the map's legibility, a notion interesting to compare with those on the readability of a text (Flesch's index, Miller, 1951; works of Javal [cf. Woodworth and Schlosberg, 1954]; Moles, 1963).

Experimental examination of human sensory channels reveals a closely analogous phenomenon, one of the most general of experimental psychology: the *dynamic rising of thresholds* (accommodation). This phenomenon reduces enormously the repertoire of fundamental, properly sensory, elements which in combination constitute the message. Accommodation appears in every sensory channel, but relatively few studies have been devoted to it. Probably the reason for this is that its instability puts it in a category scientific workers do not particularly appreciate, that of "phenomena imprecise by nature." Such phenomena do not give the worker's mind the self-satisfaction provided by good, ordinary physics.

In Chap. I we defined the elements of a sensory channel on the basis of thresholds: (a) absolute — sensitivity; (b) absolute — saturation; (c) differential.

In Chap. I, Sec. 2, we gave the acoustical sensitivity threshold of 0 dB $=2 \times 10^{-4}$ baryes, the saturation threshold of 120 to 140 dB, and the difference threshold of 0.4 to 1.0 dB. These thresholds are the results of precise laboratory experiments which place the subject in very special conditions. In particular, the subject is in the totally abnormal state of concentrating his attention on a *unique* perception.

In everyday perception, very different from this, sensation has to be instantaneous; it becomes important only by contrast with what precedes and what follows; it is part of perpetual change. Under these conditions, there is no reason for the effective difference thresholds to be the same as in the laboratory. On the contrary, the above study of uncertainty relations suggests by analogy that, since the signals are variable in time, and in fact can change rather rapidly, the difference thresholds increase considerably; that perception becomes less clear; that its very existence requires sensations which stand out better and stand out increasingly as the elementary signals become briefer.

Despite the great difficulties besetting more or less precise experiments, [page 98] this is experimentally easy to prove, at least roughly. There is a *dynamic rising* of the difference thresholds. For example, we estimate that the threshold of imperceptible variations of loudness in music, if the signal varies quickly enough, could exceed 3 dB (40 per cent), even though, after "static" laboratory experiments, we initially assumed thresholds of 0.4 dB. The question is greatly complicated by the fact that the thresholds thus given as limits are a function of the way in which the variations follow from one signal to the next.

Although the differential sensitivity of the ear to pitch is prodigious, on the order of 0.4 per cent, differences in frequency ten times as great will be imperceptible if presented suitably, that is, if, for example, transients separate them from following stimuli or if ornaments (for example, vibrato and glissando) mask them. Melodic *tolerance* can attain such values that it affects conceptions as important as major and minor; for example, by successive divergences a minor third can pass for a false major third (Tanner).

In short, the repertoire of actually differentiable elements in a message is much smaller than the repertoire of elements defined by psychophysics on the basis of laboratory experiments. It is rather variable, rather poorly determined, and seriously restricts the choice among symbols which are formed from it. For each dimension, if the difference threshold varies in the ratio of one to four, the total number of elements varies in the ratio $(\frac{1}{4})^n$, where n is the number of dimensions. From the *dynamic* elements we must draw the symbols which will serve to construct the repertoire of fundamental elements.

5. MNEMONIC FUNCTION AND THE CONSTITUTION OF PERCEPTUAL STRUCTURES

In the preceding, we have paid attention to the substance of the message properly called, to its information content, its properties, its structures, the modifications it could undergo, etc. We considered the receiving subject in the most simplistic and the most standardized way, referring implicitly to the concept of an "average individual." We were content to indicate at various points that the psychological structure of the information receptor was connected with his present situation and his sociocultural past. For example, we observed that the "apperceptual limit" is a function of the subject's education, for example, in music.

While such an attitude is necessary to the statistical understanding which is at the center of this study, especially at its beginning, we know that experimental psychology is also partly *differential psychology;* [page 99] it aims to discover the mechanisms and grounds of the divergencies between individuals' aptitudes or reactive properties. To get a better approximation to reality, we must now increase the complexity of the information-receiving mechanism which psychology uses as a model, and consider its differential properties, that is, the variations it can undergo from one individual to another. We must try discursively to explain these properties by intelligible factors, particularly by the social factors which no psychology can ignore.

In the present state of our knowledge, it would be risky to try to push this development beyond the few pieces of evidence. Studies of the receptor's manipulation of information to construct reactions, grouped under the ambiguous term "cybernetics," concentrate at present on describing a normal individual, and on the use of the most immediate semantic information. These theories are currently incapable of taking account of, for example, psychoanalytical factors, which play a preponderant role in esthetics. A mechanistic interpretation of *Homo aestheticus* would be premature.

We are interested here only in the functional properties of the receptor; we do not in any way prejudge its real structure. Any scheme, no matter how artificial, which possesses the properties displayed in the reception of information thus suits the needs of information theory, as long as there is no experimental disagreement.

The essential property of the information receptor, governing its behavior with regard to messages, is what we have called its "a priori knowledge" about the message, and particularly about the repertoire of symbols. The total a priori knowledge defines the special receptor under consideration. It is relatively easy to standardize psychophysical capacities (for example, the number of sensory elements, the capacity for pitch discrimination, the audible or visual range, etc.) and even properties of dynamic perception which can be measured by experiment (Sec. 4). But it is much more hazardous to specify the knowledge of a "standard cultural individual": Here one must differentiate structures.

In current psychology, *memory* expresses in a general way the impact of the individual's history on his present behavior, the influence of the past on the present. Current psychology emphasizes the knowledge, symbolic, statistical, or real, of the group of faculties collected under the term memory.

In fact, reviving a remark of Bergson, modern psychology distinguishes three functional types of temporal permanence, according to their extent:

(a) The minimum perceptual delay, on the order of 0.1 to 0.05 second, is perceptibly a constant, regardless of the sensory channel [page 100] used. It is directly connected to the functioning of synapses and of the nervous mechanisms. It arises directly in psychophysics, rather than in psychology properly called. We have seen the important role that the perceptual quantum played as the "length of the present" in information theory. It represents a threshold within which the term "duration" loses its meaning; only physical time persists. The mechanisms which cause it make it a quasi-absolute psychophysical constant, similar in all individuals.

(b) The *length of presence*, a sort of "phosphorescence" from immediate perceptions, varies greatly in extent, from a fraction of a second to several seconds. It functions both to create the presence of sensations and to assure the *continuity of being*, as has been demonstrated by experiments on models and on pathological cases

(Walter, 1953; Foerster, 1949, 1953). A being deprived of this elementary memory has no internal coherence. He repeats the same reflex indefinitely at such short intervals that he cannot finish an act (apraxia); along with the elementary permanence of sensations, he loses his own personality. This instantaneous memory brings about the perception of duration connected with the sensation which fills up time. It *dates* events in our consciousness while the phosphorescence of perception lasts. It makes it possible to perceive form in the course of scanning. In a message too complex to be apprehended instantaneously, it represents the elementary memory necessary to the perception of autocorrelation, the existence of which we recognized in Chap. II. Thus it conditions the perception of the temporal forms of rhythm and of melody. Its variability is reflected in the variability of the lengths of melodic phrases conceived as units (Chap. V). Fraisse has shown that the error in estimation of a duration is smallest when the duration approximates 0.8 second.

(c) Finally, memory, properly called, serves the function of permanent retention. Permanent memory cannot be dated by the conscious mind (except through reference to an external event such as a clock). However, because it is subject to accidental material degradations, it is a statistical phenomenon. What is retained and what is forgotten are not determined entirely by their content.

These three levels of memory in human beings parallel the three types of memory currently used in large computing machines. Computing machines have (a) very fast memory (ferrite cores which constitute the machine's "field of consciousness"); (b) fast memory with minimal access delay, such as magnetic drums; (c) storage memories in large number with quite a long access delay (tapes).

The individual's past experience takes effect on his present behavior through memory of type (c). This memory determines each message's structurings, symbols, statistical organization, and hence proportion of originality-banality and redundancy. Thus memory is essentially the same as the specific mental structure of each receptor. That is why it is advisable to state precisely how this [page 101] structuring is effected on the basis of the messages received: This structuring is *education*. To facilitate the argument, we shall have recourse to the classical analogy where some perceptual events — but not all — cause the manufacture of a punched card representing them *symbolically* —and not photographically, as theories of mental images would erroneously suggest. This punched card is classified without a real psychological "date." These cards obviously can be destroyed or lost, but in principle are permanent. We shall liken statistical work performed on the set of cards present in the "memory" to the progressive structuring of message symbols into organizations like those described in preceding chapters.

Our object will be therefore to state precisely how, on the basis of received messages, a statistical law about messages to be received emerges.

6. MEMORIZATION AND INFORMATION

A memorandum of a past event is constructed from the elements already selected by perception. If, for example, the past event is an esthetic message, it is assumed in objective psychology that the event will in some way be translated into a *memory;* psychophysiol-

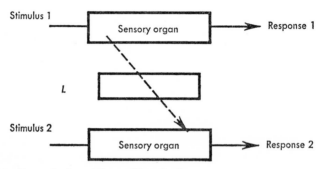

Fig. III-1. The mechanism of the conditioned reflex.

ogy will state precisely how, but this is irrelevant here. What does interest us is not so much the memory itself and the way in which it is recalled to consciousness, as the concomitant process, *learning,* which draws a general perception from a set of special perceptions.

The faculty of learning is the ability to make a general statistical, that is, not absolutely constraining, "rule" on the basis of isolated events. These rules as a whole govern the structuring of the succeeding messages and reduce their information. Up to the present this faculty has been specifically biological.

An analogy indicates how specific this capacity has been to living beings. In great automatic telephone systems, the delay necessary to obtain any phone whatever is a function neither of its distance nor of its importance for the individual who is calling, but only of a number of operations determined by the complexity of the number, which is always the same for a given central exchange. Now, as Wiener remarks (1954), one may be certain that if a biological mechanism had to call a given number several tens of times per day, a number particularly important to it, it would soon find a way to make that call much faster than calls it made only rarely; the more it made the call, the faster it would be. This is one difference between biological and physical systems: In the present state of things, the telephone exchange cannot make a general induction; it cannot learn that one number is called more often than another and hence ought to require less information.

[page 102] Behavioral psychologists, particularly K. Lewin (1951), Hull (1943), and Walter (1953), have long presented an operational scheme of conditioned reflexes based on the idea of successive coincidence (Fig. III-1).

If, in some organism, stimulus S_1 gives rise to reaction R_1 and stimulus S_2 to the reaction R_2, in general these two patterns of reaction are independent. But if the stimuli S_1 and S_2 occur nearly simultaneously (in practice, within an interval Θ shorter than the length of the present) many times, a conditioned reflex is created;

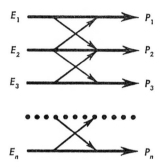

Fig. III-2.

that is, stimulus S_1 "causes" not only reaction R_1 but reaction R_2 in the absence of S_2. In other words, a special mechanism L bifurcates the stimulus by creating a liaison between two parts which before reacted independently.

In support of this presentation of elementary learning, certain authors (Walter, 1953; Shannon, in Foerster, 1953) created analog models which functioned according to this scheme.

In the creation of a conditioned reflex, the liaison which was established reduced the number of signals. While two events or sensations S_1 and S_2 were necessary to set two reactions or perceptions in motion, the liaison L makes the "well-chosen" one of the two events sufficient to create the two perceptions R_1 and R_2 appropriate to the complete signal. This results if the two signals S_1 and S_2 always — or often — occur simultaneously. Thus, on the simple level of two signals, a mechanism L prepares for a further piece of information by using the signal's redundancy due to the simultaneity of events. This mechanism L is thus an elementary memory.

We shall present the general problem of structuring by [page 103] memory analogously. For the moment, let us suppose the elements E_1, E_2, . . . , E_n of a complex signal E to be simultaneous. These elements create separately elementary perceptions P_1, P_2, . . . , P_n. We shall say that there is a *mnemonic symbolization* when some imaginable material system L — which we do not intend to explicate here — activated by the frequently repeated quasi-simultaneous presence of the set of elements ΣE_i of the signal E, provokes liaisons such that a single "well-chosen" element of E will suffice to provoke the set P of elementary perceptions. These liaisons arise between the different parts of the receptor which manipulate and convey the elements E_i to give rise to the elementary perceptions P_i. That well-chosen element will be called a *symbol* of the set of elements ΣE_i.

It is rather easy to imagine material devices which satisfy these conditions. Since this study is about information theory, we shall leave them aside. However, we shall state precisely how they satisfy the properties we have attributed to the information receptor, and particularly how they justify the existence of three types of memories (Sec. 5) distinguished by their temporal extent.

(1) We said that the set of signals E had to be "quasi-simultaneous" in order to be able to activate the mechanism L. That amounts to saying that these signals must be presented to the sensory organs (or rather to their subdivisions) within an interval $\tau < \Theta_0$ in order to be cumulated in a "common action," statistical in character. Psychophysiologists know that nervous reactions require a minimum interval of excitation, which depends on the synapses' functioning delay. Thus within this minimum delay it is understandable that there is no effective difference if the elements of sensation occur physically simultaneously or not. Thus the term "quasi-simultaneity" extends over the interval Θ_0, and we again encounter the concept of the length of the present.

(2) The integration of successive quasi-simultaneous groups of elements can continue only for a limited time interval, because eventually all the elements would end up being presented. Thus integration requires a short-term memory which certain authors (Foerster, 1949) liken to a phosphorescence of sensations that assures the continuity of being [*devenir*]. The mode of integration to which this temporary permanence corresponds is connected with the maximum extent of the length of presence (span of memory).

We have seen that the immediate perception of temporal sonic forms was the perception of autocorrelation, and that this perception demanded the existence of some kind of memory permitting comparison of the two functions of time $f(t)$ and $f(t + \tau)$. The need for an immediate memory over the length of presence thus becomes apparent from a different angle, connecting the diverse meanings of temporal extension.

[page 104] (3) Finally, the mechanism described which results in the creation of symbols possesses an undated memory, which lasts over long periods of time; it can forget because there is no assurance that the liaison established will not be destroyed later. It makes one part valid for the whole (*pars pro toto*).

On the basis of Ebbinghaus' classical results on the learning of nonsense syllables, Foerster (1949) has presented a statistical theory of memory which is essentially a theory of forgetting; the theory takes account satisfactorily of the fluctuations of memory — and therefore of the statistical symbolization which is our subject. This theory rests on the essential observation that any use of memorized data, for example, structurings of the message, is a re-presentation of them, and hence in reality a partial relearning. It assumes that the message elements are "inscribed" in cells placed in a special state which need not be specified precisely, and that they can lose that state erratically. As a result, it gives these "memos" impregnating the "cell" an average lifetime analogous to those forecasted by quantum physics of cell potentials, that is, an exponential decay in "life expectancy." There is thus spontaneous destruction of fragments of the initial message, but each use of the memorized data produces an equally erratic *reimpregnation* of additional cells. Thus the mnemonic grouping T_1 is continually transferred to the mnemonic grouping T_2, either consciously (by rememorization) or unconsciously. This simple mechanism permits Foerster to derive the experimental results of Ebbinghaus. It allows him to show the existence of a residual "absolute memory" of our past perception which is permanently inscribed in our mind. It permits him to give a satisfactory account of the everyday experience in which, several hours after an event, spontaneous memory of the event commands the memory's attention in a schematized and symbolic form (raving round and round).

What interests us chiefly here is connecting up a statistical process for retaining the information of a past message with simple cellular processes corroborated by recent knowledge of the microphysiology of nerve cells (Foerster, 1949, 1953).

The scheme just given takes a strictly functional view of the receiving subject's information-handling mechanisms. The scheme logically justifies the principal specifications required of the information receptor. It permits us to state precisely the nature of the connection between the individual value of a message and the sociocultural milieu through the intermediary of past experience. The statistical expression of past experience, inscribed in the memory, constitutes the symbolizing coding, the a priori structuring of the message to come.

Thus the scope of information theory is notably enlarged. Originally the theory treated only material messages, always in the identical form of the mechanical receptor's code. But this framework is too rigid for experimental esthetics and for perceptual theory, both of which must essentially take account of individual variations.

7. CONCLUSIONS

This chapter is devoted to the limitations on the perception of messages resulting from the receptor's structure and its dynamic variations, and to the [page 105] memory's way of constructing rules and symbols. We have the following results.

(1) The boundary of a form, in the sense of the preceding chapter, that is, an internal coherence, remains equivocal if it is not opposed to a *ground* having a different degree of coherence.

(2) An organized signal always emerges against a disorganized ground, noise.

(3) Noise can be logically defined only on the basis of *intent*. A noise is a message that someone does not want to transmit or to receive.

(4) When the receptor is an individual and the transmitter the external world, the concept of intent gives way to that of *choice*, that is, of value judgment.

(5) In the absence of other operational indications, perceptual choice favors structured forms over amorphous messages. Thus, from a statistical viewpoint alone, this choice introduces a morphological distinction between *forms* and *noises*.

(6) The study of how forms emerge in noise follows the method of experimental esthetics, namely, looking for the parallel degradations of a perception and of the message elements which caused it.

(7) The perfect morphological type of noise is white noise. It is obtained by superposing elementary erratic shocks whose frequency spectra include all possible components with the same probability.

(8) Noises of this sort compose the backdrop against which the events of the universe must stand out if they are to be perceived.

(9) The study of "coloring" white noises is the study of the minimum perceptible form in a noisy statistical phenomenon. It determines the thresholds of our perception of form due to the nature of the material constituting form.

(10) An intelligible, organized perception cannot be masked by an erratic phenomenon such as a white noise until the latter has a much higher level.

(11) Taking into account possible amplification of phenomena, our perception of the sensible world is nevertheless limited by an uncertainty principle, analogous to Heisenberg's principle, stemming from the nature of things:

Error about the signal's amplitude $\times$ error about the
signal's nature (frequency) $=$ constant.

[page 106] (12) Artificial means make it possible to reduce the uncertainty about the amplitude of a signal indefinitely on the conditions (a) that its component frequencies, that is, its form, be known a priori; (b) that an arbitrarily long time be available to observe the phenomenon.

(13) A second perceptual uncertainty principle is:

Error about the signal's amplitude $\times$ error about the signal's duration = constant.

(14) Receiving systems use the delay required to perceive a phenomenon drowned in a noise in order to integrate the ordered phenomenon and discriminate it from contingent, erratic phenomena. Ultimately, we have a weighted perception of the phenomenon's autocorrelation in comparison with noise.

(15) We may assume, as the key to the perception of forms, that the human receptor has direct perception of a signal's autocorrelation. The perception of a form can be likened to the perception of an autocorrelation among the physical elements constituting it.

(16) Redundancy allows perception of a phenomenon drowned in a formless noise with a much higher level. An important way to insure redundancy is to repeat signals for a time much longer than that strictly necessary to identify the message in isolation.

(17) The difference thresholds determined by psychophysiology in the laboratory, and the absolute difference thresholds resulting from the preceding uncertainty principles, are rarely met in normal practical messages between human beings; these messages are almost always cruder.

(18) A dynamic rising of difference thresholds significantly restricts the repertoires of elements enumerated under laboratory conditions by the different physical dimensions of the signal.

(19) The rate of information of a message is determined by the structures that the receptor perceives in the message. These structures are created by memory, which summarizes the set of messages the individual has already received in statistical rules or in symbols.

(20) The receptor is thus a developing (learning) system. Each message modifies the receptor's capacity to receive succeeding messages.

(21) Depending on their temporal extension, the functions grouped under the generic name, "memory," include (a) a perception of temporal substance of instantaneous duration (0.1 second); [page 107] (b) an immediate memory with the duration (one to ten seconds) necessary to perceive temporal structures; (c) a long-term memory, which is statistical, voluntary, and physiologically undated.

(22) The memory creates symbols by associating the set of elementary perceptions coming from a set of elementary sensations with only one or a reduced number of these sensations. The latter become the symbol. Symbolization is thus a reduction in the number of elements which results from frequent repetition of a microgroup of elementary sensations.

(23) Memory is a statistical phenomenon resulting from a statistical destruction of the recorded elements of perception. The mental structures of memory are also statistical in character.

The first three chapters are a general study of information theory applied to perception in the human receptor. In the following chapters, we shall apply these general concepts to sonic messages, and particularly to music, a typical temporal esthetic message.

Sonic Structures
and Music:
The Sonic Object

CHAPTER IV

Die in einem Künstlerhirn lebende Klangvorstellung ist das Erste und Zeugende.

ARNOLD SCHERING

Up to now, our approach to the individual's reception of messages from the external world has been primarily analytic. We have sought out the elements of the perception of messages by trying to explain analytically the concept of form, which is the essential thing in perception. Using the example of the sonic message, the studies in Chaps. II and III were primarily concerned with elementary periodicity as the basic structure. However, in qualitative perception of sonic material, we know well that messages with much more complex structurings than simple periodicity and elementary rhythm exist.

The Cartesian method would have us proceed from the simpler to the more complex. Now, along with the printed message in reading, the sonic message is the simplest esthetic message that is complete, that is, satisfactory in itself. Other esthetic messages such as painting, animated cartoons, and movies, have additional structures which are very difficult to apprehend. Hence, it is proper to study first phonetic and musical sonic messages.

Indeed, in musical messages, the large scale structures, notes, measures, phrases, and scores, are particularly clear and determinative of the work. Since the study of perception must eventually become a study of esthetic perception, a priori we find musical messages more profitable.

1. CRITIQUE OF MUSICAL THEORY

An important body of doctrine about the structures of the musical message is "musical theory," the body of instruction known as [page 109] solfège, harmony, counterpoint, fugue, and composition. It is one of the most important corpora of esthetics, with its accompanying overgrowth of historical criticism and musicology, etc. The first thing to do is to look at least for a guide here.

The scientific approach has always been deeply disappointed at each of the numerous attempts of this sort. It seems that the voluminous edifice of musical theory rests on sand. Whether conducted by physicists, psychologists, or musicologists grappling with principles, every scientific, critical study of the bases of musical theory has always led to a denial of their objective value, and often even of their subjective value, which at least had set a lower bound on their worth; their only remaining value was that of *convention*.

The most serious of these studies, Helmholtz', has been battered by all the recent theories of hearing and of integral sonic perception. The theory of scales, of consonant chords, of beats, of the articulation of a musical piece, the rules of the fugue and even of accompaniment — every one has fallen before the investigations of experimental psychology. Studies using subjects not biased by a social education have shown that all that remain objectively are vague preferences.

Of the whole immense structure, only minor fragments remain for the physicist, the psychologist, or the esthetician. The trade of making stringed instruments is a collection of empirical practices which remain valuable, but do not in any respect go to the bottom of the problem. Winckel (1960), citing Hindemith, declared: "For a long time, it has been felt that the theory of harmony conceived as an indicative arrow, sustaining musical theory until now with its indications about what is permitted and what is forbidden, is insufficient for our way of representing the musical totality; it is only a rough-edged stone to which the coherence of intervals gives some weight. Nevertheless, it proves unsatisfactory and leads to erroneous conclusions, as the practice of new music has already shown."

This pragmatic criticism of the foundations of musical theory has not proceeded only on the level of ideas, which is, after all, academic. Since the beginning of the twentieth century especially, it has been pursued on a strictly experimental level, on the level of facts, and on such a considerable scale that one cannot ignore the criticism.

Research on exotic music (Curt Sachs, Von Hornbostel) destroys the fundamental principle of universal scales, retaining only the term "scale" as a frame of reference in a sociocultural system; the incredible variety of existing scales makes it unlikely that any particular one of them is fundamentally superior. [page 110] Works of historical musicology cast suspicion on rules as fundamental as those relating to major and minor. The expansion of neoprimitive music in the modern world reveals that it is not impossible to find elements of musical convention (for example, rhythms) other than those taught classically. The dissolution of chords in dodecaphonic music, as well as their continual variation, and the sudden expansion of experimental music due to technological possibilities are experimental proofs of the weakness of the foundations of "musical theory." The evolution of music seems to be a methodical violation of previously accepted rules.

However, there is no art without constraint. To say that music is an art is to say that it obeys rules. Pure chance represents total liberty, and the word *construct* means precisely to revolt against chance. An art is exactly defined by the set of rules it follows. The role of esthetics, considered as a science, is to enumerate these rules and link them with universal laws of perception.

A hypothesis now appears. Exotic music, primitive music, modern music, and experimental music have successively transgressed musical laws without destroying the value of the music. Hence the laws transgressed were not *true* structural laws; their principles were not the true foundations of the art of modulating time. There must exist other, more secret, more fundamental, and more general laws which govern the arts of time. On the basis of a criticism of the theory of harmony, Hindemith maintains that natural laws in music will have to be as concrete as the laws of electron flow or of hydrodynamics.

Musical acoustics, though counted on by so many estheticians and physicists, has in the main failed because it is not interested in the real problems raised by the creation of sonic structures. For example, acoustics studied the rubbing of the bow on the string, when the only thing that interested the musician — not a maker of stringed instruments — was the *tone* this string produced.

Conceiving information theory as a physics of messages, we may expect the theory to explain the structures of this special message after it has accounted for some essential aspects of elementary structures. This is what we are going to try to sketch now, using a systematic change of viewpoints to establish, independent of the traditional liaisons, the existence of the sonic phenomenon per se, the sonic object.

2. EMERGENCE OF THE SONIC MATERIAL

[page 111] Transmission of music by spatial and temporal channels, particularly radio broadcasting and recording, establishes the
materiality of music. As long as music remained only an immediate perception, one was naturally inclined to approach it in an intuitive or intellectual way; nothing suggested its materiality. But when
the musical signal began to circulate in wires, in circuits, to be

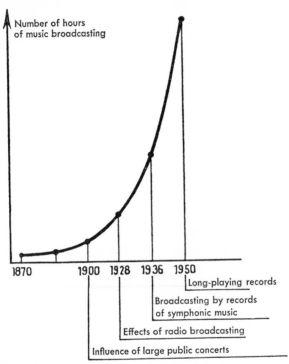

Fig. IV-1. The broadcasting of music in the modern era, expressed by number of hours
× auditors.

transmitted, stored, received, bought, and sold, its materiality increased. It became a concrete object, showing itself by its results:
The *"materia musica"* is born of recording, which puts music in the
situation of literature after the invention of printing. A musical
work is no longer unique; it is observable as a manufactured temporal item. This revolution occurred only a few years ago; the real
influence of music recording on the very conception of music scarcely
dates from earlier than 1936, the period when the broadcasting of
classical recordings of reasonable quality to a large public permitted
a shift of viewpoints about musical works (Fig. IV-1).

[page 112] Before recording, music was in the situation of every-day literature before printing; manuscripts scarcely played a socio-economic role. The popular tale, the story, the artisan's tricks of the trade, and technics were transmitted orally and existed only as re-created in the form of temporal material by a *storyteller*. The retold work was worth as much as the storyteller. Oral literature was thus reduced to a theme which, with a more or less faithful recitation, could be promoted or annihilated by the orator. Since printing, literature has become unchangeable; a text exists without changing; we speak of Goethe's *Faust* and not of the legend of Faust. This is the situation recording now imposes on music.

More than a convenient technical procedure for storing sound through time, recording in reality is mapping of *time into space*. It makes the once elusive temporal substance share the properties of space, among which *permanence* through time is the most evident.

Reproducibility is the functional requirement for the existence of a musical substance. It implies the existence of a *process*, in some form which need not be precisely specified, for retransforming the material trace of the sound into the sound itself. It differentiates *representation*, for example, the oscilloscope picture, from recording proper, for example, the groove in a phonograph record or a magnetic tape. The latter are truly sonic material conserved in space and through time. Reproducibility and permanence give the musical phenomenon "identity" and therefore bestow it with a *personality;* what is ephemeral has no identity. The ninth symphony of Beethoven recorded by Scherchen is a well-defined *objet d'art*, always the same, like all the discs printed from the same press, all the copies of the same film. It may be compared with the ninth symphony recorded by Von Karajan, making a matter of science what before could be only a comparison of somewhat gratuitous points of view.

Thus the recording arts remove one of the major obstacles to scientific esthetics. The extent of the recording arts is such that they are on the way to becoming "The Arts," addressing most of humanity.

This reproducibility, perfect in principle, this identity preserved through time, ought to be favorably received by the creative artist, because it offers him the permanence in time that he previously tried to guarantee for his work by the roundabout expedient of musical notation and of the many annotations which the scrupulous composer added. At the same time, the performer becomes essential because his interpretation of the work defines its actual form; the interpreter's field of freedom is disclosed by the judgments of the public [page 113] and of the composer himself, as long as he is alive. Thus recording furnishes the *guarantee of eternity* which is the avowed goal of every work of art.

Time is not reversible; its direction fixes the behavior of the universe, and temporal phenomena are not reversible. The musical signal, like a phonetic symbol, is conceived as having a direction of *flow;* it is *in step* with the universe. But the mapping of time into space makes time share space's reversibility: A recording is reversible, that is, it may be read in a direction inverse to that in which the composer imagined it. Playing a recording backward is an *experiment with time* which reveals the indications (Chap. V) the message gives about the direction of time's flow.

Moreover, mapping time into space by recording gives the temporal material divisibility and makes manipulation possible. The indivisible continuity of time becomes infinitely divisible; the sonic stuff which is attached to the length of a magnetic tape may be arbitrarily cut up, put together like a puzzle, mixed with other analogous temporal materials in a composition suggesting polyphonic writing, locally destroyed or modified, etc. In particular, if we divide it into fragments of length equal to the temporal perceptual quantum (1/16 second), we apprehend directly the message symbols of the repertoire.

3. REPRESENTATION OF THE TEMPORAL SONIC SUBSTANCE

Rather than by the abstract schematization of musical notation, which corresponds to nothing experimentally, a sonic message is most adequately represented by combinations of sonic elements in the repertoire L, f (level or loudness, and pitch) as a function of time. For the time being we leave aside the dimension of duration, which merges with time. Then (as we have seen in Chap. I, Sec. 5) we have two dimensions to characterize instantaneous sonic perception. (a) The pitch, corresponding to physical frequency f, is expressed in octaves or in cents (number of cents $= (1{,}200/\log_{10} 2) \times \log_{10} (f/f_0)$; there are 1,200 cents to the octave). (The mel scale represents the psychological, rather than the physical, scale of pitch.) (b) The level, corresponding to the physical intensity L, expressed in physical units of decibels (dB $= 20 \log_{10} p/p_0$). (The sone scale represents the psychological, rather than physical, scale of loudness.)

We also know that the receptor, the ear, divides these two dimensions into quanta. Thus each sonic element may be represented by an elementary square. A pure sinusoidal sound without harmonics, unlimited in length, such as an oscillator tone, would be represented by just one of these [page 114] squares, located in one place on the sonic map and lasting indefinitely in time. This map of the repertoire of elements of sonic perception is circumscribed by the border of the audible area. Above, it is bounded by the ear's "saturation" limit (around 120 dB). On the right toward the high frequencies,

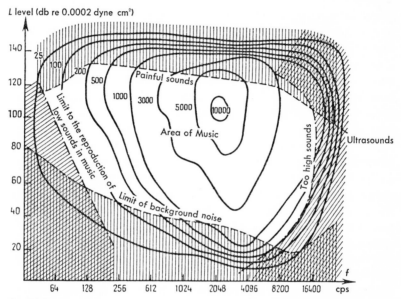

Fig. IV-2. Map of the musical domain in the plane $L \times f$. From the over-all acoustical area, we eliminate the sounds which are too weak and drown in the background noise, the sounds which are too strong and not normally usable, the sounds which are too high or low to be produced normally by instruments. The remaining area is the musical domain. The closed curves indicate the level of acoustical information (cf. Fig. I-4): the number of quantified squares $\Delta L\ \Delta f$ per unit of surface.

the upper limit of audibility (around 16,000 cps) traces the frontier of ultrasonics. On the left toward the low sounds, the area is limited by the frontier of infrasonics (around 16 cps). Finally, it is bounded below by the absolute threshold of audibility ($L_0 = 0$) which varies considerably with the pitch and reaches an absolute minimum little greater than the atmospheric background noise.

The second uncertainty principle ($N \times \Delta f = $ constant) means that, toward low sounds, the audibility threshold curve is a straight line at a $-45°$ angle to horizontal (with suitable units), and this is nearly the case.

Because thresholds quantize the continua of pitch and loudness, the repertoire is limited to some 340,000 elements. Physically, these elements are [page 115] smaller and denser toward the center of the sonic domain, where the ear is more acute. Practically, the musical or vocal message scarcely makes use of the very peripheral elements, for example, those of too weak intensity, which are too fragile in the ambient noise, or of too low pitch (large organ pipes). It seems (cf. Chap. III) that the effective difference thresholds which delimit the sonic elements are cruder than those determined in the laboratory. The map of the sonic domain appears as in Fig. IV-2.

In fact, no symbol in a sonic message is rigorously pure, as some steady tones on the flute are. In most cases each symbol is a combination of elements, that is, of a certain number of these squares, with, of course, different abscissas. The superposition of two cells over the same abscissa, that is, having the same frequency, would simply modify the level of the larger of the two. At first sight, the number of symbols seems enormous, on the order of $1,000^{1,000}$.

The elements chosen within the perceptual quantum of time constitute a symbol or a spectrum of elementary length. The ear perceives this form [page 116] in its entirety as the "timbre" of an elementary sound: *Timbre is the perception of the spectrum.*

The sonic material is thus the extension of the repertoire along the temporal dimension. Each definable temporal stage of this development represents a "symbol" analogous to a phoneme in language. Hence we represent the sonic material in a three-dimensional space by the system of coordinates L, f, and t. These axes define three planes of projection (Fig. IV-3).

(1) The plane L, f we have just considered. Following the terminology proposed by Schaeffer, we call it the *harmonic* plane, or the plane of *tone qualities* (*timbres*). The instantaneous spectrum takes shape in this plane. The spectrum generally is a continuous curve on which are superposed defined points (spectral lines or "partials" of the sound).

(2) The plane L, t represents the evolution of the average overall level of the sound as a function of time; this evolution is easy to determine experimentally. We call this the *dynamic plane.*

(3) In the plane f, t, called the melodic plane, the temporal evolution of the components of the spectrum is represented. In this plane the score would be inscribed; its staves unfold in time.

In order to study the evolution of sonic material, the definition of the length of the present Θ_0 leads us first to cut this space up in *slices* of thickness Θ_0 along the time dimension and to study the variation from slice to slice. (a) Cutting up duration according to the notes indicated in the score has almost no value if the melody has the slightest complexity, for example, if it has an accompaniment or a counterpoint. (b) On the other hand, many essential musical phenomena have a perceptual extent approximating this length Θ_0; for example,

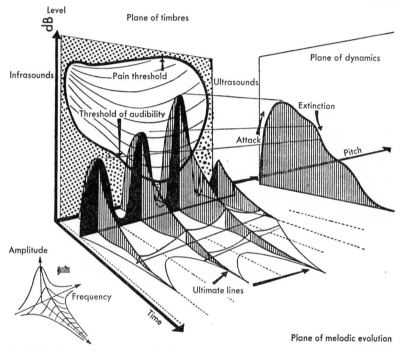

Fig. IV-3. Three-dimensional $L \times f \times t$ representation of the sonic object. In the plane $L \times f$, on the acoustic area, is projected the instantaneous spectrum of the sound. The evolution of the spectrum through time traces a volume representing the *sonic object.* Each slice with thickness the length of the present contains a recognizable "sonic symbol."

all attack or percussion transients of instruments, many *pizzicati* and *staccati,* and some consonants in speech: p, k, d, t, b.

But it is experimentally obvious that some more extended homogeneous structures are properly studied in their over-all evolution — in the dynamic plane, for example. An isolated phenomenon, for example, a chord in a reverberating empty room, is such a structure.

[page 117] By "experimentally obvious" we mean the following. Suppose we record a sound on magnetic tape and snip off sections of various lengths. If we let a "structure" be what some listening subject feels able to define perceptually, then a priori we ought to expect a uniform distribution of the lengths of "structures," that is, one length ought to be as likely as any other. But if we actually ask listeners to evaluate the "completeness" of such fragments, we find the lengths of "autonomous" or "whole" segments grouped in a vaguely Gaussian way around several privileged values, for instance, one second. These special lengths define objectively *sonic objects* having autonomous centers of interest.

A succession of forms *emerges* in the musical material; these forms are approximate units, sometimes ambiguous, but operationally definable. Phenomenological analysis of the sonic material creates an experimental unit to replace the "note" of the musical score, the operational arbitrariness of which we have denounced. We decompose the structural study of the *materia musica* into a study of the properties of these notes, then of collections of notes (solfège and composition). This is the process followed in the electronic synthesis of music, which starts from sonic objects, transforms them, *prepares* them, and recomposes them (Olson and Belar, 1955).

4. THE SONIC OBJECT

The "tone" of traditional music drew its meaning from the unique process which creates it on an instrument, since musical instruments are machines for fabricating tones. They produce small temporal segments having (a) internal *homogeneity* as to pitch and average level; (b) *individuality* acquired by the addition of "harmonics" to the fundamental, that is, by mixing in tones with frequencies that are natural number multiples of the fundamental; (c) *evolution* in time corresponding to a defined form in the dynamic plane, for example, a brusque attack, the body of the tone, a progressive decay. Each instrument furnishes a family of sounds, or more precisely, of symbols. The problem of orchestration consists in combining families of tones in order to make "complex tones" of them, often chords, operationally sonic objects. The use of many instruments, as in the orchestra, drowns the character of each instrument's tone in a higher complexity, but it is [page 118] possible to look for the same general criteria in this generalized tone which is also a sonic object.

Let us first establish harmonic and melodic laws governing the organization of symbols on an absolutely general basis.

I. Harmonic laws. Harmonic laws determine the organization of symbols from elements and the restrictions in principle which govern their combinations (Fig. IV-4).

First law: Each of the cells representing a pure elementary sound carries a certain quantity of energy. This quantity is a function of the cell's position on the map of the sonic domain: $A^2\omega^2$ or $[\log^{(-1)} L \times \log^{(-1)} f]^2$ to within constants.

The total energy transported by all the cells simultaneously clearly constitutes the energy of the sonic source. If that energy is very limited, especially as in the case of instruments of classical music, which have very little power, the source cannot create symbols *simultaneously* using many cells, or elements of pure sound. Therefore, one can create a white noise, with extended spectrum, only statistically; the procedure is to choose repeatedly, very frequently and erratically, among the elements within the temporal quantum of perception so that the choices are nonseparable. Then the elementary cells are used equiprobably and appear to be present simultaneously, since they have not had the time to vanish from perception.

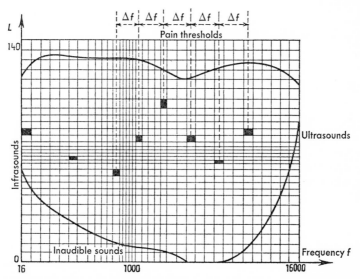

Fig. IV-4. The rule of harmonics expressed in the picture of a symbol: approximate statistical equidistance of the simultaneously chosen elements.

Second law: Even if many sources are not as simple as the vibrating elements of musical instruments, where everything has been done to concentrate the source of sonic energy in a single material body (for example, a string or air column), many sources are still more or less complicated [page 119] *vibratory systems.* Instead of having spectra — instead of creating symbols — of randomly chosen elements, these systems obey an approximate statistical law: The law of harmonics states that the frequencies of the elements of any symbol are multiples of each other or of the same greatest common divisor (partials). In other words, their pitches (horizontal coordinates, Fig. IV-4) on the map of the sonic domain will have equidistant abscissas, or will have abscissas separated by distances which are multiples of the same distance. This restriction on the choice of elements eliminates the equiprobability of symbols and limits the possible tone qualities. Thus it visibly increases redundancy while it creates periodicity. Here we find applied one of the results of Chap. II, Sec. 6.

Third law: The *law of convergence* results from the general properties of Fourier series, into which one can decompose every vibratory phenomenon with limited energy. These series, which create an equivalence between the spectrum and the form of the signal, are convergent obviously only if the amplitudes of the successive partials or harmonics decrease at least as fast as $1/n$, where n is their order, at least beyond a certain point. Thus the law of convergence says that in the graphical representation of the sonic domain, the cells representing elements used eventually fall below a straight line of slope -1. This law was formulated independently of us by Fano. (See Fig. IV-5.)

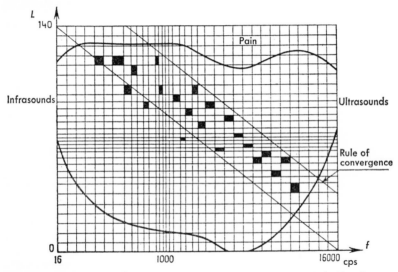

Fig. IV-5. The rule of convergence expressed in the picture of a symbol: The elements chosen are ultimately located below a parallel to the diagonal of the rectangle $L \times H$.

Fourth law: The *masking* law follows from the remark that the sonic quanta of the same pitch (same abscissa) cannot exist simultaneously without merging. Thus the sum of a quantum ($f = 1{,}000$ cps, $L_1 = 60$ dB) and of another quantum ($f = 1{,}000$ cps, $L_2 = 50$ dB) will give rise to a resultant quantum ($f = 1{,}000$ cps, $L = 63$ dB approximately). When two sound components within the same difference threshold of pitch have slightly different physical frequencies (for example, 1,000 and 1,005 cps), they give rise to beats, an envelope [page 120] vibrato. The beats are perceptible only if the sound levels are very close and the sounds last rather long.

This last law reduces to 1,000 or so the maximum number of sonic elements, discernible on the map of the sonic domain, which can be grouped together at the same time. This is the total number of pitch difference thresholds in the acoustical range.

These four "harmonic laws" govern the selection of elements which determine instantaneous tone quality (timbre). They restrict the effective repertoire of symbols of all sonic messages. In particular, these laws govern the structuring of the phonetic elements in speech, since the "phoneme" nearly corresponds to the sonic object.

By nature physically constraining, the fourth law, of masking, furnishes an upper limit to the variety of instantaneous symbols (spectra) which are available to become the sonic object at each instant. It furnishes an upper limit to the size of the repertoire of timbres. If there are 1,000 pitch difference thresholds, this upper limit will be on the order of 1,000! or $10^{2,560}$ (8,200 bits).

II. *Melodic laws* complement the harmonic laws. Melodic laws express the object's internal homogeneity and govern the evolution of symbols while the sonic object lasts.

First melodic law: This law simply expresses the repetition of symbols in time. The atomistic description of the sonic material implies a priori no memory from one symbol to another, no autocorrelation of symbols. Indeed, certain messages, for example, rain falling against a windowpane, suggest that there is *no* fundamental *natural necessity* for a correlation between successive sonic symbols. However, in the evolution of one sonic object, the successive portions separated by the ear's perceptual delay do not differ so much that there is no connection between them. Rather, they develop in time in a way which may be expressed as a sort of memory of the timbres from one instant to another — since a symbol is conditioned by the preceding symbols. This over-all evolution is connected with the existence in nature of energy dissipation in vibrating bodies. This evolution differentiates the sonic object from noise and gives it an internal coherence, a homogeneity. The homogeneity reduces the information the sound transmits while rendering it intelligible, that is, apprehensible as a *Gestalt*. To express the concept of autocorrelation, we shall say: "Each symbol cannot be very different from its immediate predecessor." Our statistical measures of autocorrelation within the sonic object (Moles, 1953a) have confirmed this law for varied sonic materials; we also showed that, with an autocorrelation interval of greater than 100 milliseconds, the autocorrelation alternately disappears with a dissolution into temporal incoherence and reappears.

Second melodic law: One may go further into this organization by trying to state precisely by *how much* the successive symbols differ from each other (see Moles, 1953a). We distinguish two categories of time intervals in the duration of the sonic objects: We call them *permanent* periods and *transient* periods. This distinction is not arbitrary, but rests on the ear's perception of variation in over-all level. [page 121] (a) In "transient periods" the over-all level L varies by more than 150 dB/sec (up to 600 dB/sec in music); for example, true consonants or instrumental attacks. (b) In "semipermanent periods" the level varies by more than several dozen dB/sec and by less than 150 dB/sec; for example, the semiconsonants of speech. (c) In "permanent periods" the level varies by less than 10 dB/sec.

The permanent periods constitute the body of the sonic object, most of its length. Here the evolution of symbols from one temporal element to another is slight (for example, as in vibrato) and the autocorrelation is great: The sonic material is defined. These periods correspond to the earlier concept in phonetics of pure vowels. They also suggest the concept of the indefinite pure tone in traditional musical acoustics. The average density of sonic elements in permanent periods is very small (20 to 100).

The transient periods often constitute a small fraction of the length of the sonic object, although certain sonic objects may be composed entirely of transients. Very generally, they are situated at the beginning and end of the sonic object. Characteristically, they combine many more elements, the number increasing as the period gets shorter. They are connected with the permanent period which follows them (or precedes them) by a progressive emergence of the elements of the latter from the many elements forming the transient symbol. A series of *refinements* or *filterings* of the elements tending to the *final elements* of the permanent system effects the emergence. If N is the number of permanent elements, the melodic law is stated thus: The average number N_t of elements present in the transient periods is proportional to the number of final elements and inversely proportional to the total length Θ of the transient period: $N_t = KN/\Theta$.

The laws governing the sonic object's internal structure thus define it operationally as an entity; they isolate it in the temporal continuum and make it a proper center of interest. The many experiments one may perform on isolated sonic objects constitute an experimental esthetics of isolated sounds somewhat analogous to the esthetic experiments one can perform with Rorschach blots. In musical tradition — which considers sonic objects only when they are assembled — the habit of experiments with isolated sounds has been lost. The perception of isolated sounds, and the many ways the individual interprets it as a function of his conscious or unconscious background, furnish a good projective test in sound which we have, indeed, used.

If one's attention is directed to an *isolated* sonic object, preceded and followed by unlimited silence, one tends to evaluate it intrinsically. Isolation implies recognition of all its dimensions starting from the center of interest which it represents in the temporal flow; in particular, perception includes estimating its duration as an autonomous dimension, *and no longer as a spatial reference point*. In perception of the sonic object, the autonomous perception of duration materializes and reveals the logarithmic law stated in [page 122] Chap. I, Sec. 2. The intrinsic coordinates of the sonic object are thus the three dimensions: (a) level = logarithm of physical intensity; (b) pitch = logarithm of physical frequency; (c) duration = logarithm of physical time. Note their homogeneity.

The presence of a center of interest "polarizes" time (duration). Prior to its existence all instants of time were undifferentiated, but this center creates a psychological state which gives rise to the sensation of duration. It differs from temporal material taken as a whole, which is a continuum exceeding perceptible duration; the saturation level of duration, as we have seen, is on the order of five to ten seconds. Physical, metrical time marks a flow with guide marks; it decomposes this flow. On the contrary, duration is psychologically perceived as a whole; it is a dimension of sensation. The esthetic procedure of isolating sonic objects is analogous to the sculptor's or decorator's isolating a marble work against a black velvet draping: This procedure directs attention to it, alone and not as one element among many in a complex framework. The study of isolated sonic objects may tempt the stringed instrument maker, the decorator, and the psychologist of time.

Originally, tones seem to have been connected with the instrument which produced them. When the instrument played alone, a tone had its own character; it was really a sonic object. Melody was born from the joining of these tones. The concept has outlived its cause; it has become artificial, incorporated in musical notation. What phenomenological meaning has an isolated flute tone in the ensemble of an orchestra? It has only an indicative, directive value for the flautist, but it is scarcely apprehensible by itself, save in the case of solo instruments. Our present study centers on the *whole* sonic message, temporal objects in the structured sequence constituting a musical composition. This assemblage will have to be studied in the context of physical time in the same way that we studied the elementary sonic object.

This remark raises the important esthetic question of the *value of the score*. If the score is an operating scheme, it is intended exclusively for the performers, but not at all for the listeners. Listeners who follow a piece in the score, wanting to know how the esthetic object they perceive [page 123] was *made*, are indulging in esthetic misconstruction. This frequent misconstruction, which we have denounced in a preceding work (Moles, 1957b), results from the confusion between *functional schemes* and *realization schemes*. Specialists in using the telephone, for example, businessmen, know absolutely nothing of telephones' electrical circuitry and construction, which interest only the service man; these specialists would find it bizarre if someone suggested to them that in order to use their apparatus well they must know its construction. Similarly, an automobile racer is not necessarily a specialist in mechanics. Closer to the esthetic domain, pictorial criticism has proclaimed many times that the painter's techniques and sleights of hand are not necessarily what cause us to understand the work. Certainly, one could not say such knowledge is harmful, or even useless; it is just unnecessary, an external aid. The artistic deed is *autonomous*, independent of its technique of construction. It may be accessible through its structures, but nothing a priori indicates that these are connected with the technique of construction.

It seems that the abusive use (at least as a reference) of the score must be attributed to two causes. One, historical, is that while music is now composed to be heard, it was initially composed to be played (for example, Gregorian chant, chamber music), that is, for participation in a collective game. The other was that until recently, no one could give a real representation of the perceived structure of the musical signal, even though numerous (timid) attempts had suggested what that structure might be.

Recent progress in the visualization of sonic objects or speech (for example, Sonagraph; see Potter *et al.*, 1947) may change this state of affairs and may give the esthetician a visual and colored representation of the complete sonic material, stripped of all reference to the operating scheme. The first attempts of this sort categorically justify the rejection of the operating scheme as an actual esthetic structure (Moles, 1954a).

Therefore, let us attempt a more direct, more phenomenological understanding of the sonic material, independent of the score.

A blind person without musical education — we may consider many radio listeners as such — perceives symphonic music not as notes, but as sonic objects, interlaced, organized in cells, in phrases, in movements, in pieces. In the sound complex that he hears at a particular instant, the listener is not interested in knowing that harmonic 13 was created by the oboe while harmonic 22 was [page 124] created in part by the violins and in part by the tuba. All *that* may interest the professional musician or the maker of stringed instruments, but not the listener; it is only of secondary value in helping him fathom the structure of the symphonic movement. From this viewpoint, the autonomous sonic object is independent of the fashion in which it was created.

Music has made up a repertoire of sonic objects, the value of which it has tested. These objects are generated by instruments constructed to amplify the vibrations of certain materials. The repertoire is limited by the possibilities for timbre, harmonic richness, and level of the instruments made by the traditional instrument-making craft, for example, strings, air columns, reeds, plates, and membranes, but ultimately nearly all sounds of traditional music group around combinations of a dozen fundamental timbres. Traditional music makes marvelous use of its repertoire, but after Wagner, conductors and composers deplored the poverty and the limitations of the classical orchestra in spite of the enrichments of men like Stravinsky and Ravel.

Recording, which materializes the sonic object and, like a musical instrument, permits us to re-create it at will, establishes no distinction in principle — that is, no qualitative distinction — among sounds. It appropriates them all indiscriminately and puts them on equal footing before the listener. But the sonic domain is, if not limitless, at the very least extremely rich in comparison with the narrow domain of musical instruments selected only because they had a sufficient sound level to hold their place in concert. If a particular "microsound" is richer than a 'cello, and we can capture it, why not use it? In fact, why not use all sounds, giving them the same status as those of classical instruments? That is the creative procedure of experimental music: to use any sonic object whatever in music which is only a dialectic of duration; to realize "the most general orchestra that exists" (Schaeffer). Schaeffer has already demonstrated some results. The recent creation of machines to fabricate sonic objects (RCA Electronic Sound Synthesizer, Meyer-Eppler, 1955) is an experimental demonstration of the interest of this viewpoint, in particular for the broadcasting of light music. The explicit goal of the RCA synthesizer, on the basis of a classification of the possible "preparations" of sonic material (Moles and Ussachevsky, 1957), is to create the most general imaginable musical sounds.

More recently, the numerous experiments conducted by Pierce, Guttman, and others on the synthesis of sounds by IBM computers, making use of the "cumulative power" intrinsic to computers, bring us very close to the actualization of those "sound cards" — providing instantaneous choice of quanta — which are described theoretically above.

5. INTERMEDIATE STRUCTURES

The scheme of the musical message which follows from the concept of temporal material as a sequence of sonic objects can be divided into levels according to the [page 125] orderings, the forms, which increase its redundancy and render it intelligible.

(1) *Elementary structures:* In these elements with temporal forms, periodicity is perceived as a quality of the sonic material. They become *symbols* within the length of the present.

(2) *Microstructures:* These periodicities connect into symbols. The development and collection of these symbols produce a perceptual form, the *sonic object.*

(3) *Intermediate structures:* The sequences of sonic objects, each lasting about half a second to a second, spontaneously break up into perceptual systems which last at most as long as the maximum length of presence, on the order of two to ten seconds. We shall call these organized systems, *cells.*

(4) *Macrostructures:* On the same scale as the musical message grasped in its entirety emerge perceptual macrostructures, often very different from those conceived by the composer. They are, on the contrary, largely a creation of the interpreter.

For the moment, we shall leave macrostructures aside, because they go beyond the logical instruments at our disposal, and shall limit ourselves to stating precisely the role of the intermediate structures, which are based on cells.

A *cell* is a system of sonic objects which are connected with each other in defined esthetic modes and are apprehensible in their entirety. It is separated from the adjacent cell, but rather vaguely, by the *contrast* of esthetic modes creating the internal connections of the two cells. It lasts approximately as long (five to ten seconds) as sensory memory conserves the presence of the events which mark it; thus it permits esthetic comparison among the events without the intervention of higher *intellectual mechanisms* (memorization). Musically, it corresponds more or less to the phrase, or to a well-defined fraction of the phrase. In spoken language, the sonic cell is the verse or the hemistich, the short phrase or the proposition.

Its limits are rather fuzzy; experimentally, cells are defined best in the plane of dynamics $L(t)$. Here, as a function of time, the level changes recognizably when one cell ends and another starts. In speech, defining cells is rather simple, and we have easily been able to isolate many experimentally in order to study their properly sonic aspects, [page 126] by methods such as, for example, inversion. One may consider the cell as a sort of micromelody inserted in the general melodic theme of macrostructures, but the constant interference of intellectual parameters (understanding of the speech or the music) and esthetic parameters proper makes it hard to study. From the strict viewpoint of a theory of sonic messages, it is easier to study phonetically a language we do not understand than a language we do understand, because we do not run the risk of mixing fundamentally distinct factors.

To study cells, we introduce an esthetic method based on recording. Much used in works of experimental esthetics, this method is the technical stratagem of inversion. Inversion may be effected by by making a record or magnetic tape turn in the opposite direction from that in which it was recorded. The principal result of this procedure is to break the normal connections of the temporal object with time, to make it recover its essential character of *strangeness*. This experiment with time breaks the temporal substance and recreates a different *presentation* of it.

We have used inversion and several other procedures (cf. Chap. V) such as cutting at random or with a periodicity approximating the size of the length of a cell, and simple repetition. Use of these procedures has shown the following:

(1) A cell is an objective, temporal sequence when it is cut in such a way that one can make a periodic theme of it. If properly recorded on a closed loop of magnetic tape with a short silence, an indefinitely repeated cell gives a sensation of periodicity without psychological "trauma" to perception.

(2) Among the esthetic modes which connect the sonic objects within one cell, a very special place must be given to rhythm, which was studied as a form in Chap. II. Rhythm organizes elementary sonic objects and normalizes their lengths to simple multiples of a rhythmic unit.

(3) Another mode of organizing cells is *fugue*, that is, progressive, often rapid, development of a repeated sonic object, until it dissolves or is completely transformed into the succeeding sonic cell.

Sonic cells are particularly difficult to study because they are vague, fluctuating units, tending to dissolve either in a particularly rich sonic object, or in a fragment of the macrostructure. Therefore, it is difficult to ascertain results other than [page 127] statistically. These statistics may rely on a systematic classification of sonic objects and cells according to a "dictionary of criteria" established empirically and refined by convergence. This classification is conceivable on punched cards, in special index card boxes, which permit families of criteria to arise by the usual procedures of classification techniques.

In view of these difficulties, we shall limit our study of cells to these brief remarks; this study has been fruitful up to the present only for phonetic messages whose individuality is easy to apprehend.

6. CONCLUSIONS

This chapter has been devoted to the sonic material and its organization. The principal method used was the *Gedanken experiment*. On the basis of a *viewpoint*, suggested by information theory, we attempted to "picture" the sonic phenomenon in a way as different as possible from the traditional, restoring to it the *strangeness* which it had lost to our eyes, too used to the viewpoint of physics or musical theory.

We considered the sonic phenomenon as a message and made an atomistic study of it. Then we re-created its structure by putting together temporal elements which were a priori isolated from each other. By its difference from the traditional method, which considered periodicity — that is, permanence — as essential, and only thereafter modified this permanence, our method has permitted us to separate the *necessary*, that is, what follows from the very nature of things (for example, the "harmonic laws"), from the *contingent*, which is only statistically imposed (for example, more or less "periodicity").

We summarize as follows the principal results:

(1) The study of the musical message from the viewpoint of scientific esthetics cannot be based upon *musical theory*. The inadequacy of musical theory is denounced by musicians themselves, and its dogmatic foundations are not confirmed by psychological experiment.

(2) A phenomenology of musical perception makes evident a *temporal sonic material*. By transforming it into an *observable object*, recording makes this material concrete.

(3) Recording spreads time over space; it is a mapping of time into space. It gives time the properties of space, in particular, reproducibility, permanence, reversibility, and divisibility.

(4) The temporal sonic substance is adequately represented by a three-dimensional diagram of level, pitch, and time, representing the evolution of timbre (spectrum) in the course of time.

[page 128] (5) The continuity of sound is subdivided operationally into *sonic objects* each possessing an autonomous center of interest. When one is isolated, a direct perception of duration as a dimension of the sonic object is organized around it.

(6) The recomposition of sonic objects from elements specified by L, f obeys restrictive laws:

— harmonic: 1: law of energy;
            2: law of harmonics;

3: law of convergence;

4: law of masking;

— melodic: 1: law of permanence;

2: law of transients.

(7) The sonic objects captured by recording are independent of their origin. There is no reason for music conceived as the dialectic of time to use only those from the a priori "musical" instruments; any sound, any noise, can take its place in a would-be "most general orchestra"; this is the first step of experimental music.

(8) The score is an operating scheme without essential esthetic value. It does not furnish the fundamental structures directly; it remains extrinsic to them.

(9) The structures of the message include

— an *elementary structure:*	the periodicity of the sonic material leading to *symbols* (*instantaneous spectra*);
— a *microstructure:*	the collection of symbols leading to the *sonic object;*
— an *intermediate structure:*	the evolution of the sonic objects according to defined esthetic modes leading to the *temporal cell;*
— a *macrostructure:*	the composition of objects and cells.

(10) Except in phonetics where the cell corresponds to the verse and is easy to grasp objectively, the intermediate structures are evanescent and difficult to study. Various procedures such as inversion and cutting provide means of fighting this transience.

The study of macrostructures, which is the object of the following chapter, requires first of all a new broadening of information theory to eliminate a paradox resulting from the concept of originality.

Semantic
Information and
Esthetic Information

CHAPTER V

The question is not what code should we use, but what code do we use.
N. WIENER

1. AN APPARENT PARADOX IN INFORMATION THEORY

In Chap. I, where we stated the foundations of the theory, we defined a message as a sequence of elements drawn from a repertoire. We defined its relative information content as proportional to its originality or unpredictability, compared to the possible maximum, which is obtained only if all the repertoire's elements are equiprobable. Redundancy reduces information; it manifests the influence of any internal organization in the message known simultaneously to both receptor and transmitter — more generally, in the case of a message from nature, known a priori to the receptor. Redundancy expresses statistically the receptor's a priori knowledge of the message. Redundancy opposes information in a dialectic banal-original, but conditions the message's intelligibility by creating an internal organization in it.

We saw that the transmitted information and the redundancy of a message are functions of the repertoire of symbols with which the receptor is concerned. Symbols were defined as groupings having a defined form known a priori to the receptor; for example, typographical characters are composed of universally accepted collections which are always topologically the same. The information symbols transmit depends on their presence in entirety or absence in entirety. The receptor is *not* interested in the details of the spots in each letter. The set of typographical signs is the effective repertoire and the information from the letters is calculated on the basis of this repertoire. Similarly, letters may be grouped into words. The words are grasped whole, as forms, and the repertoire is then the dictionary, or more exactly, the *usual* vocabulary which is effectively available to the receptor; [page 130] formal organizational structures such as grammatical rules of composition determine the information and redundancy of collected words.

A printed page has one repertoire and information content for a savage or a child — who "reads" the visible spots of black and white on the surface in a desultory order; it has another for a proofreader or a foreigner not knowing the language — who reads the letters; it has a third for the ordinary reader — who reads the words; and still another for a page compositor who "reads" the blocks of type. Each has his repertoire, and each finds his own redundancy and originality in the page; these are functions of his knowledge, of his mental habits, of his education. In practice, when we speak of the information of a written or printed text, we refer implicitly to the information gained by some "average" reader; the structure this reader supplies is a function of the general knowledge which the social group of individuals having nearly the same statistical culture is supposed to possess. Certainly, the reader is sensitive to the typography; a visible change in a character comes to his attention as an original signal, but he classes it as an error in transmission. In the same way, a change in the style of the letters gives him information on *another* problem than that of reading.

This observation leads to a hierarchy of levels of repertoires. It is always advisable to return to an analysis of levels after completing the study of a given level, because one of the principal obstacles information theory runs into in practice is the receptor's shifting of levels; the human receptor, capable of grasping extremely varied repertoires, can frequently change levels, and hence repertoires, in the course of reception, in order to find — spontaneously — the optimum level of redundancy in a given situation. That this level of redundancy need not necessarily be the highest, the level of greatest intelligibility, condemns a too hasty application of a "principle of least effort" to this problem. Indeed, there is a sort of "informational accommodation," as Frank remarks.

Thus the first rational extension of information theory is to consider successively several levels on which the receptor grasps the message. These levels give rise to superposed messages, all different, in principle, from each other. Each level has its own signs, its code, its repertoire, hence its rate of information per sign, and its redundancy. The set of information measures, $H_1, H_2, \ldots, H_n$, and the parallel set of redundancy measures at each level $r_1, r_2, \ldots, r_n$ constitute an *information blueprint* of the total message; we might compare it with the floor plans that an architect makes for a house.

One may distinguish different forms at each level of perception, and these forms may conflict more or less in the mind of the observer. Conflict arises very often in listening to music and in esthetic perception, for example, and this conflict renders informational study very difficult.

What would happen if the receiving subject, as a result of his culture, or his a priori knowledge, or for some other reason, increased his knowledge of the message transmitted to him, of its modes of structuring, of its symbols and their frequencies, etc.? The resulting originality of the message, for him personally, would diminish; the message would transmit a smaller quantity of information. The redundancy would tend to 100 per cent.

For artistic messages transmitted to a social aggregate, each individual receptor has an array of personal knowledge (sociocultural "scoreboard") which determines the information that he receives. If the receptor has complete knowledge of the message to be transmitted to him, that is, if he "knows" this message a priori, the information is null, the redundancy is 100 per cent, the message is uninteresting and banal as, for example, the pictures on postage stamps. This is all coherent and obvious.

But every collection known a priori constitutes a symbol, a defined form which can be *coded*, that is, condensed into a shorter symbol. We code the collection by eliminating the redundant elements (for example, in telegraphic style), or even by replacing it by a conventional sign just long enough to pick out the whole message from the set of other such messages, for example, the call numbers of books in a library. But there are many other ways of coding a cultural message, for example, by the title or first measures, for a symphony, by the first verse, for a poem (many catalogs of poems [page 131] have an index of first lines). Certainly, if we know a message perfectly, as we do for many artistic works, recalling the first line of a poem of Shelley may induce us automatically to recite the entire continuation. Similarly, for a veteran music listener, the title of a symphony prepares and expresses the symphony as a whole; its whole temporal development is registered in the title. If the listener knows a particular piece by heart, the first measures ineluctably imply the end, just as, if a reader knows a book, its title implies its content.

Therefore shall we say that the information it brings us is null, since "we know it already" and that, since it is pure banality, it is superfluous to retransmit such a message, which teaches us nothing? In other words, and more precisely: Does the title equal the symphony if we know the whole piece? Is the first line of the poem equivalent to the poem known by heart? And why should we go to the theater to see Hamlet performed if we know the play already?

It is perfectly evident that this is only an apparent paradox and that we never possess all the information implied by the title of the work, even if we know all its words or notes. But it will be interesting, starting from this obvious remark, to make explicit precisely how the symbol falls short of the entirety of the thing symbolized and to determine why, for example, owning a recording of a musical work is not equivalent to hearing this work. In what many ways does the hearing of a piece transcend the owning? Why is it worthwhile reviewing copies or the original of the Mona Lisa thousands of times? In other words, just what information does the message "known" a priori, the cultural message, supply? How, in the sense of perceptual psychology, can it determine one's reactions if it is already known?

2. EXISTENCE OF TWO ASPECTS OF INFORMATION

When an individual rereads a book that he knows, even if he wrote it himself, when he rehears a symphony whose themes he knows by heart, even if he conducted it, still he never knows the message so exactly, so perfectly, and in such detail that he gains absolutely nothing new from it. It is never totally banal to him. There is always something to be drawn from it, a residual information to be gleaned, because a human being's memory cannot exhaust a message of such scale. The case of an author rereading his own work and finding in it sentences that he did not know is an extreme example of this.

A receiver can try to *exhaust* the information in the message by repeating it. This process depends on the receptor's limited capacities for memory and total [page 132] apprehension. But this affirmation does not resolve the problem for two reasons.

First, the mnemonic capacities of individuals vary greatly. At one extreme is the child who "learns" a story by reading it once; at the other is the actor who can memorize tens of pages of text. Now it seems to be just such individuals as these who tend, for cultural or other reasons, to go back to a cultural message in order to exhaust it. If a theatrical play that one likes can be learned by heart, why go see it played again?

Second, many cultural messages, such as citations, short poems, everyday formulas, and proverbs — which we will not discuss here — are short enough to fall within the extent of the operating memory for signs, no matter how slight that may be. But these are not totally and necessarily *banal* simply because we know them.

Thus the rationale of *exhaustion* is not sufficient to cause the repetition of esthetic messages — note that it is esthetic messages which are repeated, not, for example, the news on the radio, the interest of which passes with its object.

Exhaustion can be a valid explanation when, for example, an individual who does not understand a piece of news on the radio needs to hear it repeated or when he rereads a newspaper article which is obscure or too rich for him (for example, texts with increasing information, nos. 6 and 7, Chap. I, Sec. 5). But exhaustion is an inadequate rationale when the terms of the message are banal (texts nos. 2, 3, 5) or when, on the contrary, they exceed the limit of the rate of information transmittable through language (for example, nos. 8, 9) without, however, obliging the reader to reread the message thousands of times. In other words, this explanation fails when the human individual is clearly looking, not so much for logical information in the message, as for an *esthetic originality* which transcends the collection of symbols in order to create an effect.

We are thus led to distinguish two viewpoints toward the message. These viewpoints correspond to two types of information.

(a) The *semantic,* logical, structured, expressible, translatable viewpoint prepares actions.

(b) The *esthetic,* untranslatable viewpoint shapes states of mind.

Until now, we made the gratuitous simplification of supposing [page 133] that the receptor was sensitive to one repertoire and *to one alone;* we assumed that in each case (for example, the printed page), he considered *only one way* of grouping the simple elements of perception to build supersigns. We supposed implicitly that the individual receptor was interested uniquely in the arabesques making up written signs, or was only a proofreader, or only a reader, or only a page compositor; we supposed tacitly that these situations were mutually exclusive.

All the evidence says this is not the case: Nothing prevents the proofreader from being able to read the text that he corrects. Reciprocally, nothing prevents the reader from having interest in the letters, in, for example, the spelling of a word or the design of the letters, as well as interest in the more or less "esthetic" arrangement of the articles and titles on the page of a newspaper. On the contrary, everyday experience leads us to believe that the latter case corresponds to reality.

Within the same material message, there is a superposition of several distinct sequences of symbols. These symbols are made of the same elements grouped in different ways. They correspond to the two most general *viewpoints* that the individual can have about the messages he receives from the external world: the *semantic* and the *esthetic*. We shall try to characterize these two unambiguously in a dialectical dipole. Indeed, in every message they define two types of repertoires, rules of organization, structures, and therefore two types of originality.

3. SEMANTIC AND ESTHETIC INFORMATION

We propose the existence of two types of information in messages generally. These types of information depend on how an observer outside the transmission channel groups elements of the message in order to relate them to repertoires. (a) *Semantic* information, having a universal logic, structured, articulable, translatable into a foreign language, serves in the behaviorist conception to prepare *actions*. (b) Instead of to a universal repertoire, *esthetic* information, which is untranslatable, refers to the repertoire of knowledge common to the particular transmitter and particular receptor. Theoretically, this information cannot be translated into any other "language" or system of logical symbols because this other language does not exist. One may liken it to the concept of personal information.

[page 135] The existence of an external observer is philosophically necessary for the distinction between those two types of information, as Cherry (1957) has shown. He makes it clear that the scheme for studying interindividual communication must appear as follows:

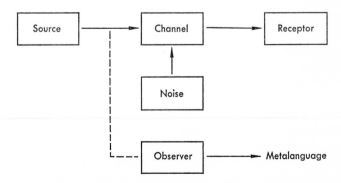

In addition to the normal source-receptor channel, the *observer* who examines the signals received from the source constitutes an auxiliary channel. This observer, considering the signals discrete and free of noise, describes them in a universally intelligible *metalanguage*.

Objective psychology takes it for granted that a perception determines a reaction. Therefore we must explain the distinction between the semantic and esthetic viewpoints in the nature of the reactions determined by these two.

The *semantic* viewpoint asks a question about the state of the external world, about its material evolution. This question must prepare *decisions* about either present or future acts or [page 134] attitudes. This viewpoint prepares the receiving subject for an external reaction. Behaviorism is interested in this viewpoint. Under the impulse of K. Lewin, Hull, etc., recent progress in cybernetics (Ashby, 1956; Walter, 1953; and others) is oriented to the search for analog models to illustrate behavioristic psychology (simple reflexes, conditioned reflexes, learning, etc.). When a regulator transmits orders to a central power station by a remote control system, it transmits semantic information. Similarly, a military order, an electrical circuitry diagram, a coded message, instructions in case of fire, a technical manual, a musical score, etc., all convey *essentially* semantic information. They prepare acts, forms of action, and in general, semantic information has a clearly utilitarian, but above all *logical*, character. It sticks to acts and to meaning. At the level of language, it obeys the laws of universal logic: It is logical in the sense that all the receptors of the message accept its rules and symbols; it becomes universal. In other words, it uses the statistical part common to all men of the sociocultural matrix. In the communication A_{ij} from any individual i to any individual j, the structural rules of semantic information (for example, those defining musical notation, mathematical notation, or road signs) use the part common to all i and j, and thus constitute a standardized code.

An important and interesting consequence is that semantic information is exactly *translatable* into a foreign language, since it follows from the symbols and laws of a universal logic common to all languages. More generally, it is *commutable* from one channel to another: The same quantity of information can be transmitted to an individual by writing, speech, radio, or pictures — often, it is true, at different rates.

But this does not exhaust the originality contained in the message. *Esthetic* information does not have the *goal* of preparing decisions; it has no goal properly speaking. It does not have the characteristic of *intent*; in fact, it determines *internal states*. At least in typical cases, psycho-estheticians or even psychophysiologists can verify objectively only the repercussions of these states (esthetic emotion, physiological works on the sensations of music, etc.). Thus the viewpoint is not at all utilitarian. "Art is quite useless," said Wilde, although it would be simple-minded to restrict esthetic information to art properly called. The reactions that it may eventually determine are neither immediate nor necessary. Esthetic information is specific to the *channel* which transmits it; it is profoundly changed by being transferred from one channel to another. A symphony cannot replace an animated cartoon; it is different in essence. Esthetic information is not *translatable;* it is only *approximately transposable,* that is, it has only equivalents, not equals.

In the process of determining statistically what the message was from its elements, the first step is to fix the logical content of the message by using normalized symbols, that is, symbols recognized by a group of some size or other, but definable by individuals whose "receptive structure" is characterized by objective statistical properties. Thus, the semantic [page 136] part of speech comes from a repertoire of sounds corresponding to the 87 vocal signs of the international phonetic alphabet. The goal of phoneticians constructing the alphabet was explicitly to make it capable of unambiguous recognition as such by 3,000,000,000 human beings. The phonetic alphabet constitutes the translation of the semantic message into another system, that of written symbols.

But a message determined by symbols of the phonetic alphabet is still not exactly determined as an acoustical signal. There is still a broad margin of uncertainty about the structure to be materialized in time by a piece of magnetic tape. This *field of freedom* leaves room for another type of message. The field can be decomposed on each temporal level into a system of quanta, of unit symbols from which a repertoire may be built up. Each unit symbol in the field of freedom can be chosen with definable probabilities, since, for example, some ways of interpreting a phoneme may be more frequent than others. Thus individual variations independent of the universal semantic content of the message may exist.

The transmitter no longer appears strictly normalized, but personalized. A message becomes personal in the field of esthetic information. With esthetic information, the channel is specified by the matrix A_{ij}. With semantic information, the channel is *universal* among individuals defined by *general* properties common to all.

Semantic information is the message carried by sequences of normalized sounds, of normalized phonemes, of phonetic words from the repertoire of the vocal dictionary, of type sentences, etc. Esthetic information is the message carried by a certain individual's preferential choice of certain frequencies and certain combinations to compose spectral symbols, of certain lengths of phonemes, of certain phonemic combinations, etc. The preferential choice follows from the constitution of his vocal tract. To each choice is attached a coefficient of relative frequency. Thus at each structural level, an objectively apprehensible rate of information is defined.

The situation is the same in the musical channel. The specification by the score of a musical interval only very crudely fixes the dominant pitch. It fixes the fundamental and a partial corresponding to the interval, in fact, two dominant lines. But we are told nothing about the spectrum to be realized in practice. The spectrum can vary within a very large field of freedom either because the orchestra score may indicate nothing about the instruments (as in reduced scores) or because an interval scored for violin and 'cello, say, is still open to the variations from one instrument to another. The study of the esthetic message is then the study of [page 137] execution (performance) based on a *metric picture* of the information transmitted at each level of the temporal scale.

Messages with exclusively semantic or purely esthetic content are theoretical limits, dialectical extremes. Every real message has some of each. Semantic information, related to the universal aspects of the individual's mental structure, is rather easy to measure and to determine objectively; hence it is better known.

On the other hand, esthetic information is randomized and specific to the receptor, since it varies according to his repertoire of knowledge, symbols, and a priori structurings, which in turn relate to his sociological background. It is very poorly known and difficult to measure. By the simplest and most valid hypothesis, we shall assume, however, that esthetic information obeys the same general laws that govern all informative messages, and that, with appropriate units, it can be measured in the same way, *mutatis mutandis*.

Part of the news on the radio is obviously semantic information; it determines the reactions of most of the public, or at least of a logically definable fraction of the auditors. This part is, for example, the weather forecast, if we want to go out the next day; the stock market reports, if we are shareholders; administrative information, if we are under an administration; laws and decrees, if we are under a government.

Another part of the news (for example, feature stories) is essentially *gratuitous*. It "informs" in the common sense of the word. It communicates anger or euphoria without determining any present or future reaction, save storage in the memory. This part is principally esthetic information.

Thus, in a speech, an orator tries to convince as much by the warmth, attractiveness, and persuasiveness of his voice as by the purely logical implications of what he states.

In a theater play, the argument, the action, the story told, as well as the grammatical structures and the logical implications, are semantic information. The movements of the actors, the warmth of their voices, their expressions, the richness of the scenery are chiefly esthetic information. The auditor obviously looks for the latter rather than for the "story" of Hamlet in the theatrical work of art.

Although materially connected, these two kinds of information, these two messages, obey independent structural laws. Without affecting the esthetic information, a theatrical play may have an incoherent, illogical, or even senseless plot, increasing its semantic originality, or on the contrary a logical, rigid, inevitable, foreseeable plot, decreasing the originality and making the play easier to follow. The esthetic information also may be too large or too small relative to the optimum amount of information which the average spectator can assimilate.

A picture certainly has a semantic aspect. The subject, the represented objects' relations of equilibrium, perspective, and anatomy are connections among "symbols," which are here the forms represented. But the esthetic aspect of the pictorial message ultimately preponderates in determining the value of the message for the spectator. This aspect also has a redundancy: adherence to a more or less pronounced traditional style of connecting forms, a dominant color of the picture so characteristic of certain painters, the brush stroke. This redundancy as a whole is a priori knowledge which defines the *style* of the painting. The original parts of the esthetic message express statistically what gives value to a particular painting within a given style; they are what [page 139] traditional pictorial esthetics calls by the vague terms *personality* of the picture, *mastery, originality,* etc. A coherent experimental esthetics must make these terms precise by capturing them in a numerical definition of esthetic originality.

Modern painting has developed from the traditional in very characteristically different ways. In general, modern paintings have considerably larger rates of originality; the quantity of information, the unforeseeability contained in the pictorial message, is incomparably greater than what it was 80 years ago. For example, the concept of "figure" which was so essential to paintings of the last century has been destroyed. But two trends share the increase of originality. Surrealism has mainly increased semantic information by breaking the "normal" connections that the world suggests to the spectator: bonds of perspective, functional bonds, traditional bonds between objects or parts of an object. Thus it decreases the structuring and increases the semantic originality by decomposing forms and their normal connections. The nonrepresentational school goes further in increasing esthetic information; it breaks down styles, traditional connections between colors, etc. (See Fig. V-1.)

This example leads us to schematize the message from the external world as transporting two types of information. From the initial symbols, the two types are simultaneously and progressively reduced, while interacting with each other as shown in the diagram on page 135.

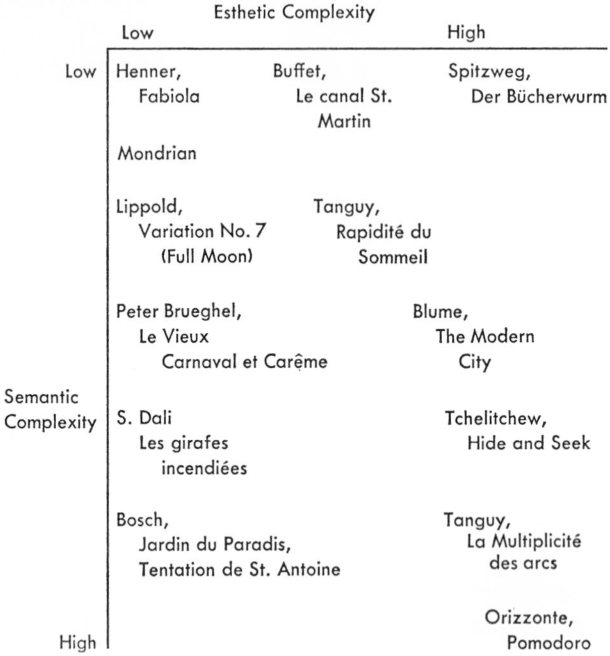

	Esthetic Complexity		
	Low		High
Low	Henner, Fabiola	Buffet, Le canal St. Martin	Spitzweg, Der Bücherwurm
	Mondrian		
	Lippold, Variation No. 7 (Full Moon)	Tanguy, Rapidité du Sommeil	
	Peter Brueghel, Le Vieux Carnaval et Carême		Blume, The Modern City
Semantic Complexity	S. Dali Les girafes incendiées		Tchelitchew, Hide and Seek
	Bosch, Jardin du Paradis, Tentation de St. Antoine		Tanguy, La Multiplicité des arcs
High			Orizzonte, Pomodoro

Fig. V-1. Dimensional classification of some works of art with regard to their esthetic and semantic contents. Several widely known works of pictorial art are arranged in this figure according to their semantic and esthetic "complexity content." It is apparent that the intelligible semantic information, which relates to the subject and known forms of the picture, varies considerably among painters of the same school from one picture to another; the artist is never the prisoner of the subject. On the other hand, the esthetic information, connected with the execution of the picture, the brush strokes, the irregularity of the spots of color, pointillism, the continuity, shadows, and unforeseeability of the motion, much better characterizes that ephemeral entity which estheticians call "style."

To make this an exhaustive classification, we would have to add at least one dimension, the emotional dimension. We have ignored this dimension entirely, although it is extremely important for the work of art, because it has been poorly explored and is still poorly known.

A representation with these dimensions, plus a temporal dimension, would reveal the leading lines of the evolution of art over the centuries.

Such an arrangement of the factors which determine the general structure of a message should be useful in experimental esthetics to determine the *subordination of structures* and the correspondences between esthetic and semantic symbols, especially in multiple messages; the scheme helps to determine the hierarchy of the symbols

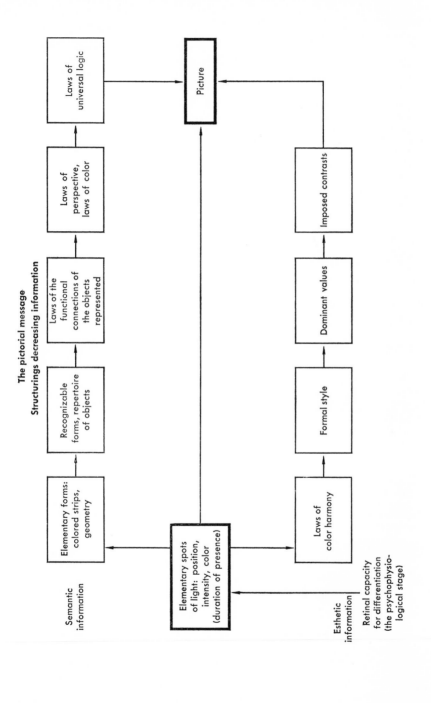

The pictorial message
Structurings decreasing information

Semantic information

| Elementary forms: colored strips, geometry | → | Recognizable forms, repertoire of objects | → | Laws of the functional connections of the objects represented | → | Laws of perspective, laws of color | → | Laws of universal logic |

→ Picture

Elementary spots of light: position, intensity, color (duration of presence)

Esthetic information

| Laws of color harmony | → | Formal style | → | Dominant values | → | Imposed contrasts |

Retinal capacity for differentiation (the psychophysiological stage) which come to the receiver's attention. In the following, we shall give some analogous schemes for several principal esthetic messages.

4. SUBORDINATION OF THE STRUCTURES OF SONIC MESSAGES

Clearly, the difference between semantic and esthetic information, no matter how justifiable logically, has no interest if it is not [page 140] operationally based, that is, if it cannot be tested experimentally.

We shall develop the distinction between the two types of information in the case of the sonic message, taken as one of the arts of time and as a model of the temporal message. (We studied the microstructure of the sonic message in the preceding chapter.)

The two principal types of sonic message, *speech* and *music*, differ notably in their relative semantic and esthetic contents, even though they are composed of the same sonic material.

We have already characterized the semantic part of spoken language as opposed to the esthetic part. Except perhaps for telephone conversations and the like, the latter is never absent from speech. Most ordinary samples of speech, however, are mostly semantic in function. Language serves primarily to exchange ideas, concepts, orders, that is, to create interindividual relations. Nevertheless, certain types of language have been turned away from serving to communicate; poetry and oratorical art have a clear preponderance of esthetic information ("étonner, émouvoir, ravir un spectateur" — Musset). In pure poetry, semantic information is only a sort of limit, a material support for intelligence. In this framework, untranslatable esthetic information, an original *tone*, contributes to the art of style, which is to suggest rather than to say. The rules which govern the art of style are precisely the laws of esthetic information. In journalism, the theory of rewriting shows that to popularize is to decrease the rate of semantic information per symbol in favor of the esthetic message.

We studied this problem experimentally in a paper dealing with the influence of speech rate, accentuation (probable dynamic range), and the frequency spread of speech. We showed the existence of "lines of force" on the acoustical chart presented in Chap. IV (see Moles, 1954b). Other studies confirming the results and stressing the same parameters have been made more recently by Lieberman on the emotional content of language (*J. Acoust. Soc. Amer.*, 34[7]:922).

In music, the semantic message is rather slight. It is whatever is "intelligible" in the musical message, whatever constitutes a net of logically or symbolically apprehensible relations. The essential part of the semantic message of music is the *scheme* of the music, the score, a translation into universal symbolic language of often complex operations. The structural rules and laws governing most scores constitute the doctrines known as solfège, melody, harmony, counterpoint, and orchestration. These doctrines are dogmatic without a very solid experimental foundation, as we remarked in the preceding chapter, but they are at the same time very complex and very rigid. In other words, the semantic information of music is very slight; its redundancy is great. At least for specialists who know the symbolic code of [page 141] musical notation, it is a message that is very foreseeable and easy to reconstruct. We estimated the semantic information in Chap. I, Sec. 10.

On the other hand, the esthetic information of music is great. First, as the preceding chapter suggests, its set of symbols is infinitely richer than that available to notation; it extends beyond and transcends notation, which is only a scheme for performance. Second, the structural rules that it obeys, though still little known to us, seem very slight. The discretionary margin of musical originality is very great.

On seeing the score, which he usually knows only superficially, the layman too often believes that music is an entirely precise, defined art, which allows no arbitrariness or variability. The contrary is true. Marc Pincherle denounces the imprecision of musical texts thus: "Let us avoid the simple-minded idea . . . that written music is a precise, complete language such that its realization in sound is perfectly assured by the double mechanism — a reflex in an accomplished virtuoso — of sight-reading and instrumental performance: [if that were the case,] there would be one type of performance with which said virtuoso would necessarily have to end up. Opposed to that are the thousand divergencies among the physical persons of artists, as well as among their instruments . . . to the point that one would search in vain for two performers capable of furnishing two entirely identical versions of any significant fragment. But the notation itself does not have the imperative perfection that the uninitiated are wont to attribute to it."

Relative to the scheme of the score, several "degrees of freedom" are available to the musical signal, to the *materia musica*.

(1) There are the *imperfections of the score* itself. The score cannot notate precisely, for example, modes of attack, in spite of efforts over the centuries to improve it (staccato and pizzicato notation, trills, orchestral indications). A recent effort, the Klavarskribo, represents an enormous effort to rationalize and increase the precision of notation. But even the most recent do not claim at all to be perfectly precise.

(2) *Variations in orchestration* can modify greatly the sonic ma-

terial, which depends on the distribution and use of the instruments, without changing the score. Each orchestra has its own special instrumentation. At best, one might imagine a notation, for an instrument with fixed sounds such as a piano, in which the symbolizations have some quantitative agreement with the sonic substance they sketch. But it would be illusory to claim as much for an orchestra or even a simple string quartet.

(3) Because of the *variations in the construction* of instruments, there are no two identical pianos, no two identical violins. The variations can be enormous: Think of the difference between Bach's *Klavier* and the piano on which we perform Bach today. A [page 142] very special instrument very often ignored is the resonator, the concert hall itself, which does play a role in the music.

(4) Above all, there are the differences or latitudes in *interpretation* which arise from the instrument (or orchestra) and the performer (or conductor). In the case of the richest sonic signal, that of the orchestra, the latitudes can attain such fantastic values, particularly in the length of performance, that it is impossible to speak of a symphonic work without at least referring to a particular performer, if not a particular performance. Such a reference would have been illusory 50 years ago, but is meaningful now because of recording, which defines a performance adequately.

Even now, a musical work is systematically collective. It has at least two authors who participate nearly equally: the composer, who furnishes the operating scheme, and the performer, who "realizes" (Scherchen) the scheme. Unlike Wagner, composers are rarely the best performers or conductors, and vice versa. Only in very special cases can the work be attributed to a single author. However, in experimental (tape) music, the composer himself manipulates, transforms, and prepares at leisure the raw sound recorded on magnetic tape; without using either score or interpreter, he creates directly in the studio with scissors and splicing tape (for example, Meyer-Eppler's "authentic composition").

In short, the signal has much freedom relative to the semantic message. The musical message is composed principally of esthetic information obeying very poorly known rules. One of the tasks of experimental esthetics is to determine these rules. The innumerable divergencies and latitudes in interpretation nevertheless obey rules which are all their own. Thus, a *crescendo*, a *rallentando*, follow certain metric rhythms from one instant to the next; within each tenth of a second they do not vary at random. All the statistical rules together create the effective structure of the esthetic message by restraining its arbitrariness and determine its effective information output.

We can estimate quantitatively several of the factors in esthetic information, using the concept of a permissible deviation from the indicated norm for each parameter defining the sonic object. The norm might be, for example, the score.

Loudness levels or dynamic contrasts for music range between 30 and 100 dB. The musical score notates:

	1	2	3	4	5	6	7	
	ppp	pp	p	mf	f	ff	fff	
dB:	20	40	55	64	75	85	95	(Stokowski)

[page 143] Given 12 notated pitch levels, musical practice allows a deviation of *one* level if it is progressively brought in, say over a period longer than one second — 10 to 15 quanta of duration.

The absolute speed (metronome speed) in performances of classical symphonies easily varies by 15 per cent in comparison with the normalized value.

LENGTH OF THE DIFFERENT PARTS OF BEETHOVEN'S NINTH SYMPHONY (in minutes and seconds)

Conductors	Allegro	Scherzo	Adagio	Finale	Whole
Furtwängler	17.35	11.50	19.35	24.50	73.50
Scherchen	17.20	12.20	16.10	26.00	71.50
G. Wand	16.25	11.20	17.15	23.50	68.50
W. Goehr	14.15	11.55	17.20	23.55	67.25
Kleiber	15.45	10.15	16.50	23.30	66.20
Hörenstein	15.10	11.20	14.50	23.20	64.40
Karajan	14.50	10.00	15.55	23.55	64.40
Toscanini	13.15	13.00	14.05	23.05	63.25

The variation in the short-term tempo in relation to a uniform measure can be considerable (Moles, 1953a). Within an interval of several (for example, ten) seconds, the length of a measure may vary by a factor of nearly two.

VARIATIONS IN TEMPO OF THE NINTH SYMPHONY (M.M.)
(Averages over 30-second samples)

Conductor	Allegro ma non troppo		Scherzo	Hymn to Joy	
	Beginning	Measures 50 to 60		Beginning Measures 92 ff.	Tutti
Score	88	88	116	80	80
Furtwängler	60	57	113	52	68
Scherchen	64	64	106	56	72
G. Wand	56	58	116	76	80
W. Goehr	76	76	123	60	64
Kleiber	76	71	115	64	68
Hörenstein	72	72	114	68	76
Karajan	72	72	126	70	73
Toscanini	72	80	122	76	80

[page 144] Harmonic divergencies normally do not exceed one to two commas (5 to 10 cents). Exceptionally they reach a quarter tone.

Melodic divergencies (in successive notes) are connected to harmonic divergencies only in instruments with fixed sounds (piano, harp, harpsichord, organ). In the orchestra, where the instruments are only statistically dependent on each other, the average deviations decrease as the interval of integration increases (easily 12 cents for a 30-minute symphony).

With some solo instruments, the deviations are even less limited. The systematic "false" playing of certain instruments (for example, the harpsichord) is clearly part of the esthetic information (for example, in the recordings of Wanda Landowska).

Finally, with the instruments themselves one must introduce the effectual concept, ignored in musical doctrine, of the *inharmonicity* of instruments: for example, piano (Seashore, 1938), organ (Olson and Belar, 1955), and violin (Moles, 1954a). Musical doctrine ignores the increasing deviations of the harmonics of the notes these instruments furnish from the nominal frequency that they would have if the law of harmonics (Chap. IV) were rigorous and not statistical. It is now recognized that these deviations are needed for musical expression, just like the "false notes" on the harpsichord and certain other instruments. These deviations are responsible for the factors which formerly were vaguely called "color," "life," "warmth," in performance.

For instruments as complex as the whole orchestra, the timbres themselves and their variations remain practically incalculable; they have not even been approximated. For example, the octave distribution of certain polyphonic parts is left practically *ad libitum* to the conductor or to the score copyist.

The maximum possible esthetic information could be determined theoretically by analysis of the dynamic differential deviations (cf. the rising of thresholds, Chap. III, Sec. 4) of the factors listed above and by an estimate of the number of combinations of these "esthetic elements." One would thus obtain the *field of freedom* of the musical signal in comparison with the score. The real information could be deduced from the *structuring* of the esthetic message into strict or statistical organization. At present we do not have direct, accurate results on the real information, but various experimental results affirm that esthetic information in music is relatively large, redundancy low (20 per cent).

The very approximate figure (Fig. V-2) compares the distributions of esthetic and semantic originality in different sonic messages. These distributions refer to the "normal use" of these messages by "normal" individuals. This double abstraction restricts the scope of these schemes.

[page 145] Not so much because its semantic information is low as because its esthetic information is considerable, does the richness of the musical message appear to exceed the receptor's capacities.

Although the musical message is for the most part esthetic, there are

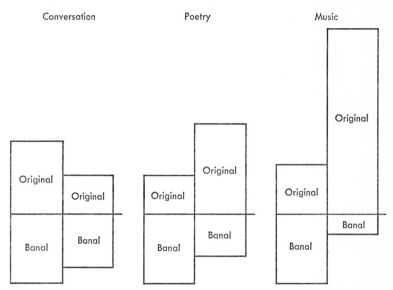

Fig. V-2. Approximate comparison of semantic (left) and esthetic (right) information in conversation, poetry, and music.

some for whom the semantic part has a preponderant importance and value. Many professional performers are almost exclusively interested in the semantic part of a musical message; their concern is to perform from the operating scheme. In short, one may almost say that these special receptors (the performers) "listen to the score" instead of listening to the music. As a result, they tolerate the most extraordinary deformations of the musical signal; for example, a bad hall, faulty retransmission, noise, etc.

Moreover, some musical messages can assume an almost exclusively semantic value. Such messages, frequently and universally repeated, exhaust their esthetic originality and become synonymous with a logical statement. An example is the *radio theme song*. Thus, hearing the William Tell Overture by Rossini is practically equivalent for the American listener to the formula: "The Lone Ranger rides again. Hi-ho Silver." By a preliminary coding set up in the listeners' minds, music assumes the role of speech, of meaning. It is expedient to call this "situational coding"; it corresponds to rules of constraint imposed by common situations. Nevertheless, this is an exceptional case. If we say that music has the form of a language, because it has structurings, we should emphasize that in general music is a "language without meaning."

[page 146] Analysis of the different relationships coming into play in the message structures permits us to specify the following scheme of ordinary phonetic and musical sonic messages. (See diagram on p. 142.)

5. DISTINGUISHING THE TWO TYPES OF INFORMATION

The study of the different degrees of freedom of esthetic informa-

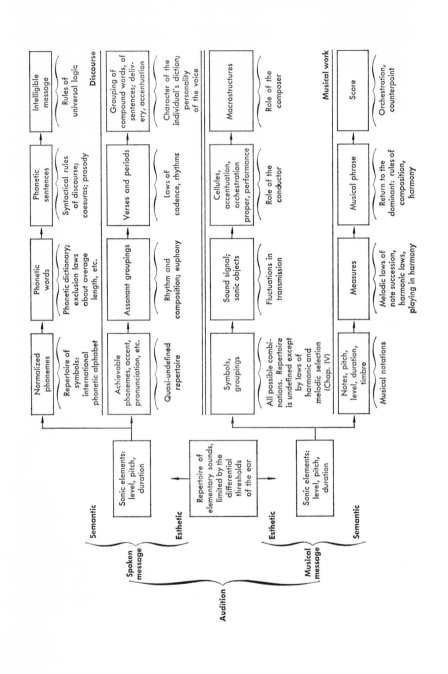

tion (Sec. 4) suggests that many of the "parameters of deviation" which determine esthetic information are connected with the *level* (dynamics). Among these "parameters" are timbres, attack transients, the distribution of the elements in the sonic object, *sforzandos*, etc. As a result, any systematic alteration of the "level" will very markedly degrade the esthetic message. Recalling how little the "technicians" of semantic information listen to the esthetic message (Sec. 4), we find a method of "filtering" semantic information by selective destruction of the esthetic part of the message.

Essentially, the method consists in degrading progressively the dynamics, that is, the contrast of intensities or of levels, $L_{fff} - L_{ppp}$ $= 20 \log_{10} (p_{max}/p_{min})$, to the point of destroying the artistic value of the message. This operation will cause esthetic information to disappear first. We have studied this operation, known as "clipping," with music (Moles, 1953a), and various other authors have studied it with speech (Miller, 1951). The studies imply that it is possible to reduce the dynamics, that is, the "expression" of the signal, to the neighborhood of zero (infinite clipping) without notably altering the intelligibility of the sonic signal, that is, while conserving nearly all of its semantic information. The semantic information of speech is particularly easy to measure, because it is proportional to the experimental value called intelligibility, that is, the per cent of sentences correctly understood. For speech, the overall intelligibility remains greater than 90 per cent.

When the signal is reduced to a succession of binary digits (0 or 1), all the harmonics of the signal are destroyed and only the "fundamental" or the "dominant harmonic" is left; all dynamic expression is crushed. The sonic object reduces to a narrow band of constant width evolving in the melodic plane. The symbols have a single constant level — whatever the pitch, that is, whatever the abscissa in the graphical representation of Chap. IV. Of the esthetic part, all that remain are the properly temporal elements, variations in length and rhythm, deviations from the nominal values of the notes, that is, finally, an infinitesimal proportion of the message's immense esthetic potential. [page 148] In short, infinite clipping selectively destroys esthetic information and, from a practical point of view, leaves only semantic information. Thus it "filters" the two kinds of information.

The survival of the intelligibility of speech is quite remarkable if one reflects on the extraordinary alterations induced in the signal's form. Analogously, the very many experiments that we have performed on this subject have shown us that music's "intelligibility" survives in the following sense:

(1) Any listener possessing a sufficient knowledge of the musical repertoire can "recognize" the piece thus transformed and can define the conditions of performance, such as with piano, orchestra, etc.

(2) Any professional musician can rewrite the melody of the piece presented and can reconstruct an approximate orchestration or accompaniment.

What remains physically perceptible in this succession of identical pips is the *modulation* (inflexion) *of duration* that they represent. These pips are a materially sensible partitioning of time; on the microscopic scale, they are an elementary rhythm.

Thus *semantic information is strictly connected with the modulation of duration*, with the infinitesimal perception of rhythms. In fact, our knowledge of the mechanism of general auditory perception would suggest this (Stevens and Davis, 1938). Naturally, the signal emerging from this transformation has lost all euphony; "esthetic information" closely follows "esthetic value" and this justifies the name adopted.

If we wanted to isolate the esthetic message, we would have to destroy the semantic part. But that is much more difficult because, as the preceding experiments showed, the semantic part is connected to the division of time and it is impossible to suppress this division without suppressing the message itself. Nevertheless, it is possible to repress this division of time by transforming it in such an unusual way that it becomes unrecognizable, without perceptibly modifying the materiality of the objects and of the sonic sequences. The process to use is *inversion;* it furnishes a different, unusual view of the message.

We have systematically applied inversion to musical and phonetic messages, using magnetic tapes or disc recordings. Here are the essential facts:

(1) Inversion *totally* destroys the sense and the normally accepted value of speech, rendering it totally and definitively [page 149] incomprehensible. But inversion destroys only an infinitely smaller proportion of the value of the musical signal. Although the musical signal becomes strange and unusual, it remains intelligible in the sense that an articulation of the sequences of the sonic objects remains perceptible; the sonic objects retain distinct identities, and their esthetic "value" very nearly subsists.

The essential distinction thus established separates music from language in a way that their differences in structure would scarcely permit. It demonstrates what we said above about the relative distributions of semantic and esthetic information in the two types of messages: If music is a language devoid of meaning, then inversion of music cannot destroy its meaning.

Poetry, especially that furthest developed toward the sonic object (*lettriste* poetry, for example) in inversion becomes situated between speech and music esthetically. This is just what one would predict from the diagram of the preceding section.

(2) Complete destruction of the meaning of speech does not completely destroy the qualities of the sonic objects. While they are unintelligible synthetically, they keep their properties analytically: The vowels (providing tone quality of the sonic object) are recognizable, but the transients are entirely destroyed or transmuted into other transients. Certain true consonants (k, d, t, p, g, b) are transmuted into other consonants. The false consonants (s, f, ch, r) are not transmuted. This process suggests an objective distinction between consonants and vowels to replace the conventional distinction between traditional consonants and vowels.

(3) As a result, the (true) vowels convey a larger part of the esthetic information than the consonants. The consonants carry the greater part of the semantic information in their ordered, temporal forms. Several ancient (in particular, Semitic) languages recognized this: Their written forms include only consonants.

(4) Inversion transforms an attack transient into an approximate final consonant, for example, $pa - ap$. It is possible to construct sentences out of phonemes which give intelligible sentences when recorded and mechanically inverted; for example, "zemenof a zarf" inverted becomes "phrases à phonèmes" in French. (One may even find specially trained people who can perform the inversion.) In this counter-experiment, most of the semantic message is reinjected artificially into the final message. The experiment shows on what the variations of esthetic information depend in [page 150] inversion; it directs attention to the indicative temporal pointers, the decay transients, which are statistically slower than the attack transients. These pointers are part of the signal and give it its irreversibility.

(5) The audition of classical music — that is, very well-known music, with very familiar rules of semantic organization — shows that the factors considered essential by musical theory, such as the resolution of chords, the return to the tonic, are of secondary importance to artistic value. Inverted music, in which these factors are destroyed, is not notably affected by the loss. In a very complex musical signal which exploits all the resources of the orchestra in order to increase the richness of the sonic object, for example, works

of Stravinsky, this richness remains totally intact and becomes essential; it practically drowns the preceding orientational factors, so that a significant fraction of young listeners, sixteen to twenty-two years old, can prefer inverted music to straightforward music in suitably chosen cases. Thus, a curious uncertainty is created about the value of the direction of temporal evolution in the music.

(6) Temporal inversion is accepted only when the texture of the sonic objects, which is naturally connected to the instruments which create the objects, obeys some simple laws. The principal laws are: (a) weak attack transients (< 80 dB/sec), as in, for example, the violin, 'cello, organ, and other bowed string instruments; (b) duration of the decay transients as close to the duration of the attack transients as possible; in other words, sonic objects tending to have some symmetry with respect to their center; (c) rather extended delays in the resolution of chords.

These laws amount to avoiding pointers which indicate the flow of time. In this form the result becomes an obvious banality.

These laws exclude struck stringed instruments (for example, a piano) or plucked instruments (guitar), but allow glissando and certain percussions without decay (for example, the accordion).

The requirements (a) through (c) permit a priori determination of the esthetic value which a piece will retain under inversion. They show the interest of the concepts of *materia musica* and "sonic object" for the direct understanding of musical sensation.

(7) Finally, temporal inversion reveals the cultural and social aspect of musical structures. Inversion suggests that the "laws" of musical theory [page 151] are only the traditional and cultural dogmas of one civilization. We applied inversion systematically to pieces of music of the following types: (a) classical, before 1900; (b) modern, after 1915; (c) experimental; (d) European; (e) exotic, beyond the Moslem cultural frontier. More or less musically formed European subjects perceived increased esthetic information from (a) to (b) to (c). These tests bring out the importance of a much broader and more systematic use of the possibilities of the orchestra (for example, in the domain of timbres) accompanied by a progressive dissolution of the dogmatic rules imposed by classical composition. In case (c), inversion reveals the exact nature of the interest present-day musicians have in experimental music: They hope to increase the richness of musical material in the form of increased esthetic information or originality, which appears as an autonomous value.

The experiments with exotic music were performed with subjects of varying musical education who were, however, all European. The experiments show that, where the subject does not know, from education or the sociocultural milieu, the structural rules of what he hears, his appreciation of the *materia musica* proceeds directly on the esthetic level, that is, he does not indicate any preference, nor even any clear ranking, between straightforward and inverted exotic music. Occasionally he shows very clear opinions about music when he possesses its code of semantic rules. But when the semantic part of the message is hidden from him, he perceives, with difficulty but directly, only the esthetic part.

The results from systematic use of inversion extend very broadly beyond those summarized above. This extremely fruitful procedure will likely have to take its place among the great methods of the experimental esthetics of the arts of time. It is one of the methods of *Gedanken* variation suggested by phenomenology. By shattering the normal view of the temporal object, it aims to rediscover an intrinsic appreciation forbidden to us by our mental habits.

The two methods, clipping and inversion, are essentially means of observing semantic and esthetic information. They may be considered as *information filters*. Neither one produces a perfectly dichotomous, absolute filtering; [page 152] rather, each effects only a statistical filtering. In this regard the first, though less rich, is more rigorous than the second. Inversion has many other applications; for example, it can be used to create new sonic objects from speech by ridding it of its superfluous or irrelevant semantic information. The objects renovated by this preparation can then be used in musical compositions. Already this is an established procedure in experimental music.

It is very hard to *measure* the separated kinds of information in the sonic message, in the present state of our knowledge. The following rather artificial procedure is probably the best at present:

[page 153] (1) Estimating the maximum possible information H_{max} of the sonic message by determining the capacity of the channel; that is, the number of symbols and the number of possible arrangements of them.

(2) Measuring the average redundancy of the signal. The average redundancy may be determined experimentally in all types of channels by the procedure (Chap. I, Sec. 13) of random suppression of the signal's elements, here symbols, until semantic or esthetic understanding is completely destroyed. While semantic understanding is rather easy to define objectively, esthetic understanding remains particularly difficult to grasp. In temporal channels, the mes-

sages develop randomly in time. We know that the product of a random phenomenon, with a degree of order ω, and a regular phenomenon, with a degree of order 1, is a random phenomenon with a degree of order identical to the first: $\omega \times 1 = \omega$. Therefore experimentally this procedure consists in a periodic chopping of the initial message; the length of the periods being suppressed depends on the temporal symbols forming the repertoire. In the most general case of the sonic message, the study of over-all information will proceed by starting with pips taking at least 1/16 of a second to decay, that is, the length of the present, and increasing until the message is destroyed. The information from the symbols, sonic objects, and cells can probably be analyzed with pips whose periods of decay approximate the expected lengths of these repertoire units. This method has already been extensively applied to speech by Licklider and Pollack (see Miller, 1951), and by Meyer-Eppler, but is still only beginning in music. The several experiments we performed with periods of decay on the order of half a second led to a destruction of the message when approximately 65 per cent of the length of the message was obliterated. The messages used were piano pieces by Liszt and symphonic orchestra works by Mendelssohn. This result is interesting when compared with that for language; it verifies that sonic objects last much longer in music than in speech.

The intelligibility of speech is lost when pips lasting 1/10 to 1/8 second destroy approximately 70 per cent of the length of the message. This last result should be compared with that obtained in Chap. II, Sec. 6: There in *ordered* cuttings approximating 80 per cent, hence even more pronounced, we preserved the consonants and a sampling of the vowels. The difference between the two results reflects the difference between the processes, namely, the selectivity in destroying [page 154] structure. From the theoretical viewpoint, this difference is due to the random deviation (in a Gaussian distribution) of the lengths of sonic objects from their average length of 0.08 second in normal speech. This result has an interest for the theory of language.

Our experimental method of separating the semantic and esthetic information of phonetic and musical signals was the method of concomitant variations using *polyphonic filters*. Such a filter is an electrical system incorporated in the reproduction channel. It divides the acoustical range into, for example, 29 bands (each a third of an octave wide) whose gain is controlled at will. Numbering these bands arbitrarily 1, 2, 3, . . . , 29, we may thus eliminate the reproduction of all even bands, 2, 4, 6, . . . , or of all odd bands, or cut up the acoustical spectrum at will. If we have series of subjects listen to sets of systematic variations, then an estimate of the contribution of the different bands to semantic and esthetic information emerges from the value judgments obtained. The results obtained with these methods are represented in Fig. V-3.

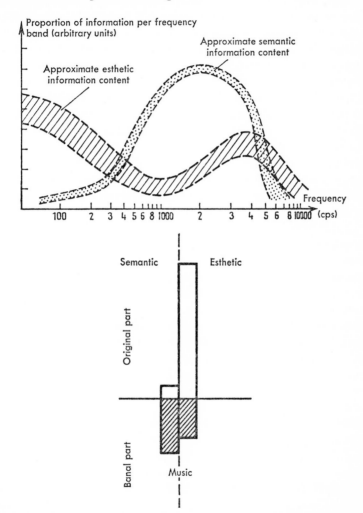

Fig. V-3. Approximate distribution of semantic and esthetic information over the range of acoustical frequencies for music. The results for esthetic information have a considerable spread.

The field opened by these experimental methods is very broad. The few fragmentary and approximate results presented here have no value other than to give an idea of the sort and the scope of the experiments to which these methods can give rise.

6. MELODIC MACROSTRUCTURES

In describing sonic cells, which represent the simplest of melodic forms, we noted (Chap. IV, Sec. 5) the difficulty of delimiting the cells precisely. Their borders fluctuate; they overlap; and from the purely morphological viewpoint which we adopt in this study, they are rather poorly differentiated from the sonic mass. The *Gestalt* theory of von Ehrenfels, Koffka, and Köhler, etc., has precisely defined the notion of form in the temporal field for "simple melodies." Information theory must go back to the studies on this subject, most of which assume the existence of scales as the basis of the melodic structure.

By way of preliminaries we note the following:

(1) Melody is only one element in the organization of the musical signal. It is not at all essential to the modulation of duration, which may proceed in many ways, in particular by using the sonic material per se, in the style of coloring (Schönberg's *Klangfarbenmelodie*), or in the style of dynamics, which can be either rhythmical (for example, jazz and certain exotic music, such as Javanese) or arhythmical (some pieces of experimental music).

[page 155] The melodic part is distilled from the sonic mass when the message and the instrument are simplified to the rather flat style of oscillator tones, which represent the most elementary form of melodic phrase, a sort of asymptote of banality, deprived of deep esthetic interest. Esthetic interest seems to be synonymous with the *richness* of the message. Melody impoverishes a message while making it intelligible: In the limit, a pentatonic melodic phrase of a few notes is not more than a skeleton of music. The "arrangers" of light music buy this skeleton and dress it with harmonic forms, timbres, and variations in order to make it consumable.

(2) Melodic forms are far from the essential elements of intelligibility when they are included in a structure that is even slightly complex. We have established (Moles and Frances, 1952) that recognition of a fugally treated theme was far from dependent on a melodic structure which the composer conceived as evident. The perceptual structure constructed by listeners, even by musicians, often rested on factors specifically attached to the morphology of the musical message (level, transients) and not on the melodic theme.

Even the professional musician depends on the simplest phenomenological perceptions, to a degree varying with his culture. In the experiment cited (Moles and Frances, 1952), only two out of ten professional musicians were able to recognize correctly the detailed structure of a very classic fugue of Bach. The reasons they adduced at times referred to the simple viewpoint of the listener; they were based on the dimensions of the sonic object (particularly the dynamic development).

(3) Nevertheless, to information theory in its present state, melodic forms, transposable musical phrases which can be repeated and subjected to fugue and variations, appear very *elaborate* in comparison with those considerably simpler forms studied in Chap. II, including only periodicity of sonic material grasped as a quality, the most unadorned rhythm, and certain kinds of symmetry. Here progress can be faster for the visual, spatial message than for the temporal message.

Some general concepts stated in Chap. II can, however, give us a few pointers. The essential theme developed earlier is the correspondence established on an elementary level between form and *autocorrelation*. We held that perception of form should be understood as direct perception [page 156] of the proportion of autocorrelation of a message for different values of the interval τ; form is perceived as a statistical predictability of the future on the basis of the past, the affirmation of a regularity in the external world reflected by a state of expectation. This squares well with experiments, such as those on the completion of figures in the theory of form.

This essential concept continues to guide research in the more complex domain of melody considered as a sequence of simple "tones" ("chords"). The chords are defined as "approximately simple relations" of frequencies or of pitches. If we examine an isolated melody without accompaniment or harmony, where the sonic objects become identical with the tones, some simple mathematical operations on the autocorrelation function, for delays corresponding to two or more successive notes with frequencies in an integral ratio, reveal an autocorrelation for these periods which is clearly greater than the values which would be obtained if the two tones did not have these frequency ratios. But these autocorrelation values depend greatly on the spectral structure of each sonic object — of each note; namely (a) on its simplicity or absence of random phenomena; (b) on its purity, defined as the existence of a dominant frequency (often called the "fundamental" by physicists but better called the "main harmonic"); (c) on the mutual resemblance of each of the two or more sonic objects whose autocorrelation is studied. Calculation shows further that though, as is generally true, the frequencies of the "harmonics" fluctuate around their nominal values (cf. the concept of inharmonicity, Sec. 4), the autocorrelation function keeps a high average value. Calculation also shows that a too rigorous accuracy of the frequencies in relation to their nominal values implies, on the contrary, a decrease in the autocorrelation of the temporal function from tone to tone, because of other inevitable fluctuations (phases). Here the "harmonics" are the frequencies n times greater than the fundamental where n is integral; they constitute the permanent symbols lasting through the sonic object.

From this semitheoretical analysis we have the following results:

(1) In order for a melody to be clearly perceptible as a form, each successive tone must originate from sources or instruments with very similar harmonic contours, not from sources extremely different in spectrum.

(2) These sources must have a very obvious dominating frequency which stands out clearly from the other elements of the symbol.

(3) Finally, as a consequence of (2), the sonic objects must not be too short: If the sounds are too short, the relation $K/\Delta\tau = N$ between the number of elements N in the symbols and the minimum time for perception [page 157] multiplies the extent and the complexity of the spectrum and drowns the dominating component.

In short, sonic objects must have simple and similar structures in order to appear as a satisfying form. These theoretical deductions are verified by orchestral practice, which in general entrusts the melody — with perhaps a few addenda — to a single instrument or to a group of matched instruments. When orchestral practice entrusts the melody to instruments with complex timbres or when it has a counterpoint or a polyphonic structure accompanying the melody, it takes care to make the melody emerge very clearly from the orchestral mass by making the melody louder. These empirical remarks thus corroborate the viewpoint developed here.

In presenting melodic form as an autocorrelation we consider the existence of "simple" ratios as theoretical justifiable. But we are especially cognizant of the fact that the strongly statistical nature of the ratios lets the "form" subsist in spite of significant degradations in the ideal exactness of its parts. This essential point justifies the empirical character that the physicist's critical analysis imposes on the concept of a succession of simple ratios. It is very clearly opposed to musical doctrine strongly impregnated with the Pythagoreanism of its Hellenic origins.

Clearly the brief analysis presented here can be considered only as a basis of argument, for this analysis is quite insufficient in its simplistic form to explicate the whole concept of melodic phrase.

In interpreting the relations between the semantic message and the esthetic message, we translate the concept of *form* as *foreseeability*. This foreseeability restrains the choice among symbols assembled in sequences of defined sonic objects. We note that this foreseeability amounts to increasing the redundancy of the semantic message; one can interpret the existence of melodic forms as the statistical perception of the reduction in information transmission. Esthetic information is also reduced to the degree that the choice of timbres, that is, of internal structures of sonic objects, is reduced, and we have just seen that this is the case. Thus a certain — very lax — connection is established in melody between the two types of messages: an over-all impoverishment of information transmission due to a greater intelligibility. Melody, and especially monodic melody, becomes intelligible in relation to polyphony or to the couplings of musical phrases.

Infinite clipping of very complex orchestral messages showed that the passages where instruments stated the melodic theme were always grasped first as characteristic, while passages of orchestral coloring were harder to perceive and were more easily drowned [page 158] in the "quantification noise" (the artifact responsible for the form of the clipping).

Finally, these same experiments made obvious an alternation between the two types of information, semantic and esthetic. While this alternation is essentially irregular, its irregularities follow precisely those of the sonic material perceived as a whole, that is, they follow the behavior of the sonic objects assembled in cells, of melodic phrases or of their "codas," etc.

These experiments suggest the existence of a sort of semantic-esthetic counterpoint. The two kinds of information diminish together in certain periods, particularly around melodic themes, then vary independently or oppositely in certain other periods, in *information packages* irregularly distributed in time.

This remark gives us access to the macrostructures such as arise from large-scale composition of the musical message.

7. INTERFERENCE BETWEEN TYPES OF INFORMATION AND MACROSTRUCTURES

For clarity in the scheme of the subordination of structures presented in Sec. 4, we separated the semantic and esthetic messages. The preceding experiments suggest that this separation is an excessive simplification and does not correspond sufficiently to the nature of things. In reality, the two kinds of information interact. This is easy to conceive because they are carried by the same elements; the *receptor* groups the elements in different repertoires of symbols. The study of this interaction, of this *semantic-esthetic counterpoint*, ought to give us access to the general macrostructures of the message beyond the melody, beyond the extent of the immediate span of memory (Chap. III, Sec. 5).

By way of preliminary, we shall present as a law a simple consequence of the fundamental formula of information measurement.

The law of repetition: When a perception (a group of symbols, sonic objects, cells) is repeated n times, the rate of information yielded per unit of time decreases as the binary logarithm of the number of repetitions increases:

$$\Delta R = - K \log_2 n.$$

This law governs the organization of the sequences forming the musical message; it governs *repetition,* one of the essential procedures of composition.

One may now interpret repetition as a means [page 159] of diminishing the over-all originality of the message. The logarithmic law makes evident the importance of the *first repetitions* of a sonic object or a sonic cell. It is interesting to recall here the role of simple symmetry (repetition once) and multiple symmetries in the perception of forms, like Rorschach blots, and the kaleidoscope: There is a connection between the intelligibility of perceived forms and their degree of symmetry.

In any temporal message, perfect repetition of a cell or of a sonic object is an ideal limit. In practice in music, "repetitions" always vary: At the very least there are random variations due to the performance and, more generally, variations occur in the operating scheme, the score.

We may classify several of these variations in order of complexity or increasing richness: (a) simple repetition of symbols with random variations in performance; (b) repetition with change of pitch (transposition, change of octave); (c) repetition with structural variation in the sonic cells (repetition of a theme by different instruments); (d) repetition with variation in accompaniment; (e) repetition with contrapuntal variations of the second voice; (f) repetition with modification of the theme by development (fugue); (g) variations on an initial theme; (h) repetitions separated by the insertion of another theme.

[page 160] In this nonexhaustive list, the very fact of repetition fades away as the originality added by variation compensates for the redundancy caused by repetition. "Repetition" disappears still faster when several of these procedures are combined. If we suppose the unit of form has a sensibly uniform duration and if we graph, as a function of time or of the number of repetitions of the unit form, the variation of information starting with an original unit form, then we have a diagram like Fig. V-4.

The unit form we started with carried initially a certain package of over-all information. This information is a function of its harmonic structure, of its complexity, of the richness of the form that

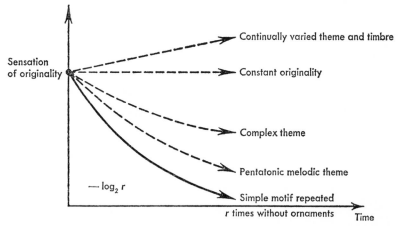

Fig. V-4. The originality of a theme repeated r times in the course of time decreases as minus the binary logarithm of the number of repetitions. If the theme is complex or is varied during the repetitions, its originality decreases more slowly.

it uses effectively. In the same way, we may attempt a classification of macrostructures as follows, according to: (a) the number of tones or of sonic objects implied in the cell forming a melodic phrase; (b) the complexity of the scale of pitches used: fifths only, pentatonic scale, 7-toned scale, 12-toned scale; (c) the complexity of the second voice or accompaniment; (d) the richness of the sonic objects used to state the theme, that is, the richness of the orchestration, the complexity of the orchestra, the number of timbres; (e) the existence of ornamentation or micromelodies; etc.

It is very easy to compare the original themes of symphonic fragments, which occur at the beginning of pieces, in order to make the preceding factors in originality evident. An experimental tape we made of examples of musical messages with increasing information rates, analogous to the text samples given in Chap. I, could be considered as an empirical scale of informational complexity in music, the complexity of other works being determined by a comparison process.

On a graph analogous to the preceding, where the vertical axis represents the rate of information, the initial points of the lines, which express the variation of information with time, will be located at different heights. We define the instantaneous rate of information

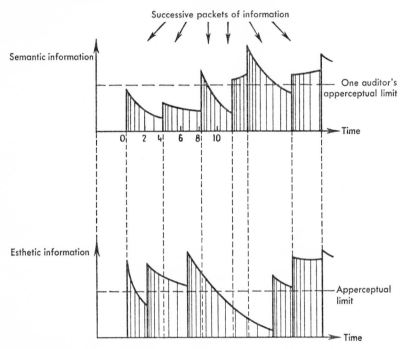

Fig. V-5. The successive packets of information presented to the auditor, either semantic (above) or esthetic (below), must be judged in comparison with his apperceptual limit (dotted line). Figure taken from Hiller's work on this topic.

as the information transmitted in the quantum of time equal to the length of the present. If one examines a simple musical message composed of more or less evolving sonic cells, each repeated several times before the following one occurs, the information transmission as a function of time behaves as in Fig. V-5. The figure obviously corresponds to a very schematized case.

Recently, L. A. Hiller, at the University of Illinois, working on the Illiac computer, made a whole set of measurements of information rate in works of Mozart and Schönberg (cf. Cohen, 1962).

A fundamental principle in applying the general theory to the individual receptor (Chap. II, Sec. 2) may be expressed thus: The *individual* [page 161] *receptor has a limited capacity H_0 for the apprehension of information* (originality). This limiting capacity is not instantaneous but bounds the information transmitted over an interval of psychological integration linked with the instantaneous memory — on the order of five to ten seconds (a time we have encountered repeatedly). This memory corresponds to the individual's continuity time lag; it excludes the faculty of discursive memory properly called. This limit is a function of the receptor's over-all knowledge of the structure of messages; his knowledge is in turn a function of his education, of his sociocultural milieu, etc.

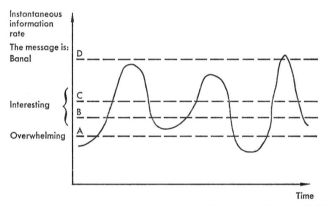

Fig. V-6. The variations in the auditor's apperceptual limit (dotted lines A, B, C) delimit assimilation of the message and, correlatively, the interest it has.

If the effective information rate of the message is greater than this limit, the message is *too rich*. In practice, the musical message is in general *overwhelming*. The receptor assimilates not the whole thing, but fragments chosen either randomly or according to rules whose general form will be made explicit later.

The above remarks lead to the concept of the *limitation of the information density*. Suppose on the preceding graph we represent the limiting rate of assimilable information [page 162] by horizontal dotted lines located at various heights (the apperceptual limits) for various individuals A, B, C, D, according to their level of "musical culture" — a vague term.

Several cases are possible (Fig. V-6):

(1) On the whole, the curve of information density remains above the apperceptual limit (for example, individual A). The message is *too rich* for this individual; it overwhelms him; he feels himself

"drowned" and loses interest in it except during a few instants of isolated attention.

(2) The function of information transmission oscillates around the individual's apperceptual limit (cases B and C). This is the general case. The individual perceives the packages of information which overwhelm his perceptual capacity; then in the course of successive repetitions and in spite of their variations, he apprehends them or a part of them more or less completely. In any case, the musical message is beyond him *on the whole;* he does not succeed in exhausting it and has to try to achieve familiarity with it in the course of many rehearings; familiarity permits him to exhaust it. All this agrees well with the everyday sociological facts of the audition of music.

(3) Finally, it is possible (case D) that the individual receptor's apperceptual limit is above the function of information output. This event may have two causes. (a) The individual may have an integrated, total knowledge of the complex musical message. A priori this must be exceptional, because the most perfect virtuoso or conductor always retains a residuum of uncertainty, of unpredictability, about a message so rich that it can never be exclusively redundant. (b) Most frequently, the simplicity of the message or the number of repetitions of it reduces [page 163] it to banality; for example, radio theme songs, simple rhythmic melodies, certain popular melodies. "Light" music or *"Unterhaltungsmusik"* is defined precisely by the fact that it is entirely apprehensible by most auditors.

The scheme presented here of the perception of a series of simple, repeated musical themes, based on the evolution of originality in the course of time, has only a heuristic value. Its field of validity is small, since it ignores counterpoint, polyphony, etc., but it already covers a good number of the disparate facts of the audition of music by receptors having varied musical culture. In particular, it introduces a quantitative understanding of sociocultural and socio-esthetic facts; it suggests, for example, the possibility of defining indices of intelligibility — more precisely, of audibility — to be attached to each piece of music by methods analogous to those suggested by Flesch (Miller, 1951) for written texts, average indices of musical culture valid at the very least for rather broad musical styles (classical, modern, sacred). All of these would facilitate the complex task of socio-estheticians.

We may come closer to reality by replacing the dotted horizontal straight line representing the apperceptual limit, which is only an abstraction, by a variable line to take account of the fluctuations of attention or of sensitivity. These fluctuations are well known in experimental psychology and over a long time are vaguely periodic. (Cf. tests of the auditory thresholds as a function of time [Woodworth and Schlosberg, 1954], periodic variations of the output of errors in tests of concentrated attention or in Kräpelin tests [Lewin, 1951].) Fatigue and relaxation are reflected by depression of the apperceptual limit.

More important is discrimination between semantic and esthetic information, because it broadens significantly the rather narrow field, series of repeated themes, in which we started. At the end of the preceding section, various experiments led us to present the evolution of a piece's originality as governed by a semantic-esthetic counterpoint. The fundamental separation of these two types of superposed messages, on the basis of their organization and their different symbols, implies that the principle of apperceptual limitation is valid separately for each of the corresponding structurings; for example, many performers possess a large apperceptual capacity for the operating scheme composed of the symbols of the score, without necessarily being sensitive to the originality of the performance. On the contrary, the vague terms, "finesse," "audacity," "vigor," etc., often used to describe the playing of a performer or of a conductor, reveal that the nonperforming listener's apperceptual limit [page 164] may be high on the esthetic side without in any way prejudging the semantic originality or banality of the piece. In fact, the auditor is ignorant of much of the piece's semantic content, since he does not know how or care to distinguish Mozart from Liszt *on paper:* His viewpoint is different.

The graph of information evolving during the message is then divided in two parts, with two nearly independent apperceptual limits. These parts correspond by superposition, as indicated in Fig. V-5.

The role of the law of repetition, while perfectly clear for semantic information, is less obvious for esthetic information. When there is a repetition of the melodic theme, the orchestral timbres, and the transients of the sonic objects are often also repeated. However, a "package of esthetic information" may result from a change in the playing of the instrument which is not readily visible in the semantic message. In fact, the term *counterpoint* means precisely that there is a reciprocal, but randomized, determination of the two messages, that is, some kind of correlation, in a diversity of ways which is a very element of the information.

The rule of limiting information density stated above plays a preponderant role in the audibility (facility of exhaustive understanding or apprehension) of the musical message. An overly rich timbre, an overly complex sonic object, too brutal transitory periods composed of many acoustical elements grouped according to very lax laws of harmonic or melodic connections occur, preferably in isolation: either between silences or in a simple semantic context, in cells which are changing only slightly. They are frequently repeated before giving way to others.

Reciprocally, if the transmission of overly predictable elements is banal to an auditor who no longer finds sufficient diversity, diversity can emerge either from enrichment of the sonic object or from the structural complexity of the cell.

Starting from this limitation of the average originality:

$$\frac{1}{\theta} \int_{t}^{t+\theta} H(t) \ dt < H_0$$

in the interval of maximum extent of presence, $\theta_{max} = 5$ to 10 sec, one may speak more precisely: In order for the musical message to remain entirely intelligible to a listener of capacity H_{max}, the semantic plus esthetic information in this interval must be lower than H_{max}. This creates a certain compensatory alternation, a dialectical interplay between the two types of information.

The scope of this rule is limited by the assumption about the integral intelligibility of the message. In reality, this assumption is rather gratuitous, for concern for intelligibility is rather secondary to the composer. Recent music in particular deliberately goes farther and farther beyond the [page 165] auditory capacities of the "average public." Except in special cases the creator is guided by essentially artistic imperatives, generally very much above the apperceptual capacity of the potential listeners. Film music, music for animated cartoons, and "educational" music are exceptions.

Only in these cases will the rules of composition that one could extract from applying the principle of apperceptual limitation to the counterpoint of the semantic and esthetic messages really interest the musician. Practically, in order to go further in the formulation of laws or of rules, the study ought to bring in *value judgments*, but since these must remain foreign to scientific esthetics, they limit its field of action.

In general, because the rule of intelligibilty plays a secondary role, the laws of counterpoint remain difficult to capture closely; they will require a laborious study of many musical compositions. Nevertheless, there are important cases where auditory apprehensibility is important, for example, in multiple messages where the musical message itself follows and sustains another type of message, either sonic (the words in recitative, opera, etc.), or visual (theatrical or movie action). Then music is not a pure art, but part of the over-all message, with the elements of which music itself must enter in counterpoint. Thus the music becomes subject to important supplementary requirements, among which audibility is not the least. We shall discuss this type of message in the following chapter.

8. THE INFORMATIONAL ARCHITECTURE OF THE WORK OF ART

We showed above that any message from the external world, of which art is a special part, to the individual is composed of a finite number of superimposed messages. The repertoires R_1, R_2, ..., R_n and the codes C_1, C_2, ..., C_n of these messages constitute a hierarchy of levels defined by the observer. These repertoires of signs are superimposed in the following sense. At each sign level, stereotyped subroutines for assembling the signs compose valid "supersigns" as simple signs on the repertoire level immediately above. Each assemblage, made into a stereotype through certain code rules, is the material of signs evaluated as simple by perceptual integrating mechanisms; this process is repeated at each successive level.

The set of repertoires is, by definition, known to the "perceptor." This set is the community of sign repertoires shared by the mind of the transmitter (when the transmitter is a man or a creative microgroup) and the mind of the receptor, which conditions the message's apprehension. The rules for assembling signs constitute the successive codes. Greater or lesser knowledge of these rules determines, not only apprehension, but *comprehension* of the message, at least at the level considered.

Comprehension is possible on the level considered only if the redundancy of the message is large enough, that is, if the originality is diluted and packaged in enough signs that they may be separated with respect to the delay for apprehension. The redundancy of the message measures the relative excess of signs in comparison with the number which would be strictly necessary if the signs were utilized optimally.

The delay necessary for apprehension is determined by the physical mode of apperceiving the message (scanning, reading, grasping over-all, etc.). In other words, assuming that the human mind cannot absorb more than around 16 to 20 bits of originality per second, the message, on the level to which our attention is directed, must be redundant enough to have approximately this rate of originality in order for the message to be perfectly apprehended and understood. If the message's redundancy is very low, the information or originality is then too great; the receptor's mind "rejects" it and eventually moves to more accessible levels. On the other hand, if the redundancy is very high (too little information, overly banal), the mind loses interest and eventually moves to another, more "interesting" level.

The ontological goal pursued by the work of art is always to give the receptor "a little too much" information, a little too much originality; this "too much" is what is called the perceptual richness of the work of art, but the excess must be moderate.

Consider a simplified, elementary message proceeding on just one hierarchical level, having a single repertoire of elements. The message's *artistic value* is bound up with a decreasing function $f(|H_1 - H_1'|)$ of the deviation $|H_1 - H_1'|$ of the potential originality H_1 offered by the emitter, that is, the work or the artistic message, from the optimum H_1' characterizing the receptor (see Figs. V-7–V-9):

$$\text{Value} = f\left(|H_1 - H_1'|\right).$$

But a real message such as a work of art is characterized by many signs superposed in a hierarchy. We remarked earlier that the redundancies $r_1, r_2, \ldots, r_n$, or the quantities of information $H_1, H_2, \ldots, H_n$, relative to the repertoires $R_1, R_2, \ldots, R_n$, constitute an actual metric description of the message, like an architect's scale drawings for a house. The characteristic values of apprehension in the receptor's mind $A_1, A_2, \ldots, A_n$, relative to the repertoire levels $R_1, R_2, \ldots, R_n$, represent the receptor's structure.

A correspondence, an adjustment between the A_i and the H_i, is established if there is apprehension at every level in the work, precisely to the degree that each level in the work is directed to a special integrative structure in the receptor's mentality (Walter). The originality must exceed the receptor's capacity at each level, but by a very critical quantity, ΔH, which is directly connected with the feeling of over-all artistic value.

Specifically, consider the hierarchy of repertoires $R_1, R_2, \ldots, R_n$, with their respective codes for assembling signs, on the one hand, and the corresponding repertoires of the levels of apprehension $R_1', R_2', \ldots, R_n'$, with their normal codes for associating signs. The relative unbalance or disequilibrium at each level creates a certain contribution $V_1, V_2, \ldots, V_n$ for each level to a value V which may legitimately be called artistic or perceptual; V is a weighted function of the differences $H_1 - H_1', H_2 - H_2'. \ldots$

We shall assume (as a rough approximation) that the partial values are additive: $V = V_1 + V_2 + \ldots + V_n$. Then there can result a compensation between levels of apprehensibility which is one of the fundamental rules of art. For example, someone examining an artistic picture almost spontaneously dissociates these different

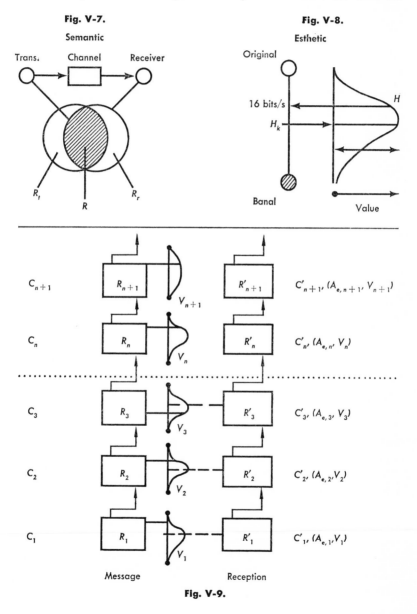

Fig. V-7.

Semantic

Fig. V-8.

Esthetic

Fig. V-9.

levels; particularly when the picture is not perfectly satisfying on one level, the examiner spontaneously deflects his attention toward another level where he finds a special satisfaction. It is possible experimentally to define the levels by such techniques as blacking out a picture with grills having meshes of varying thicknesses. For the sonic or linguistic message, research on these levels proceeds by periodic cuttings in defined rhythms as outlined above.

There are thus several ways of apprehending (grasping) a message, of attributing value to it, and these ways are mutually compensatory. It is legitimate to think that what everyone agrees to call a "masterpiece" corresponds to a suitable adaptation to all of the levels of the hierarchy of information surpluses, supplying simultaneously the richness of renewal, of repetition, and the fullness which characterize a masterpiece.

We must remember that in order for this analysis to be valid, it must apply to each dimension of the message, in this case the work of art, particularly to the semantic (universal) dimensions and the esthetic (sensual) dimensions. The analysis ought to be carried out in these two dimensions for each of the hierarchies which may arise:

$$V_{s_1} + V_{s_2} + \ldots + V_{s_n} = V_s \text{ (over-all semantic)},$$

$$V_{e_1} + V_{e_2} + \ldots + V_{e_n} = V_e \text{ (over-all esthetic)},$$

$$V_s + V_e = \text{over-all value.}$$

All these values add by dimensions to give the over-all semantic or over-all esthetic value of the work; moreover, they add by levels to give a hierarchical value for each level.

There may be semantic or esthetic compensations for a surplus of originality; this compensation is at the basis of several fundamental rules of composition. From this architectural description of the artistic work, composition appears to be a compensatory interaction between the various hierarchies of originality with the goal of permitting the receptor always to have some minimum access to the message presented to him. Examples of this procedure are extremely frequent in music and film, which are probably among the arts which have gone furthest in the theory of "composition." Specifically, think of the dialectic of timbres and durations, Wellek's dialectic of polar and linear perceptions, the action or play between melody and harmony, and all the structures of the sonic message which are governed by a dialectical compensation between two categories of messages, corresponding to two different types of repertoires.

9. CONCLUSIONS

At the end of this study of the perception of musical structures, we may try to answer the question posed initially as a paradox. A record of music can be cataloged in a repertoire under the symbol of a title or a number, and an individual can know the meaning, and thus the content, of this symbol. Why then is the title not equivalent to the symphony? And why listen to or see the work of art, which is essentially a *repetition?*

The answer supplied by this chapter calls first for a critique of the expression "the individual knows the meaning, and thus the content, of the symbol" (that is, the title of the symphony). Indeed, without serious restrictions, one cannot liken the individual to a machine provided with memory. Human "memory" must include a distinction between (a) the durable, precise, memorizing memory, which can be likened to the permanent memories (Chap. III, Sec. 5) of machines, but which [page 166] plays only a fragmentary and irregular role in artistic experience; and (b) immediate memory, a sort of phosphorescence of perception whose extension in time appears limited to the same order of size as the saturation interval for our perception of duration. We explained the latter by noting that duration is marked only by being filled with sensations; memory (b) assures the continuity of the individual.

Only the second kind (b) affords a permanence and a stability in the individual. It is memory (b) which allows us to liken the individual to an information receptor provided with a memory of limited temporal extent (Chap. III, Sec. 6).

We can now resolve the paradox.

(1) While the individual can assimilate the whole of a slogan or of a musical theme song, the first and the most obvious reason why he cannot liken the title to the symphony, the poem to its first line, is simply his limited mnemonic capacity. No matter how well he knows a play, because he does not know it enough, he will go to see it again in order to extract a supplementary information about the vicissitudes of the action. But this motive is too obvious to retain us long; there is nothing to learn here.

(2) The second apparent motive to repeat a message results from the important distinction between semantic and esthetic information. Because these kinds of information are apprehended through different symbols, the title of the symphony or of the play codes the restricted and narrowly structured symbols of what is predictable in the message, principally the semantic part. But the esthetic message remains almost entirely unforeseeable. Under the title of a

work is understood implicitly only a constant collection of symbols. But the *realization* of the musical work differs each time and constitutes the *field of freedom* of the work, even for those works which appear to us to be the most stable through time, for example, variable lightings of one portrait. Only recording can notably reduce this renewed originality, but in the limit the variations of the *receptor himself* come into play: The receptor does not remain rigorously the same all the time, but undergoes little variations — which, from a methodological and ideational viewpoint, are more conveniently incorporated in the variations of the message.

(3) The third reason why the work transcends any memorizable coding stems from the extent of the field of freedom of esthetic information. While the work's semantic information may be exhausted and eventually memorized, *the peculiarity of the work of art is that its richness transcends the individual's perceptual capacity.* Thus, the normal goal of the reproduction of a work of art is to permit us to exhaust it; at the very least it is oriented toward this exhaustion. A symphony, a pictorial work, a film, an [page 167] animated cartoon, are messages of practically unlimited information richness in comparison with the apperceptual capacity of the human being. He must rely on repeated reception in order to lower their originality and assimilate a significant part of the information that they contain, or in order to lower the information rate so that he can assimilate what he perceives.

This is just the role played by the recognition of a work of music, which is expressed in the well-known rule of the sociology of music: The public is interested only in works that it knows.

We have just sketched three reasons why the work of art exceeds the receptor's recollection, no matter how extensive. Do these three exhaust what is different about the esthetic point of view? E. Souriau observes that the concept of mental image at the basis of the preceding arguments does not take account of the exhaustion of esthetic sensation, whether the image be coded (for individuals with symbolic thought, (1) and (2)) or whether the image tends to a representative richness asymptotic to that of the work itself (image-thought type, (3)). A residue of the perception remains, and this residue is *presence,* which is very prominently sensualistic.

An image can be constructed by imagination, by symbolic coding (Langer, 1957), or by fragmentary perceptions calling forth and founding the image on concrete elements. No matter how complete a mental image, it cannot reveal the phenomenological content of reality. No matter how perfectly I know the furnishings, the topography, and the tiniest details of the pieces of the room where I live, no matter how exactly I exhaust them mentally, I cannot re-create the sensation of presence that I would have on entering it, in the sense that "all is happening as if ——." Now there exists an esthetic pleasure proper to even schematic recreation: It is the pleasure of whistling a melody, of reading a score while humming it, of making a rough sketch of a picture, of recopying a passage from a book one owns. This is an autonomous esthetic value independent of those cited above: It is the pleasure of "resensualization."

We only mention this problem here, which is closely connected to the definition of presence. To treat it in the spirit of the present work would require a basic study extending the scheme of the indi-vidual as receptor which we have systematized most summarily. Such a study falls in the domain of cybernetics, not information theory, or, in any case, it is proper to a psychology other than be-havioral. From the experimental viewpoint, it would clearly demand pushing the enriched mental images furnished by certain drugs (for example, mescaline) to their extreme limit, while basing these images on a combination of well-chosen, suggestive elements of the esthetic message. [page 168] One would have to exploit the latent contents of memory which our mental mechanisms cannot ordinarily use.

We summarize the principal results of this chapter as follows:

(1) The inadequacy of symbolic coding (for example, by title) of a known message shows that, particularly in a work of art, the re-ceptor is looking for a kind of information different from the one we have considered up to now.

(2) One must distinguish in every message a human receptor re-ceives (a) a semantic message, expressible in symbols, determining translatable, logical decisions; (b) an esthetic message, determining interior states, untranslatable.

(3) Each of these messages, transmitted by the same elements in different groupings on different levels of perception, possesses its maximum information, determined by the extent of its repertoire, its real information, and its own redundancy. The two messages are often nearly independent.

(4) All messages include semantic and esthetic parts. In speech, the two parts seem to play nearly equivalent roles. In music, the esthetic message is infinitely richer in elements and carries more information than the semantic message. The latter has a very high redundancy because of the numerous, and moreover arbitrary, log-ical connections which create in it scales and rules of composition.

(5) The rules which order the organization and the repertoires of symbols of a given type of message determine the structures of the message. To find them out is the first step of an experimental esthetic study of structures based on information theory.

(6) Esthetic information represents the *field of freedom* of the musical message in relation to its operating notation (the score), which is only a schematization of the music.

(7) Poetry stands between speech and music in its distributions of the two types of information.

(8) It is possible experimentally to distinguish between the two types of information by filtering. (a) *Infinite clipping* retains most of the semantic information and obliterates esthetic information. [page 169] (b) *Inversion* retains most of the esthetic information and removes the part of semantic information resulting from unrolling in time.

(9) From experiments performed on speech and music, we have the following results: (a) Semantic information is connected essentially to the modulation of duration and to the quantification of time into microrhythms. (b) Music and speech behave very differently under inversion. Inversion destroys nearly all the semantic information of the second but alters the first much less. (c) Inverting speech permits separation of true consonants (transients morphologically perceived) from true vowels (perceived by the quality of their sonic material). (d) True vowels carry most of the esthetic information, and true consonants most of the semantic information. (e) Our perception of the direction of the flow of time rests principally on indicative pointers supplied by transients, since this perception disappears when the transients do. From this one may extract rules about the invertibility of musical messages. (f) Temporal inversion reveals the sociocultural aspect of musical conventions. Inversion of exotic music, whose conventions we do not know, does not create a significant difference in artistic value.

(10) The method of inversion is one of the great methods of experimental esthetics. It can furnish many results because it constitutes an experimenting with time.

(11) It is possible to measure in aggregate or separately the amounts of information transmitted by a message by determining: (a) the maximum capacity of the channel from a psychophysical study of its dimensions; (b) the effective redundancy of the messages by destroying the symbols found, until the message is also destroyed.

(12) The sonic forms which constitute melodic structures are per-

ceived directly as the magnitude of an autocorrelation based on empirical ratios of numbers corresponding to what musical theory calls scales.

(13) The perception of melodic structures is governed by the concept of maximum extent of temporal presence, which has the same order [page 170] of size as the saturation threshold for the perception of duration. Presence assures the continuity of being [*devenir*]. The melodic phrase, the sonic cell, are perceived in their entirety only within this duration.

(14) The repetition of any sonic event, object, cell, or melodic phrase, decreases its originality as the binary logarithm of the number of repetitions.

(15) The musical message as a whole appears as a succession of packages of originality of varying size. Its originality decreases more or less slowly depending on the number of repetitions and the complexity of the variations introduced in the repetitions.

(16) An apperceptual limit on information transmission in each individual receptor, a function of his musical culture and his sociocultural surroundings, governs the apprehension of the musical signal. Apprehension is more or less complete depending on the size of the limit in comparison with the information transmitted by the signal.

(17) There exists a counterpoint between semantic and esthetic information. They determine each other in an irregular alternation. In order for the musical signal to be "intelligible" in the sense of integrally perceived, the average transmitted information, integrated over the maximum extent of presence, must be on the order of the limiting rate of apperception. If it is much lower than this rate, the signal seems uninteresting; if it is much higher, the signal overwhelms the listener and destroys his attention. The listener then can only exhaust the message by many repetitions (learning).

(18) To the degree that the criterion of intelligibility is important to the music, for example, in multiple messages (theatrical recitative, opera, film music), there is a compensatory alternation between semantic and esthetic information.

(19) These structural rules may constitute some ground rules for "authentic composition" practiced in experimental music or *musique concrète*, where the essential problem is to assemble sonic objects in a sequence sufficiently ordered to be intelligible.

Multiple Messages and Structural Esthetics

CHAPTER VI

La parole est un bruit dans lequel le chant est enfermé.

GRETRY

1. EXISTENCE AND CLASSIFICATION OF MULTIPLE MESSAGES

Until now, we have focused attention on messages from the external world which reach the individual through a single sensory channel (vision, audition) and, within one of these sensory channels, through a single mode of communication defined in one of two ways:

(1) By its dimensions, as sketched in the classification of the arts (Chap. I, Sec. 1): (a) printed text (L); (b) pictures (L^2), for example, drawing, photography, painting; (c) moving pictures (L^2T), for example, movies, animated cartoons.

(2) By its structuring and symbolic repertoire: (a) speech; (b) poetry; (c) music.

The mechanisms defined in the preceding chapters are either general mechanisms governing the message (Chaps. I, II, III) or particular applications of these mechanisms to temporal, and especially sonic, messages (Chaps. IV, V). As a whole, these mechanisms deal with sending *only one* of these messages to the individual at a time, as well as with the reactions of the individual.

These mechanisms approximate numerous aspects of reality quite adequately when the individual communicates with the surrounding world by *concentrating his attention* on one aspect of it, for example, the visual or auditory aspect. Many artistic messages, especially the traditional, such as photography, drawing, and music, belong to this category. In receiving them, we consider that the accidental simultaneous presence of several sensory excitations disturbs each. By an effort of the will, we try to obliterate certain excitations [page 172] in favor of others on which we concentrate our receptivity. This seems to be one condition of the esthetic situation: If we listen to a radio concert (and do not hear it passively), we do not have free attention for the printed page, and vice versa.

Recent works on the sociology of radio music all denounce, from the strictly artistic viewpoint, the diffuse *marginal attention* that the individual has available for any message whatever. When there is truly simultaneous reception of several distinct and unrelated messages, it seems established (cf. Silbermann, 1954) that attention fluctuates: Sometimes it concentrates on one (music), sometimes on another (reading), sometimes on a third (speech in conversation). Altogether the receptor collects a *mosaic* of various perceptions, with which he approximately reconstitutes each of the messages. Each message suffers from this treatment.

Complete perception of one of the artistic messages demands attention excluding the others more or less efficiently, depending on the strength of one's sensory interest.

General esthetics teaches us, however, that besides simple messages interfering more or less with each other, there are *multiple messages* in which several channels, or several modes of using a channel in communication, are used simultaneously in an esthetic or perceptual *synthesis*. Here we no longer have interference, but correspondence and agreement between the logical meanings transmitted by the different modes. The most banal multiple message is our perception of other people: The human being is not represented by a unique message, as on the telephone, but by many manifestations. To apprehend the message of "another person" is to apprehend his totality, and the receptor's mind will reflect any disagreement in the "counterpoint" of the messages that another person sends him by an *alarm* signal.

Many arts are grounded on multiple messages, some of them belonging to distinct channels:

(1) The *theater,* a presentation of others or of ourselves, includes a sonic message, speech, and a visual message of attitude.

(2) The *movies* (L^2T), like any artificial channel, are particularly instructive, because they separate the materials from which pictures and sound are generated.

(3) *Television* we shall consider for the time being only as a mode

of communication, and hence as an extension of the movies, until autonomous laws are found in the procedures of television.

(4) *Total cinema* (cinerama) is mentioned here, for the time being, only for the sake of completeness.

[page 173] (5) *Ballet* is very interesting to esthetics, because its two component channels, visual and sonic, usually are of equal importance.

(6) In *opera,* at least three messages are superposed: visual, vocal, and musical.

Other multiple messages come in just one channel *used in different ways.* Among them we shall emphasize the temporal arts; for example, *radio opera* and *recitative* are the superposition of a spoken or poetic message on a musical message.

Having made a special study of the most important of the temporal arts, we now try to find out how the broad concepts of information theory can contribute to the esthetics of the multiple-message arts. Presently, the study of these arts is extremely fragmentary; until now it has been only literary or documentary, without even entering the framework of scientific esthetics.

2. STRUCTURINGS OF MULTIPLE MESSAGES

As we saw in Chap. IV, the first step of scientific esthetics, starting from the intelligible-original dialectic, must be to determine the subordination of successive structures defining the symbolic repertoires which act on the information (originality) furnished by the message. Corresponding to each way of grouping the symbols is one such structure. Each structure ought to be determined separately, with equal regard to its semantic and esthetic aspects.

As a rule (Chap. V), we know the structural laws of the semantic part of each simple message better than we know the laws of the esthetic part. The reasons for this are evident; they stem from the symbolic structure of the human mind, which apprehends defined symbols more easily than statistical rules. For example, a study of the musical message suggests that the structures of esthetic information are primarily statistical rules which restrain choice, while the structures of semantic information are primarily symbols which may be repertoried and transcribed. The latter are easier to grasp than the former; the structures of semantic information obey logical rules which are quite easy to make explicit.

In a complex art such as *ballet,* under present economic circumstances, color movies alone offer the possibility [page 174] of development and renovation. Three partial messages join in ballet:

(a) purely temporal music (T); (b) movement (L^3T); (c) fragmentary colored vision (L^2). Ballet is created by a social microgroup: composer, *maître de ballet* (choreographer), and set designer.

It is easy to inventory approximately the successive repertoires of symbols of the semantic part of each of the partial messages. We have examined the repertoire of music in Chap. V. For movement, the subordination of structures is roughly the following:

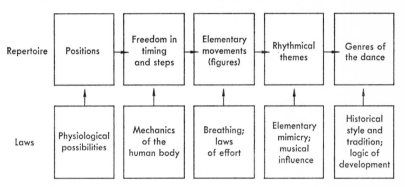

For vision, the subordination of structures is much more complex. The scheme below indicates only a few of its elements:

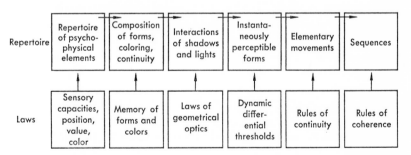

Given these conditions, one may present a rather crude scheme of the subordination of semantic structures as shown in the figure on pages 174-175. In this diagram, the vertical correspondences indicate the temporal connections between parts in the over-all composition of the message.

An interesting application of these schemes [page 175] would be to use them to program a computer to realize an *analog model* of perception. Indeed, in the spirit of cybernetics, one of the most direct methods to study perception would be to create a *model* in which the successive repertoires of symbols would be incorporated

Repertoire

Musical message

Laws

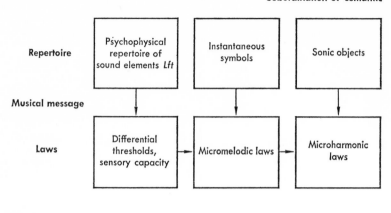

Repertoire

Message of the dance

Laws

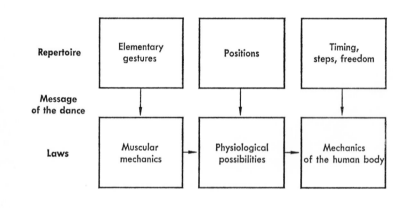

Repertoire

Visual message

Laws

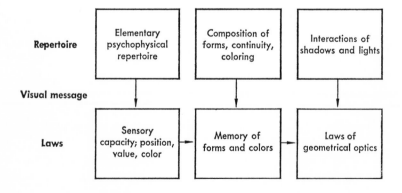

structures in ballet

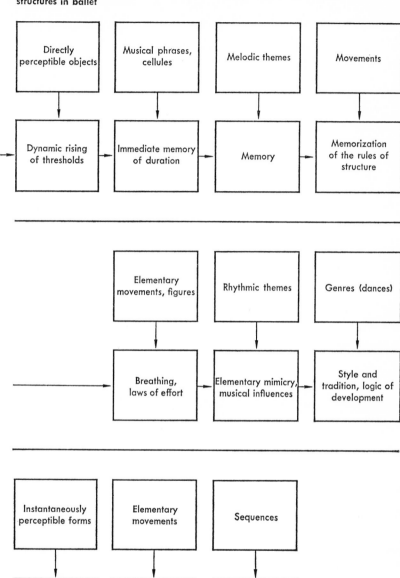

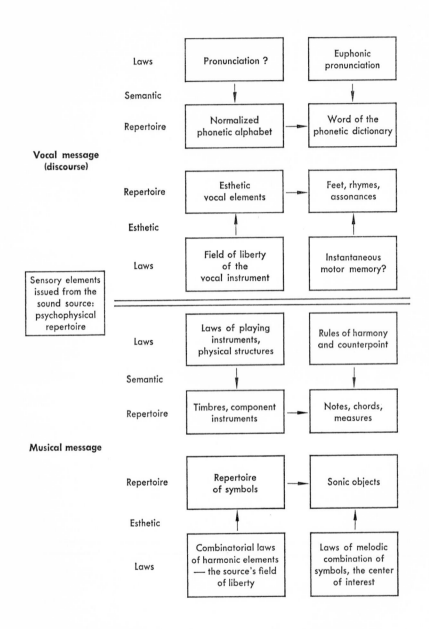

Recitative

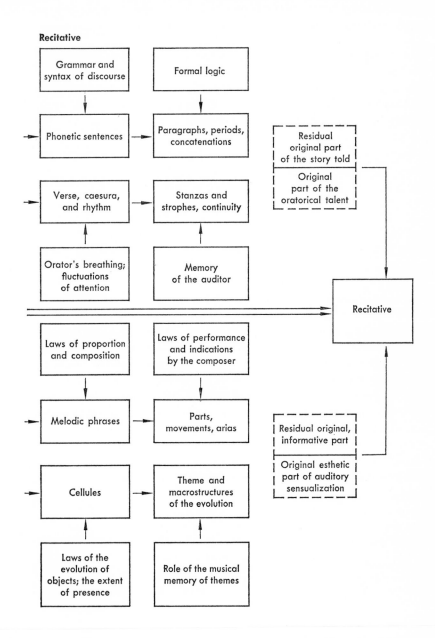

in the calculator's memory. The message, suitably coded at input, would be applied to the different stages which follow the laws of each repertoire. The whole model would be divided into two parts, one for the esthetic, the other for the semantic, part of the message. One objective of the study would be to determine the statistical fluctuations of attention, another to grasp the impact of social constraints on the content of the repertoires at each level of the hierarchy.

As an example, we shall study the sung message accompanied by orchestral music as, for example, in radio opera; that is, we consider the lyric work conceived for or adapted to radio or records and hence supposed to be self-sufficient without the addition of a visual message. Such a message is possible, at least for short works. We shall call this special type of message the *generalized recitative*. This name extends a term used in opera to designate the singing parts where the orator tells a story: In the limit, a whole opera is a story sung to music, that is, a distension of the recitative. For this example, we shall first try to find out how the musical-vocal counterpoint composing the unified message is effected.

Using earlier studies (Chaps. IV and V), we present the structure of this message as shown on pages 176-177. This structure more or less synthesizes the two messages, phonetic and musical, studied separately in Chap. V.

In this inventory of message structures, we must pay much attention to the structural correspondences between the different components, that is, to the symbolizations having nearly the same temporal extents. These correspondences play a considerable role in fusing the components into a harmonious signal. The inventory, which ought to arise spontaneously from the experimentally evident sonic structures, thus does not have to exhibit an artificial symmetry nonexistent in the sonic material; hence the inventory will not attach a real existence to imaginary divisions indicated, for example, by the score or by the text. Each real structure results from a law or property of the receptor mentioned in the diagram beside each repertoire, and each repertoire is the set of symbols in each real structure. Thus we have a general diagram of the phenomena which come into play in the organization of multiple messages, and this is most important for esthetics.

Certain laws governing a particular subordinate structure may be less restrictive than those governing the corresponding structure in another partial message. [page 180] Under these conditions, one of the structures might intrude on the other and dominate the signal.

For example, a very intelligible melodic theme might intrude and, in vocal music, entirely dominate the vocal structures. The latter then have to submit to the temporal contours of the sonic objects. The result is a deformation, a destruction of the vocal organization at that instant. Examples are the accentuation of silent *e*'s in singing French, latitudes in pronunciation in English, elisions and compressions of German syllables. The restricting force of the laws (governing a subordinate structure) is represented by the probabilities of connection with the elements of the repertoire preceding the subordinate structure. If the structuring reveals very different laws in corresponding structures, then experimental esthetics ought to study the way in which one or the other of the partial signals emerges in attention and the reciprocal relations between them.

3. STRUCTURAL LAWS OF MULTIPLE MESSAGES

The essential problem posed by multiple messages is the fluctuations and modalities of the receptor's attention. How does the receptor perceive the different kinds of information transmitted to him by the message, and what laws govern the direction of his attention to each kind?

Attention is an over-all state of the individual. It is not attached to a particular sensory channel: There is no auditory or visual attention. The receptor's attention is directed to the sensory messages from the external world. It can either spread over all of them or be directed to just one.

Recalling the law of maximum rate of perceptible information, the law of the "apperceptual limit" (Chap. III), we are led to deduce an equilibrium action between the kinds of information from the different messages. This result transposes our development of semantic and esthetic information in Chap. V.

In the present case, this law is expressed thus: The sum of the originalities (measured by the quantities of information), both semantic and esthetic, of the different partial messages constituting a multiple message must not exceed a certain maximum average value H_{max} within an interval on the order of the maximum extent of presence (a few seconds) in order to be apprehensible to a particular individual. The value H_{max} is a function of (a) psychophysiological laws; and (b) the sociocultural past of the individual considered.

As in the case of musical structures, the value of this law depends on the importance which is attached to the *apprehensibility* of the signal. The important point is that, for multiple messages, the apprehension value, the intelligibility of the message, plays a much more necessary role and becomes an essential esthetic value. The reason for [page 181] this is that the multiple arts are all *collective* arts. They carry their message, not to a private individual, but to a group of some size.

The technical reasons are even more evident: If the artist is an individual endowed with gifts which are statistically exceptional with respect to the average, the probability that a single individual possesses the different, and sometimes contradictory, gifts which go into composing a multiple message is infinitesimal. Multiple messages are from more than one individual, from a *creative microgroup*, to a generally larger number. Opera, film, ballet, theater, are collective: They are addressed to a social group. In the group is created a *field* of interpersonal relations which condition reception of the message (K. Lewin). At the other extreme, drawing, photography, painting, sculpture, and literature are addressed to a mass of isolated individuals and to the most intimate part of their being.

Other reasons, principally historical, have made the general intelligibility of multiple messages essential. Thus the messages rely on an "average normal receptor." Reification of such a receptor is better justified here since multiple messages are for a receiving *group*, while the single-channel arts rely on the infinite capacity for apprehension of a *mass* where each isolated member directs the best of his attention to receiving the message. In all multiple arts, from Greek theater to the movies, intelligibility is essential: They aim to *mean*. For the time being and within the framework of our hypotheses, unintelligible theater is out of the question.

From the general rule about saturating the receptor, we have some obvious consequences:

(1) On the whole, partial messages, whose counterpoint constitutes a multiple message, are simpler, less rich in information, more redundant, than they would be if they were isolated and the sole object of attention. In general, the libretto of an opera does not develop abstract concepts, complicated sentiments, or an unlimited richness of poetic evocation. The acts and sentiments of the heroes of the Tetralogy are simple: They are stated in everyday vocabulary and in a logical syntax. Conversely, with a musical theme overloaded with polyphony, too rich in varied timbres, having many dissonances and orchestral textures, it seems difficult to construct a recitative which simultaneously follows the elementary laws of syntax and logic, no matter how limited.

This is, indeed, one of the fundamental laws of composing opera. In the arias, everything gives way to the vocal message, which imposes its rhythm and its breathing (phrasing) on the instruments; the orchestra is often reduced to an accompaniment.

(2) In order to compensate for the signal's loss of esthetic richness, recitative and opera systematically alternate originalities (in sonic messages, *brilliance* is often connected with the [page 182] structural originality of the musical substance). The musical message and the vocal message alternate their outputs of maximum information; these outputs are distributed in successive "packages" and force themselves on the attention successively. Here we have rediscovered the traditional structure of the opera from a viewpoint better for intellectual understanding than for empirical rules of writing.

This rule of alternation, well known in esthetics, is valid not only on the large scale (arias and orchestral reentries, choruses and solos); it is also valid in the intermediate structures. This law is characteristic of the details of numerous arias, duos, or quartets, where groups of one or two verses are repeated, stressed, and accompanied by orchestral ornamentation at nearly periodic intervals. While in fact this results from the breathing of the singers, it equally conditions the attention.

(3) The rule of intelligibility governs a third important aspect of multiple messages, their evolution in the course of a civilization. All realizations of multiple messages are, as we noted above, extremely social, both in their creation and in the total receptor to which they are directed. They therefore tend to a continuous evolution in which each work is based on the preceding more exactly than are simple messages for individuals (painting, sculpture). A play, an opera, a film, take advantage of accumulated experience not only in the properly technical domain of details concerning procedures and style, but also in the more fundamental domain of structure and internal organization. That is, the workers in multiple arts tend to outdo each other consciously and critically. They stand on earlier work and look for the richest expression. In the multiple arts, there is a conscious search for a richness of increasing originality, rather than for an original style properly called, as in painting; there are, for example, the typical cases of the music hall and the scenery for an opera.

Subjected to the imperious law of over-all intelligibility, and very much aware of it, the creative microgroup (for example, in opera: composer, librettist, decorator, set designer) tends spontaneously to increase the contrast in alternations of information output among the component partial messages. This is very obvious in opera:

Evolving from a homogeneous mixture, relatively understandable (Monteverdi's *Orfeo*), the vocal and musical message in opera gradually separated. Each tends to seize hold of the listener's attention for a few instants to the detriment of the other; and we have the birth of the *aria* separated by orchestral themes.

In short, the multiple message is *unstable*. In the course of its historical development, its constituent parts [page 183] tend to dissociate. Instead of fusing more and more homogeneously, the parts tend to separate into alternated simple messages. This development is visible in arts such as ballet, which has evolved from an extremely coherent mime on simple musical themes toward alternations of "figures," nearly pictorial scenes, and music.

Film music offers the story in a nutshell of a multiple art in the course of a civilization. The first idea in film music was to back up a masterpiece with a masterpiece, namely, to use tested works of classical music, for example, symphonies, for a supposedly equally great visual or motor message. It then appeared very quickly that the sonic message *intruded* abusively on the listener to the detriment of the visual message; it interfered arbitrarily with the visual message, whatever its intrinsic value. It appeared further that, while it was not forbidden to use the informational riches of symphonic music in order to enhance the brilliance of the cinematographic message, it was absolutely required to locate such music only in the *dead periods* of the film. If necessary, the vacant intervals of the sound track became filled with a deliberately colorless musical substance, which was either overly redundant, for example, consisted of many variations on a very meager original theme, or was removed from the receptor's attention by a low sound level.

4. THE EVOLUTION OF THE RECITATIVE AND INTELLIGIBILITY

Let us state the mechanism of this evolution for the "generalized recitative." This case includes religious hymns, choruses with orchestra, and singing in the opera. Musicologists generally present the recitative in a purely historical way, saying very little about its internal economy. The diagram in Sec. 2 suggests the progressive elaboration of a complex message from distinct repertoires which correspond to each other in time. The diagram emphasizes the strict parallelism between the organizations of the two component messages. This strict parallelism leads to a merger of speech and music by considering the voice in the limit as a very special instrument: It has a more restricted range than many instruments, but a richer temporal structure. Thus it yields a supplementary originality which the orchestral signal cannot give. The "phonemes" (sonic objects) of the orchestra possess a much more restricted repertoire of modes of attack (consonants).

"Recitative" uses the expressive identities between music and speech by shaping both of them in the same temporal sequence, playing on contrapuntal combinations of the foreseeable and unforeseeable, and creating a double dialectic of duration stemming [page 184] from the duality of the source. From the crude viewpoint of the immediate sonic object in Chap. IV, one could present this dialectic as a supplementary resource of instrumentation.

However, the importance of recitative is sufficient to earn it a separate place in the register of "orchestral" combinations, since it is one of the most expressive genres of music since the fourteenth century. In *its* original form, whether religious hymn or naissant opera, recitative presented the equilibrium or balance between semantic information and esthetic information, alternately increasing the richness of the repertoires from which the sonic objects were drawn. At the same time, at least in principle, it conserved "logical" intelligibility — in the broad sense. This logical intelligibility allowed it to *tell a story* to the listener, particularly in opera. In other words, it allowed the composer an economy of means, combining the predominance of the esthetic and sensual value of the musical signal with the intelligible value of the vocal signal, which is more appropriate to transmit narrative information. The great composers of opera, from Monteverdi to Mozart and Wagner, relied heavily on this sung story.

In the synchronization between the orchestral system and the sung phrase, the third consequence in the preceding section implies a struggle for preeminence in the listener's attention. In this dialectical struggle, the opposition becomes the essential fact, as in the purely instrumental concerto. When the multiple message is destroyed, either the orchestra, the singing, or the solo instrument automatically triumphs. This unstable equilibrium owes its artistic value to very precise use of the structural analogies sketched above: The over-all message, which results from the superposition of the two special "instruments," vocal and orchestral, combines the respective foreseeabilities and unforeseeabilities resulting from the laws governing each sequence. This combination *must* ideally be contrapuntal, that is, this combination must increase the semantic intelligibility of each of the partial messages by stressing each of them alternately.

In fact, it is very difficult to make this equilibrium last throughout the message: Too many constraints ought to come into play to be really satisfied. The message's intelligibility, in the ordinary sense of the "story told" to which the microgroup (composer-librettist) or poet attach a positive value, may be increased, for example, when there is a coincidence between the alternation of loud and soft parts (sonic objects) of speech and loud and soft parts of the instrumental signal. Such a coincidence emphasizes the rhythmicity of each of them, by giving them a higher degree of periodicity, and hence makes them better apprehensible. In most cases, however, the intervention of another superposed signal, by creating interference between corresponding structures, reduces the intelligibility of the semantic part. This is one of the most important criticisms of all time directed [page 185] to this type of multiple message.

We saw in Chap. V that the major part of what, in the common sense of the word, is called the "meaning of the text" is carried by the consonants, or more exactly by the transient modulations of the vowels. In fact, there is little resemblance between "musical consonants" and phonetic consonants; the length and the temporal form of the instrumental attacks are quite different from the initial and final consonants which limit the phoneme and constitute the semantic framework of speech. It would be more proper to speak of the "transients" and "cotransients" intended to support the "musical consonants," rather than of consonants and vowels. Musical attacks are more rapid than consonants; musical decay transients are much slower. The "body" of the sonic object, which would correspond to vocalization of the phoneme, is sometimes nonexistent. Thus there is little likelihood of rhythmical and sequential agreement between the musical and the phonetic signal. The semantic intelligibility of the multiple message is therefore usually low. On the other hand, this releases a wealth of esthetic resources, the essential interest of the multiple message.

Thus this analysis almost automatically puts the accent on esthetic value. Intelligibility, any inclination of the signal to narrate a story, to transmit a logical message, becomes of secondary interest and naturally loses all importance. In an average concert hall, the average semantic intelligibility over a rather long period of operatic singing is not greater than 40 per cent. That is, properly speaking 60 per cent of the phonemes are unintelligible. And this is true under the most favorable circumstances, when the listener is familiar with the language in which the recitative is sung and follows the story told him with the aid of the redundancy of his mother tongue,

and when in addition he has the help of the visual message, normally eliminated by radio broadcasting or recording.

Everyday practice verifies this fact: Whether the message is a religious recitative or operatic singing, easy tests show that very few listeners rely on the intelligibility of the message which reaches them in order to construct the story. If the stories interest them, most make considerable use of a written libretto or of their previous knowledge of the dramatic action or text sung.

The most efficient procedure to increase the intelligibility of sung discourse is to compensate for the increase of unforeseeability by repetition, according to the rule of Chap. V, Sec. 7: Intelligibility increases as the binary logarithm of the number of repetitions, all other things being equal. Repetition is a very widely used procedure in religious singing. There the entire structure is based on [page 186] simple fundamental statements, and it is one of the best examples of functional esthetics: The esthetic "canon" results directly from adaptation to a goal. The very loud reverberations in religious edifices condition similarly the length of the notes and the melodic and contrapuntal rules defining Gregorian chant.

The problem of intelligibility in recitative makes it dependent on the special phonetic characteristics of the language used. One of the most important quantitative characteristics of the language is the relation of transient phenomena (consonants) to the permanent phenomena (vowels). Languages having a small number of distinct vowels used abundantly in comparison with the true consonants, that is, languages having sentences with a relatively homogeneous dynamic texture, with only slight variation in levels of loudness, must be more favorable to recitative than languages in which very numerous modulations form the fundamental framework of intelligibility.

This remark explains the success of the recitative in languages favored by the wealth and clarity of their vocalization: Italian has only six pure vowels, but English has many semivowels and diphthong vowels, and conveys the majority of semantic information in the sequence of consonantal transients.

Peculiarities of language also explain the fundamental esthetic difficulty encountered by adaptors of opera who try to translate the coincidences between elements of the vocal message and those of the unchanged score. These attempts at transposition are always extremely perilous, and in the rigorous sense they are theoretically impossible. Hence the current tendency to present opera or religious recitatives in the original language, French, Italian, German, Russian, Hebrew, or Latin, and deliberately to spurn their phraseological meaning in order to keep their essential esthetic value.

The golden age of the operatic recitative, around 1860, ended up in a partial dissociation of the multiple message into *arias, orchestral parts,* and *recitative* in the strict sense. Since then, the recitative has evolved toward an essentially esthetic value, more and more neglecting the logical comprehension intended to tell us a story; we are supposed to know this story otherwise from a visual message or text, etc. The voice tends more and more to be considered as a very special instrument of the orchestra, both in its singing passages properly called and in the recitatives. In the latter, the fundamental rhythms, for example, of breathing, serve as a common envelope of the verse and of the melody. The ultimately illusory attempt to make the details of attacks and extinctions coincide is abandoned. Such a coincidence is realized, [page 187] and then very imperfectly, only in a few cases of popular melodies or of imitative song, where the accompaniments gradually give way to the vocal instrument.

While in practice the unity of the sonic message seems to be the principal care of recitative, in this case the semantic message must be sacrificed to the esthetic part. As a result, vocal characteristics are adapted to those of the instruments. For example, purely euphonic texts are composed in which the proportion of vowels to consonants is higher than in intelligible language; the laws of grammar, syntax, logic, etc., which have only a negligible interest, are abandoned, and only the properly esthetic laws of structure and essential poetic values are respected. Poetic values are values of form (assonance, caesura, meter) combined with a selection of evocative syllables and key words, placed by the composer at the points of the melody where their intelligibility suffices for them to retain an effective, evocative role in the over-all message.

While this method of structuring the message is a little cavalier with regard to syntax, recent results in the theory of language justify it. Our apprehension of sensory messages is indeed a lacunary structure: Less at will than according to a *Gestaltist* scheme, the mind grasps a puzzle of pieces of perception which it puts together according to the forms furnished a priori by the association of ideas; it does not rely on a logical construction which it does not always have time to create. Where syntactic considerations are unnecessary, the structure of the vocal message may assume the lacunary form of perception itself, broadening the field of freedom of the message in favor of the esthetic part.

The normal outcome of this evolution is that the semantic value of the language or of singing totally dissolves, and the vocal phenomenon is reintegrated into the music as an instrument supplying sonic objects on an equal footing with other instruments. While the small pitch range and the traditional specificity of the phonetic structure of language or singing opposed this progress until recently, as least regarding the dissolution of semantic content, the procedures for *preparing* sound developed by experimental music liberate language. Attempts to use the phoneme from the strict viewpoint of the sonic object have given sufficiently interesting results to justify the formula of Grétry: "Speech is a noise in which song is confined" (Moles and Ussachevsky, 1957).

5. ANOTHER EXAMPLE OF THE MULTIPLE MESSAGE: PANTOMIME

Pantomime is the art of successive positions, of stereotyped and fixed simple movements performed in a relatively constant rhythm. Pantomime would appear to be one of the purest cases of message and repertoire, offering an easy schematization of the semantic information contained in an artistic message.

Pure pantomime stems from the works of the school of Decroux; most of the pantomimes now in the world come from his school. We recall Decroux' remarkable statement: "Actors are gods who want to reconstruct man and begin directly with his hat, instead of with his bones." And we recall the difference between the stereotyped and and symbolic gesture presenting quanta of movement, and the fluidity of the gestures of Pierrot in his flowing garments. The various procedures for writing down dance suggest a method of writing mime (Labanotation) which indicates movements with information signals or markings. This method lends itself easily to statistical study using information theory.

Frank has called attention to both motor and perceptual difference thresholds. We know that the structure of a channel is determined by the perceptual difference thresholds of the receptor, because the variations of the message within the threshold are negligible by definition. The set of difference thresholds thus determines the message's repertoire. From this repertoire, the actor or mime extracts some signs, elementary positions or movements, and assembles them. Here the individual's average capacity for information has an upper limit of 16 bits per second. Frank shows that in every case, the action of the mime is adapted to this informational limit. The methods of adaptation are diverse and sometimes subtle, for example, "out of the sheer habit of motor movements directed by the medulla." Accounting for such adaptations gives rise to a theory of pantomime. If limited information capacity is essential to the human operator, the nature of the channel involved matters greatly. From this theory can be built a strictly objective informational esthetic of sign movement, theoretical or experimental in character. (Frank has developed an outline in *Cahiers d'Études de Radio-Télévision*, No. 24, 376-387, 1961.)

6. FROM ESTHETICS TO THE PHENOMENOLOGY OF PERCEPTION

From methodological reasons, we have restricted this sketch of multiple messages to works of art, and more particularly to sonic messages. At the beginning of a theory, the thing to do is to restrict the field under investigation as much as possible, to go from the particular to the general, from the simple to the complex. A "work of art" appears autonomous; it may be circumscribed within limits and isolated in our field of attention. From this [page 188] viewpoint, it is easier to study and more easily detached from the complexity of reality.

But the work of art is only a typical, easy-to-define case of the perception-reaction cycle, which constitutes the essential problem of experimental psychology. In the case of the work of art, the perception properly called takes precedence and is manifested more objectively than the reaction. In this sense, it is simpler and easier to approach. But the etymological origin of the word esthetics ($\alpha\iota\sigma\theta\eta\iota\omega$, sensation) goes considerably beyond the problem of art. Esthetics in the broad sense studies our way of experiencing the surrounding world; it studies the position of the individual in his environment. For this reason, this dogmatic presentation of the dialectic originality-intelligibility should normally lead into the vaster frame of the relations between the human being and his world, of the phenomenology of perception. In practice, the latter problem is more fluctuating, more subjective, and more complicated by the individual's viewpoints, which govern his attention and obscure the more general problem. That is why we shall stop this study of perception, for the time being, within the frame of scientific esthetics, within the limits of the message of art.

7. CONCLUSIONS

We summarize below the principal results of this chapter, which is devoted to extending information theory to multiple messages.

(1) In addition to simple messages conveyed by a single sensory channel, the external world sends multiple messages to the individual. Multiple messages use several transmission channels simultaneously or several ways of using these channels.

(2) Each simple constituent message obeys the general information theory studied earlier. Each includes a subordination of structures which determines its information rate.

(3) The correspondence between the subordinated structures of the semantic and esthetic parts of each of the constituent messages, as a function of their temporal extent, defines the configuration of the multiple message.

(4) The receiving subject can apprehend the set of partial messages as a whole only if the over-all average information rate is lower than a certain maximum, the "apperceptual limit."

(5) Establishing subordination schemes for the repertoires of symbols and their respective contents prepares the way for programming [page 189] digital computers, functioning statistically, to realize *models* of the perception of sensory messages.

(6) Artistic multiple messages are generally collective messages transmitted from a creative microgroup to a larger group of receiving subjects situated in a field of common influence. The preceding condition on intelligibility is more imperative here than for simple messages addressed to a mass of isolated individuals.

(7) In artistic multiple messages, there is a sort of polyphony of the partial messages. The counterpoint they create determines the greater or lesser intelligibility of the over-all signal.

(8) The limitation on over-all information rate is analogous to the limitation found in Chap. V. It implies (a) a greater simplicity and a higher redundancy in each of the partial messages; (b) a clearer alternation of the original parts of each partial message; (c) a historical instability of the different genres of artistic multiple messages, resulting in either a dissociation of their constituent parts or a total subordination of all but one of the parts to the remaining one.

(9) "Generalized recitative" is a multiple sonic message composed of a voice or singing superposed on an orchestral message. It is strictly governed by the condition of over-all intelligibility: It attempts simultaneously to *narrate* a story and to *present* a sonic *structure*. Religious hymns and opera are characteristic examples.

(10) As the genre evolves, semantic intelligibility tends to lessen. The message moves toward the artificiality of a series of arias separated by orchestral statements.

(11) In practice, in the course of evolution, the intelligibility of sung discourse tends systematically to become of secondary importance in order to augment the field of freedom of the esthetically predominant musical parts. The recitative abandons the claim to narrate a story in music, and contents itself with supposing that the story is known a priori; it tends toward program music.

(12) At the end of this evolution, speech is reintegrated into mu-

sic; it is considered as a special sonic object. [page 190] In an esthetic normalization which destroys intelligibility, speech must adapt its form to increase the richness of the orchestral message.

The theory developed here for multiple messages offers an understanding of the collective arts. The ultimate extension of the theory leads beyond works of art, which are the proper object of esthetics, to more general messages from the environment to the individual. Perception of these messages constitutes the individual's "presence in the world" in which he lives.

The Philosophic
Value of
Information Theory

CONCLUSION

Dass jeder sieht die Welt in seinem Sinn
Und jeder sieht recht, soviel
  ist Sinn darin.

GOETHE

1. MATERIALITY OF COMMUNICATION

The viewpoint characteristic of this work is that communication is material. In order to be appreciated exactly, this viewpoint must be returned to the historical circumstances which gave rise to it. What differentiates man from animals is essentially his capacity to communicate widely with his likes, and it is not an overstatement to say that what characterizes modern man is the use of artificial communication channels. Admittedly writing and optical or acoustical telegraphy, which are among the most rudimentary artificial channels, date from a relatively remote period of civilization. But the conscious realization of the materiality of communication is extremely recent. Not so long ago, the ideas transmitted by interpersonal messages were so obviously essential that they overshadowed the material aspect: The ideas "transmitted" caused the transmission to be forgotten.

For Plato, Bacon, and Spinoza, the materiality of writing was only an accessory contingency from which, properly, thought should be emancipated; the myth of the frozen words in the third book of *Pantagruel* was only a pleasant tale without philosophical value. Alone among the ancient civilizations, the Chinese and the Hebraic, by a semimystical route, approached the materiality of writing as an intrinsic value. The Chinese long considered it a sacrilege to destroy any writing whatever, no matter how uninteresting, and the Hebrews founded a finespun interweaving of logical and theological doctrine on respect for "The Book" (*Torah*).

The invention of printing led the materiality of writing to be discovered; a continually growing *economic* value has taken the place of the value of *respect*, which has been pulled to pieces. The increasing *quantity* of signs, however depreciated by their very multiplicity, made [page 192] evident the concreteness of the signs' existence, independent of the ideational value they represented.

In the invention of other channels for communication through space and time, for example, telephone, radio, sound recording, picture and motion recording, *Homo faber* preceded *Homo sapiens* even more. It was necessary for these channels to be invented for people to perceive that an aliquot part of materiality, namely, the *symbol*, transcends the piece of paper or the telephone cables; to conceive, in short, the existence of a materiality of communication no matter what the mode of communication. The importance of the "ideality" of communication in the conceptual presentation was modified when it was joined by its materiality.

While in the school of Erasmus it required a mental effort which could have passed for hair-splitting to examine materiality, in the century of newspapers, radios, records, and films, materiality is pragmatically imposed:

before artificial communication channels: ideality   materiality

after artificial communication channels: ideality   materiality

In the modern world there is a whole class of individuals who *handle* the material support of ideas: not only printers, booksellers, messengers, and telephone operators, but also *communication engineers*. The communication engineer sees the vector *signal*, carrying ideas he does not know or care to know, pass in the telephone wires, circuits, and amplifiers. He must deal with the problems of "crowding" wavelengths, of the delays in use of lines, or still more concretely, with the rates to be charged for each word telegraphed as a function of the distance. The quantitative aspect of information foists itself upon him.

The mass circulation press first discovered the esthetic consequences of the materiality of ideas in a new art whose very conception was foreign to traditional techniques. In the art of assembling communicated messages, the synthetic art called *page composition* or layout (for example, of a daily paper), the artist looks for an esthetic value in assembling fragments of communications that he *does not make* himself. The clear dissociation between editing and composing and the irrelevance of what is composed make evident its materiality.

Discoveries in other modes of communication confirm that this was not a fortuitous circumstance, but a general property of the materiality of communication. Everything considered, this materiality is just the classic choice the artist makes between composition and fabrication: composer and musician, painter and color fabricator, architect and contractor.

[page 193] Generally, the artist does not fabricate the material with which he works. Modern techniques have *revealed* and *promoted* to their true places as artists a series of "composers": the page compositor, formerly an obscure collaborator in the printing workshop; the cutter-editor who is often the real scenarist of the movie; the sound engineer of radio and recorded music. Modern techniques have emphasized the *independence* of the roles of the maker of the material (the author followed by the typographer, the musician, the maker of colors, the scene designer followed by the photographer) and the synthesizer (the page compositor, the orchestra conductor, the painter, the stager or producer).

A new esthetics created on the basis of this remark must first essay a systematic study of the materiality of communication, in contrast with the study of ideas which was the spirit of classical esthetics, especially in certain domains, for example, literature. Consonant with information theory, this new esthetics ought to point out that every communication process has a common element, a *metrical* one: information per se, independent of the shape of the message, of the channel it uses, and of the reactions it provokes.

The viewpoint adopted here and the objective of this work fall into place naturally in the modern state of communication and derived arts: Historically, they are at the point of understanding the generalized theory; more particularly (esthetics in the narrow sense), they try to study the messages from the external world most easily *isolated: works of art.*

2. CRITIQUE OF THE THEORY PRESENTED

It is perfectly clear that such a theory is subject to many criticisms, on the grounds both of its hypothesis and of its results. Its results often leave out what appears essential to depth psychologists and deal nearly exclusively with points that appear obvious to them. Numerous criticisms have already been directed at the theory (Ruyer, 1954).

But it is not within the scope of this book which states a thesis, that is, a point of view, to examine whether one or another of these conflicting points of view is closer to "reality," because to do so would imply a discussion of the philosophical notion of "reality," which is certainly irrelevant to the present exposition and probably illusory. On the other hand, it seems useful to present some obvious formal criticisms in this last chapter.

(1) The information theory of perception adopts the fundamental hypotheses of all objective psychologies; within the framework of these, it develops and deepens behavioristic theory. It is thus subject to all the criticisms of behaviorism, [page 194] particularly of its narrow materialism. The most obvious of these criticisms is that the theory ignores all the aspects of psychoanalysis which certainly play an essential role in perception. However, a few timid attempts have been made to fill this gap (see Foerster, 1949 *et seq.*).

Information theory is a *structuralist* theory; it claims that the observer chops up the world, or at least the messages from the *Umwelt* to the receptor, into simple elements which form the repertoire. Following certain rules, the theory tries to reassemble these elements in a certain order, so as to reconstruct a likeness of "reality" which is as exact as possible on the observer's level of observation. The set of assembly rules, collected in a code of constraints, represents what may be called the *structure* of these messages. This procedure has the enormous advantage of being perfectly operational; indeed, this virtue is intrinsic to the structuralist theory. But the arbitrariness of this atomistic chopping-up is usually held against the theory, even if such chopping is only an algorithm of scientific reasoning.

(2) The general theory of behavior has become much more tractable since the historic works of Pavlov and Watson. More recent and less polished than this general theory, information theory is obviously *simplistic* in dealing with esthetic perception. Lacking nuances, it studies a few of the grossest, the most obvious, and especially (or at least often) the most trivial aspects of perceptual behavior, while leaving aside other, equally obvious, aspects.

Thus it is *insufficient* within the very framework that it assumes. In the mechanistic model of the "information-receiving subject" that it suggests, it ignores the prodigious "mutability" of characteristics which emerges so clearly from study of man's psychophysical apparatus. For example, an attentive subject can see a candle ten kilo-meters away at night (a few photons) or can hear a sound scarcely stronger than the agitation of the molecules in the atmosphere. But this same subject can perceive an extremely extensive complex of forms, colors, and sounds in the crudest way in one-sixteenth of a second, still retaining instantaneously what is identifiable in the complex.

In its present state, our theory suggests nothing about this adapt-ability, which is unequaled by any physical apparatus (such as warning radars). This arbitrary choice, a function of its explica-tive possibilities, is common to all sciences in the process of forma-tion. From a strictly methodological viewpoint, it is clearly suffi-cient that none of the aspects neglected by the new doctrine prove irreducible to the terms of the basic hypotheses of the theory. That result is still a question of time, but it appears that the doctrine discussed here will become more tractable rather rapidly, judging by its partial success in interpreting the concept of form which originally appeared rather to contradict the very bases of a scanning theory (cf. Chap. II). There still remains to be found a satisfactory treatment of "category perception" which some scientists have re-cently considered as essential to perception.

(3) Aside from its failings in its own domain, one must deplore the theory's external weaknesses. Certain concepts to which the theory appeals, for example, intent (Chap. III), as determinants of perception ought to be developed in the same spirit as the theory; at present, such a development would seem laborious or premature. With this viewpoint, some cyberneticians such as Walter (1953) tried to make a census of the "proper functions" of living organisms; this work is still unfinished and ambiguous.

[page 195] Similarly, in the esthetic field, the theory suggests nothing about the intrinsic pleasure of internal re-creation and of presence at the sensualization of the work of art, a pleasure whose importance we pointed out (Chap. V).

(4) Finally, it would be superfluous to emphasize the mechanistic character that information theory inherits from its technical origins, but this is perhaps less a criticism than a declaration. The important new terminology introduced by information theory reflects the tendency to a *synthesis*, an essential trait of the theory the necessity for which philosophers have emphasized with envy. Some of its terms, such as fidelity, channel, transmission, distortion, background noise, losses, reactions, signal, and periodicity, introduce previously unknown concepts into philosophical psychology, and these concepts

are part of the universe on an equal footing with the abstract concepts inherited from the introspective psychology of past centuries.

Reciprocally, concepts such as memory, length of the present, duration, choice, intent, history, and foreseeability or predictability, have been introduced by means of information theory into scientific or technical domains. The latter did not know of them or regarded them suspiciously, simply because, as a result of a kind of mental deformation which deliberately disregarded certain aspects of reality, they did not see the concrete phenomena to which they applied. Traditional physics lived in continuity and linear and reversible phenomena, all viewpoints which are really abstractions; it ignored the buckets that were emptied and not refilled, the pieces of glass that were broken and clearly remained broken, the pawns moved in a game of chess, the cards perforated in a tabulating machine. Physics contented itself with studying the "laws" of water flowing at the edge of pails, the "laws" of the distribution of forces in glass, the "laws" of the friction of the pawns on the chessboard, or the "laws" of driving punches into cardboard. It prudently limited its study to this side of the moment at which the phenomenon changed character so much that it became *another* phenomenon.

Doubtless, however, the extensive and disparate terminology of information theory is an immediate difficulty blocking its inclusion in psychological and philosophical research. In this volume, we tried to alleviate this difficulty in part by listing the terms used and the passages in which they are defined in the index.

Information theory appears to be a great scientific theory, in the sense that philosophers have given this expression, joining the company of gravitational theory, atomic theory, electromagnetic theory, general relativity, etc. It attempts to assimilate many facts and special laws in an integrative synthesis. Certain of these facts [page 196] and laws are so obvious as to be banal; others, in the leveling of values characteristic of scientific theories, are entirely new. If it leaves aside facts, or ignores or is opposed to more classical theories, one must remember with R. Aron that "the goal of science is not universal reconciliation, but ever renewed progress."

3. THE FUNDAMENTAL RESULTS

The fundamental point of departure of this study, following naturally from the materiality of communication, is that *information* is a *measurable quantity* which characterizes the process of communication. To communicate, near or far, is to transmit something. What is transmitted is *complexity*. Information differs essentially from meaning: Information is only a measure of complexity. To transmit a message is to make more complex the space-time surrounding the point of reception; it is to produce a microreplica of the complexity created at the origin of transmission.

Meaning rests on a set of conventions which are a priori common to the receptor and transmitter. Thus it is not *transmitted;* potentially it preexists the message. Only complexity is transmitted from the transmitter to the receptor; it is precisely what is not present at the receptor; it is what is *unpredictable.* The measure of information no more depends on the number of symbols transmitted than on the effects of these symbols; rather, it measures the *originality* of the grouping of the symbols, as opposed to the *banality* of the foreseeable.

Originality is thus among the fundamental values of the theory. In the perception of forms, *originality* opposes *intelligibility,* because only *forms* are intelligible and they reduce unpredictability, hence originality. The cleavage between the values of originality and intelligibility makes intelligibility the operational synonym of banality in the message. The etymological meaning of the word intelligence, *interligere,* justifies the assertion that what is most intelligible is what has the most bonds (liaisons), and is thus what is most often encountered in the networks of thought. The most intelligible is at the same time the most banal; the position of the mind between intelligibility and creativity is only a transposition of its position between banality and originality. The concept of originality appears necessary to the human mind as one of its *central concepts,* the existence of which structuralism postulates and Belin Milleron has pointed out. It is understandable that development of this concept should give rise to a great scientific theory.

The study of form as the union of predictable perceptual elements, either in the length of the present, or discursively in a scanning process, has led us, by connecting form with some kind of *trace* of the present in duration (instantaneous memory, immediate memory, or memorization), to consider the perception [page 197] of form as the epiphenomenon of a *direct perception of autocorrelation;* the study has led us to give autocorrelation an importance which psychology has not emphasized until now. A message is a complex *form,* and its rate of information measures the complexity of the form. Information theory furnishes us a ranking of forms. The message transfers complexity from one point of the world to another.

Certain *forms,* which reduce originality by making the message assimilable, are permanent. They may be *normalized* and *reper-*

toried; they are *symbols.* Many symbols exist potentially in the psychophysical elements of the message; those which exist actually depend on the modes of grouping which the conventions conserved in the individual's memory find in the message. Other forms are only statistical, approximate, and inform us no more than does a *wager* about the future of the perception on the basis of its present and past state. These statistical forms are expressed by structural rules which replace the preceding symbolization.

Among these forms, one of the most important is *periodicity,* less an absolute property in the mathematical sense than a measurable quantity. Periodicity measures the regularity of the spatial or temporal development of the perception, whether or not there is a conscious *scanning* of the message. Our perception is dominated by two sorts of physical time: one rather well defined; the other more fluid, more variable, the extension of the immediately perceptible duration; the latter is the temporal "field of consciousness." With regard to the periodicity of physical phenomena, the "length of the present" separates perception of the degree of rhythmical regularity, periodicity, as a *quality of the perceived substance,* temporal or spatial, from direct perception of *rhythm* or of a foreseeability of future events.

The periodicity of an audible sound is a necessary concept in acoustics. But periodicity in the physical sense is *not known* as such by perception; rather, it is conceived as a directly apprehensible quality of the *sonic substance (Klangstoff)* which fills time, similar to the color of a visual impression. In the domain of sound, this analysis makes pitch an important special feature of timbre *(Klangfarbe)* when the latter has a stable dominant for longer than the length of the present. Periodicity is perceived only if it affects durations which are themselves apprehensible: Rhythms, melodies, measures, etc., considered as cyclical phenomena, have been practically neglected until now by physical science.

From the properties of symbols and rules of form in the dialectic of information, it follows that the *successive subordinations* of these symbols and rules represent important knowledge about the structure of the message. Each further restricts the repertoire of primitive elements by increasing its redundancy. Any theory of messages, in particular of artistic messages, must [page 198] determine these subordinate structures, their laws, and their repertoires. This will be the goal of a "message physics," a component of experimental esthetics.

Sonic messages and musical messages in particular provide the clearest example of this message physics. The musical message must be approached in its immediate materiality, not through the artificial operating scheme of the score, which interests essentially only the performer. Phenomenological study of the message, which ought to be descriptive, reveals the existence of the successively subordinated structures, which in fact characterize the most general message. The structures are built from the psychophysical elements of hearing. Assembled according to "harmonic laws" which include operationally the concepts of harmonics and timbre, these elements compose symbols, present within the quantum of duration, whose temporal evolution constitutes the *sonic object*, an experimentally separable entity. Within the extent of the immediate memory, the groupings of sonic objects constitute sonic cells, perceived as *forms* which enter into the macrostructures. The latter irregularly alternate banality and originality.

The analysis of message structures offered by information theory suggests the possibility of creating models of sensory perception by using computing machines functioning statistically, programmed as a function of these structures.

The musical message is typical of the real artistic message. Often *repeated* to us, yet without losing its value, this message leads us to examine how the subordination of symbols is effected in several artistic messages. The musical signal shows that in reality there are two distinct and simultaneous structurings of the psychophysical messages furnished by the message, and hence two partial messages:

(1) The translatable semantic message, with universal symbolization, prepares acts and obeys an internal *metalogic* (whatever this logic may be). Information theory was originally intended for this message because the semantic part constituted an object of thought to transmit for the purpose of determining reactions in the receptor. (See Cohen, 1962.)

(2) The *esthetic* message has symbols unknown to us and rules often little known; it is untranslatable and unique.

Each of these two messages conveys its own complexity; each obeys autonomous structural laws. They are both present in different kinds of messages, in proportions depending on the roles that the messages must play. A telegraphic message is mostly semantic information. A spoken message appears in general to include equivalent proportions of these two *aspects* of information. As for the [page 199] musical message, while its semantic part (musical notation) is very structured, and hence conveys a small amount of information, its esthetic part is extremely rich in information which, as a general rule, *overwhelms* the individual receptor.

Reception of the esthetic message is conditioned by the existence of a limiting information rate, both semantic and esthetic. This limit is a function of the past and memorized *culture* of the receptor, as well as of his *attention potential*. In order for a message to be intelligible to us, the complexity that it conveys must, on the average, not be *too rich*. However, artistic messages are practically always too rich. Consequently, the receiving subject is obliged to *exhaust* these messages by successive re-presentations.

If not completely determined by this condition on intelligibility, the structure of the artistic messages is nevertheless conditioned by it and must create a counterpoint between the two types of information. The two types assert themselves on the receptor alternately and irregularly in successive packages of information; the message evolves progressively toward banality in the course of time or of the scanning of the message. For example, a very rich musical message makes great use of repetition, which progressively diminishes the rate of information.

The receptor's apperceptual limit, which introduces the condition on intelligibility, plays an essential role in the complex and interacting structurings of multiple messages. Multiple messages, in a sort of concerto, are those which use different sensory information channels (sound movies, ballet, etc.) or exploit these channels in different ways (recitative, opera, illustrated books, etc.).

The materiality of communication implies that communication must obey the fundamental physical laws governing all objects. Among the first of these is the *approximation* caused by the quantification due to perceptual thresholds, and the *destruction* caused by noise, which creates uncertainty in the message.

Noise constitutes the ground against which we perceive messages from the surrounding universe. These messages must stand out sufficiently from the background to intrude upon our perception. The perpetual and disordered agitation of this background implies two *uncertainty principles* in perception:

(1) The first connects our extreme threshold of sensitivity to our a priori knowledge of the qualitative nature of this perception, namely its frequency: Uncertainty about the perceptible signal $\times$ uncertainty about its frequency = constant. Thus, we can perceive a very weak sound only by making it emerge from the background noise *and* on the condition that we have an a priori idea of its pitch or timbre.

[page 200] (2) The second connects the perceptible signal to the minimum interval required to perceive it: Uncertainty about the signal $\times$ uncertainty about its duration = constant.

These universal rules play a role in the perceptual framework analogous to the uncertainty principles of Heisenberg in the framework of the material-object world of physicochemistry.

4. ESTHETIC METHODOLOGY

The conceptions developed above state or suggest *methods* of experimental esthetics. Among them are the following:

(1) One of the most general heuristic procedures of esthetics, based on the *materiality* of the work of art, consists in progressively *destroying* the work by known, perceptible quantities, and in following the variations in esthetic sensation, value, and knowledge as a function of this destruction. This is a method of concomitant variations.

The method of destruction used will be a function (a) of the nature of the artistic message (sonic, visual, etc.); (b) of the a priori knowledge one has about the message (forms, subjects, etc.); (c) of the factors one is trying to discern (regularity, originality, semantic content, etc.).

The procedure for destruction depends on the individual case, but we point out the following two: (a) Distortions act on any dimension whatever of the transmission channel and make evident the perceptual parameters relating to that dimension; for example, elliptical distortion applied vertically (flattening) to a picture by El Greco; horizontal optical distortion to a Daumier; trapezoidal distortions creating false perspectives or displacing the apparent normal viewpoint of the picture; distortions by monochromatic lightings which filter the colored information received; cutting frequency bands in the sonic spectrum of the musical signal, etc. (Moles, 1954b). (b) *Noise* is the statistical destruction of elements; for example, spraying black spots at random with an air spray on a copy of a picture; masking the phonetic or musical message with a white noise.

(2) Derived from this very general method is the method of *periodic destruction* [page 201] in time or space, which we must mention separately in virtue of its importance. With this method, one chops up the esthetic message by periodically removing it from attention. This procedure has a very general value, since it does not profoundly alter the order of the message's presentation. We used this method to determine the redundancy of written messages (Chap. I) and of

temporal signals (Chap. V). In the case of the visual message, it might consist in superposing a grillwork or net (a periodic black or grey screen) on a picture; by varying the separation and the width of the bars of this grill, one could study the resultant esthetic variations. The method requires certain precautions in use: In particular, one must avoid having the receptor direct his attention selectively to the pips of chopping (or the bars, etc.) instead of to the message.

(3) The procedure of partial or infinite *clipping* (Chap. V, Sec. 5) is more connected with the methods of distortion. It methodically dichotomizes a temporal or spatial message. We have seen that this operation affects semantic and esthetic information very differently; it filters out and preserves the first. We applied clipping in the sonic domain. In the visual domain, the method would be applied, for example, by the procedure of photographic supercontrast, creating from a picture masses of blacks and whites, thus making the composition of masses important; the method should be companion to the study of lines of force in composition (*Wahlen*).

(4) *Inversion* is an autonomous method applicable only to the arts of time. It degrades nothing of the artistic material, but presents it under different and unusual circumstances; it upsets the perspective. We have emphasized its applications in studying esthetic information, but it has a wide field of application in all arts of time where perception partakes of a sequence of temporal events in an *order* (film, ballet, animated drawing, etc.). It is literally an experiment with time.

(5) The *transposition of messages* is based on structural analogies often emphasized throughout this work. On the basis of a law, experiment, or result obtained for a given type of messages, we look systematically for what would be their equivalent if each of their elements were translated into another message; we try to find how this experiment or result would be expressed and whether it might be true.

More than an esthetic method properly called, this is a *heuristic* method. It offers possible experiments rather than affirms the value of their results. It raises the question: Since such and such a structure exists in the sonic channel, with some law for selecting elements, what corresponds to it in the visual channel, for example, in a picture or a film sequence?

[page 202] (6) A special application of the preceding method, which served us frequently in studying music, is looking for correspondences between vocal and musical messages. The musical mes-

sage transports esthetic information, the laws of which are very hard
for us to define. Each time a serious difficulty arises, it is advisable
to look for the elementary and structural correspondence in the phonetic field and to determine how the analogous difficulty appears
there. If music is language without meaning, the study of language
with meaning can give us indications — always subject to caution,
a point never to be forgotten — about the morphology of the former.

(7) Finally, among the general heuristic methods in the domain
of perception, we must class the procedure used constantly throughout this work, *recourse to artificial communication channels.* This
procedure is historically at the origin of information theory. In objective psychology, every perceptual problem implies the existence
of a mechanism to resolve it. It is wise to look at least for an
inspiration about this mechanism to the technical channels created
in order to extend perception beyond the limits set by psychophysiological possibilities.

Looking for such inspiration should in *no way prejudge the identity between artificial mechanisms and natural processes.* This point
could not be too much emphasized, because ignorance of it seems
to have caused innumerable errors, notably in the general public.
In the behavioral sciences the existence of mechanisms realizing a
functional analogy plays the role of *existence theorems* in logic.
Without telling us anything about the real solution, it demonstrates
the existence of *at least one* objective scientific solution to the problem posed. Recourse to the telegraph for the study of codes and
symbolizations, to the telephone for the transmission of speech and
music, or to television to get ideas about scanning or *Gestalts* has
enlightened us many times. Thus it is advisable to turn to artifices
as a way of conceiving psychological mechanisms. We should place
this indirect manner of thought among the heuristic methods.

The triple objective of this book is to state a *problem* (Chap. I),
a *development* (most of the book), and a *program.* The brief outline
above of the contribution of message theory to esthetic methodology
naturally suggests a program of researches continuing and developing the results presented. Among these results some are technical,
others theoretical. But clearly experimental researches are too much
bound up with each other for one of them not to react on each of the
others, and it would be superfluous to try to define a coherent order
in these developments; it will always remain arbitrary. So, we
[page 203] shall limit ourselves to enumerating a few of the most
obvious of these developments:

The determination of the repertoire of elements of the visual channel has important technological effects on the reproduction of paintings, as well as on the search for the laws of format regarding the optimum use of the visual field. This research has been only sketched by certain works of American psychologists and estheticians (cf. Woodworth and Schlosberg, 1954).

The difficult study of the dynamic rising of thresholds, accommodation, either auditory or visual (Chap. III, Sec. 4), is very important theoretically, because it touches on an essential mechanism of perception.

Penetrating more deeply into esthetic structures, one may determine the redundancy and the semantic information in film and animated cartoons. To do so, we *invert* sketches where the action is well defined and of which it is easy to gather a sensibly uniform group, and we suppress progressively an increasing number of pictures. (a) We may perform this suppression systematically, ultimately accelerating the action. The perceptual threshold or the upper limit of acceleration will inform us directly about our perception of time. We know already that suppressing one picture out of 24 cannot be sensed either from the sound track or from the unrolling of the film. (b) Or we may suppress *selectively*, achieving a telegraphic style of action, the extreme limit of which corresponds to the residual semantic information.

The search for an index of intelligibility for music, to play a role like that of Flesch's index of the readability of texts, is also directly connected with semantic information, but includes an important sociocultural aspect.

The realization of an analog model of perception, with internal organization answering to the successive structures of the sensory messages such as they have been set forth (Chaps. V and VI), the study of interaction between levels of symbolization, and the use of these studies to program digital computers to compose music (Hiller and Isaacson, 1959), where the purpose is to make a certain degree of order emerge from an unintelligible disorder — all these are further developments.

5. CONDITIONS ON THE VALIDITY OF AN INFORMATION THEORY IN PSYCHOLOGY

Current psychology oscillates between two clearly opposed propensities which generate value judgments on most publications in this area. The first is the strictly experimental propensity, which in the limit would reduce psychology to a series of well-performed and well-controlled experiments in well-known and entirely objective fields of operation. The second would aim exclusively at finding mechanisms to produce entities which could be more or less mathematized as analytic functions; from these mechanisms would derive the independent and foreseeable protocols of the contents of particular experiments.

In any case, current psychology appears as an objective science, accessible to all and susceptible to application.

Now, a theory is an instrument of the mind, a viewpoint, an integrative system, and a way of communicating. Since every theory is a system linked together by reasoning, every theory exhibits the contrast between the fragility of each of its elements and the relative solidity of the whole. The function of a scientific theory is to connect up as many separate facts as possible in a unified perspective (cf. Nash, 1963). The specific role of a theory is to introduce coherence into disparity.

A theory may be evaluated by two types of criteria:

(1) *Methodological criteria.* A theory must account for the experimental facts in the order of their a priori importance. This importance is determined by the position the facts occupy in the mass media of communication in scientific society, that is, by a scientific analysis of the contents of journals, monographs, books, etc. From the start, a theory must neglect some facts insofar as the neglected facts do not contradict those retained by the theory. The explicative strength of the theory diminishes in proportion to the residue of unexplicated facts. Initially, the theory will pay attention only to facts which actually contradict it, by reexamining the interpretation and the language (definition) of such facts, since by these facts the theory may ultimately be destroyed.

The history of science shows that very often a theory can absorb facts which contradict its initial form after a laborious digestion which changes the theory significantly. This digestion sometimes leads the theory to increase its basic entities (for example, the factors used to account for a phenomenon). But such a result is always dangerous to the economy of thought which is one of the essential goals of a theory.

The theory will also have to digest or classify the facts which appear to be neither for nor against it, as soon as the theory is extensive enough to justify, to those concerned, the labor needed to make such facts relevant. In certain extreme cases, a theory declares, pure and simple, that the facts were wrongly or poorly observed, especially for dimensional or even irrelevant reasons, and the theory goes on in spite of them. Though this is a dangerous procedure, there is no gain without risk.

(2) *Values* constitute the second type of criterion: A theory must have some value. The value may be one of (a) rational order, and economy of thought in particular, gained by providing mechanisms which establish a redundancy in the semantic message that makes up the theory. The value may be one of (b) heuristic order, to the extent that the theory suggests evocative language. Thus a word may suggest an analogy between several completely distinct disciplines, each having very different habits of thought. The value of a theory is connected with (c) the foreseeability of a structure, the

possibility of constructing a form or of completing an intellectual network. The theory proposes verifications to perform and further information to acquire.

These three elements concur in determining the value of a theory. None separately suffices to judge a theory. A theory is all three: a mental form, a style of expression, and a path covered.

These criteria do not include the criterion of "truth," which is an arbitrary invention of certain schools of philosophy who refer to a "real universe," hidden and by definition inaccessible — a universe to which science would be only a constantly changing approximation.

In principle, a theory does not produce new facts except in entirely theoretical sciences such as mathematical physics. In other sciences, psychology, for example, a theory cannot do without experimental nourishment — and sometimes forced feeding, depending on how the beast is fattened. But it is of the essence of a theory to suggest experiments leading to new facts. Facts are a theory's most concrete by-products, and apostles of experimentation tend to judge a theory by these facts. As Bruner remarked humorously at the Fifteenth International Congress of Psychology: "Truth has no place in psychology."

All these observations appear in the context of a political economy of thought: Where facts are rare, they are all the more valuable. But in sciences such as experimental psychology where one is gorged with facts to the point of indigestion, the value of a theory will hang much more on the intellectual devices that it puts forth to organize the chaos than on the additional facts which the theory suggests be established.

Information theory, especially in psychology, presents itself as a new department of learning. It proposes an attitude of mind which may be construed as a principle of analogy: We will be satisfied with a functional analogy, that is, with one reproducing the behavior of the phenomenon studied, rather than with a structural analogy which reproduces all the elements the observer sees, whether or not they are relevant to the phenomenon observed.

A theory determines its criteria for completion, which are not necessarily the criteria for termination. Without worrying at all about taking account in detail of the masses of psychological data, an informational theory assumes that it is fulfilling its goal if it provides a graph, an organogram, sufficient to establish the specifications and the programming of a machine, entirely man-made, whose external behavior, on the level of precision of the supposed observer, is dominated by the actions of the organism under study, whether man or animal.

The ultimate goals of an informational theory, for example, of a theory of perception, will be to produce an organogram, to describe the repertoires contained in the records and the memories of this organogram, to define the methods by which these repertoires are filled, to define the level of observations and precision taken, and to analyze the interaction between the different hierarchical levels of observations.

Such a theory always proceeds by successive approximation. It constructs increasingly complex, increasingly abstract models on levels of observation increasingly close to those of psychology. However, the complexity of the model is not necessarily related to the complexity of the theory itself. The theory must satisfy criteria of accessibility and of economy of thought and must be simpler than the observations, since any system of experiments is by definition obviously a model of itself. The theory as a whole cannot be larger than all the elements of the experimental message; in practice, it must be considerably smaller. This is Occam's razor.

It would thus be senseless to criticize a theory or model on one level of observation on the basis of remarks or experiments which partake of another level of observation. Ripples, waves, and tides are different phenomena which all take part in modifying the level of the sea at a given point. Orderly thought will always refute objections based on a level of observation other than that assumed initially.

These remarks establish what may be legitimately expected from an informational theory in psychology based on the realization of an analog mechanism. The purpose of this model is not to discover new facts, but to suggest attitudes of mind capable of leading to new actions.

Science gives us measurements and forms. The role of the scientist is to maintain in the crowding of his mind a proper equilibrium between the quantity of measurements and the quantity of forms, for his final goal is to understand.

6. PHILOSOPHICAL VALUE OF INFORMATION THEORY

The object of this book was essentially to *present* information theory, first rigorously, then in with some immediate *developments*, and to apply it to some of the simplest and most concrete aspects of esthetic perception, taken as a special case of ordinary perception.

In a general way, we have adopted the Hegelian method in this

book. We tried to find dialectical oppositions by characterizing the
two poles sufficiently to make the contrast between them stand out,
then by presenting a rapid and incomplete synthesis; we tried to
find in this synthesis one of the terms of new opposition and to bring
forth its opposite pole. By this mechanism, overtaking and passing
beyond the initial dipole, we tried ceaselessly to enlarge the initial
viewpoint.

In conjunction with the fundamental dialectic order-disorder inherited from thermodynamics, information theory suggests a number of similar *dialectical dipoles* deriving from the first:

Order	Disorder
Predictable	Unpredictable
Banal	Original
Redundant	Informative
Intelligible	Novel
Simple	Complex

Each of these dialectics focuses attention on a new field of application remaining to be explored. Such a development is the task indicated for the philosopher.

As we appropriated it from communication physicists, information
theory was essentially atomistic and exploratory: It decomposed
messages from the environment into simple elements [page 204]
which it assumed, in some way not clearly stated, to be taken one
by one; it followed the example of the mechanical systems which
inspired it. In this form, the theory was suitable only to mechanistic
psychophysics, the fecundity of which must nevertheless be emphasized. In this book we tried, in developing the concept of form, to
make the theory integrative and *Gestaltist*.

The theory claims the role of a great scientific theory. Its synthetic power allows us to apprehend many disparate facts. In its
development, it rediscovers some banal facts as landmarks; others,
unexpected (for example, the uncertainty principles), justify it as a
method of presentation.

Philosophy consumes scientific concepts in order to draw universal concepts from them; for this reason it is interested in any
synthesizing theory. Although information theory, like any just beginning, remains clearly systematic, putting more emphasis on internal coherence than on agreement with other theories, the very
large number of experiments and results that it can bring together
in a logical perspective classes it beyond arbitrary systems.

In fact, the theory appears as a huge *Gedanken* experiment, attempting to re-create the strangeness of communication by making evident its material aspect. It was specifically this point of view which led us to the concept of sonic objects (Chap. IV).

Communication theory still raises more problems than it resolves. While it attempts to synthesize, it is also a program. Ultimately, its *heuristic* value justifies it from the philosophical viewpoint. Whatever the criticisms which can be addressed to it, and even were its essential values rejected (for example, the materiality of communication, the value of originality, the opposition between the intelligible and the original), the fact remains that like the great theories which preceded it, information theory furnishes an unlimited field for research. For this reason, it seems, necessarily, to impose its point of view in a definitive way, making acceptable the picture of the universe given by the individual's perception with all its uncertainties; it concretely returns man to the material world. In this picture, man becomes the very condition of knowledge of the world, instead of becoming asymptotically eliminated as in the science of the nineteenth century — the science which saw in an immense thermodynamics, conceived by an omniscient being, the ultimate description of the universe.

Bibliography

[The following is based on a revised bibliography drawn up by Dr. Moles. I have checked every item except those starred (*) with the original publication, the Library of Congress National Catalog, or the Harvard University Union Card Catalog. I have added numerous recent references which are relevant. — *Translator*.]

*Alsleben, K. *Aesthetische Redundanz*. Schnelle Verlag Quickborn, 1962.

Ashby, W. R. *An introduction to cybernetics*. New York: Wiley, 1956.

Attneave, F. *Applications of information theory to psychology*. New York: Holt, 1959.

———. Stochastic composition processes. *J. Aesthetics & art Criticism*, 17:503-510, 1959.

Ayer, A. J., *et al. Studies in communication*. London: Secker & Warburg, 1955.

Bense, M. *Aesthetica*. Stuttgart: Deutsche Verlags-Anstalt, 1954.

Berlyne, D. E. *Conflict, arousal and curiosity*. New York: McGraw-Hill, 1960.

———. Effects of complexity and incongruity variables on G.S.R. investigatory behavior and verbally expressed preference. *J. gen. Psychol.* 71:21-65, 1964.

———. *Measures of aesthetic preference*. Proceedings of the First International Colloquium on experimental aesthetics. Paris, 1965.

Bernhart, J. *Traité de prise de son*. Paris: Eyrolles, 1949.

Birkhoff, G. D. *Aesthetic measure*. Cambridge: Harvard University, 1933.

———. *Collected mathematical papers*. New York: American Mathematical Society, 1950.

Brelet, G. *L'interprétation créatrice*. Paris: Presses Universitaires de France, 1951.

Brillouin, L. *Science and information theory*. New York: Academic Press, 1956.

Broadbent, D. E. *Perception and communication.* New York: Pergamon Press, 1958.

Burris-Meyer, H., and Cole, E. C. *Scenery for the theatre.* Boston: Little, Brown & Co., 1938.

Chase, G. *America's music.* New York: McGraw-Hill, 1955.

Cherry, C. *On human communication.* Cambridge: Technology Press of MIT and Wiley, 1957.

————, ed. *Information theory — 1955 London symposium.* London: Butterworths, 1956.

Cloudsley-Thompson, J. L. *Rhythmic activity in animal physiology and behaviour.* New York: Academic Press, 1961.

Cohen, J. E. Information theory and music. *Behavioral Sci.,* 7:137-163, 1962.

Combarieu, J. *Music, its laws and evolution.* London: K. Paul, Trench, Trübner, 1910.

Copland, A. *What to listen for in music.* New York: McGraw-Hill, 1957.

*Cube, F. von. *Über die Entropie von Gruppen.* Schnelle Verlage Quickborn, 1963.

Diderot, D. *Le paradoxe du comédien.* In A. Billy, ed. *Œuvres.* Paris: Gallimard, 1946.

Drever, J. *A dictionary of psychology.* Rev. ed. Harmondsworth, Middlesex: Penguin, 1964.

Dudley, H. Remaking speech. *J. Acoust. Soc. Amer.,* 11:169-177, 1939.

Einstein, A. *A short history of music.* London: Cassell, 1953.

Fletcher, H. *Speech and hearing in communication.* New York: Van Nostrand, 1953.

Flesch, R. F. *The art of plain talk.* New York: Harper, 1946.

Foerster, H. von, ed. *Cybernetics, transactions of the conference* (6th-10th). New York: Josiah Macy, Jr., Foundation, 1949-53.

Folgman, E. E. E. An experimental study of composer-preferences of four outstanding symphony orchestras. *J. exp. Psychol.,* 16:709-724, 1939.

Frances, R. *La perception de la musique.* Paris: Librairie Philosophique Vrin, 1958.

*Frank, H. *Grundlagen der Informationsästhetik und erste Anwendung auf die "Mime pure."* Ed. J. Hess. Waiblingen, 1959.

Fucks, W. Mathematische Analyse von Werken der Sprach und Musik. *Physikalische Blätter,* 16:452, 1960.

Garner, W. R. *Uncertainty and structure as psychological concepts.* New York: Wiley, 1962.

Guilbaud, G. T. *What is cybernetics?* V. MacKay, trans. London: Heinemann, 1959.

Guiraud, P. *Bibliographie critique de la statistique linguistique.* Utrecht: Editions Spectrum, 1954.

————. *Problèmes et méthodes de la statistique linguistique.* Paris: Presses Universitaires de France, 1960.

*Gunzenhäuser, R. *Ästhetisches Mass und Ästhetische Information.* Schnelle Verlag Quickborn, 1962.

Hegel, G. W. F. *The philosophy of fine art.* F. P. B. Osmaston, trans. London: G. Bell, 1920.

Herdan, G. *Language as choice and chance*. Groningen: P. Noordhoff, 1956.

Hick, W. E. On the rate of gain of information. *Quart. J. exp. Psychol.*, 4:11-26, 1952.

Hilgard, E. R. *Theories of learning*. New York: Appleton-Century-Crofts, 1956.

Hiller, L. A., and Isaacson, L. M. *Experimental music*. New York: McGraw-Hill, 1959.

Hindemith, P. *The craft of musical composition*. New York: Associated Music Publishers, 1945.

Hofstätter, R. *Einführung in die Sozialpsychologie*. Stuttgart: A. Kröner, 1959.

Hull, C. L. *Principles of behavior*. New York: Appleton-Century, 1943.

Jackson, W., ed. *Communication theory — 1952 London symposium*. London: Butterworths, 1953.

Jakobson, R. On the identification of phonemic entities. *Trav. Cercle linguistique de Copenhague*, 5:205-213, 1949.

Jakobson, R., Fant, G., and Halle, M. Preliminaries to speech analysis. *MIT Acoust. Lab. Rept.*, 13, 1952.

Jeffress, L. A. *Cerebral mechanisms in behavior*. New York: Wiley, 1951.

Langer, S. K. *Philosophy in a new key*. 3rd ed. Cambridge: Harvard University, 1957.

Leibowitz, R. *Schoenberg and his school*. D. Newlin, trans. New York: Philosophical Library, 1949.

Leipp, E. *Les paramètres sensibles des instruments à cordes*. Paris: Thèse, Faculté des Sciences, 1960.

Lewin, K. *Field theory in social science*. New York: Harper, 1951.

Locke, W. N., and Booth, A. D., eds. *Machine translation of languages*. Cambridge: Technology Press of MIT and Wiley, 1955.

Mathews, M. V. An acoustic compiler for music and psychological stimuli. *Bell System Tech. J.*, 40:677-694, 1961.

Merleau-Ponty, M. *Phénoménologie de la perception*. Paris: Gallimard, 1945.

Meyer-Eppler, W., ed. *Gravesano; Musik, Raumgestaltung, Elektroakustik*. Mainz: Arsviva Verlag, 1955.

———. Some problems of reproduction of electronic tape music. *J. Acoust. Soc. Amer.*, 28:791, 1956. (Abstract.)

———. *Grundlagen und Anwendungen der Informationstheorie*. Berlin: Springer, 1959.

Miller, G. A. *Language and communication*. New York: McGraw-Hill, 1951.

*Moles, A. L'emploi de l'auto-corrélation dans la mesure du signal musical. *J. Physique*, 12(11):64, 1951a.

*———. Le théâtre antique — exemple d'esthétique fonctionelle. *Études Philosophiques*, No. 1, 77-91, 1951b.

*———. Comment peut-on mesurer le langage parlé. *Folia Phoniatrica* (Zurich), 4(3):169-199, 1952a.

*———. An informational theory of animal languages. In *L'Étude acoustique des signaux animaux*. Amsterdam: Elsevier, 1952b.

*———. *Physique et technique du bruit*. Paris: Dunod, 1952c.

————. Structure physique du signal musical. *Revue scientifique*, No. 3324, 277-305, 1953a.

*————. Studium und Darstellung der Komplexer Ton in der Musikalischen Akustik. *Funk und Ton*, No. 6, 277-287, 1953b.

*————. Sur la coloration minimum des bruits blancs. *Onde électrique*, 286, 1953c.

*————. Essai de classification des méthodes de préparation du signal musical. *Annales des télécommunications*, 9(7-8):204-210, 1954a.

*————. Rôle des facteurs dynamiques dans la caractérisation physique du discours. *Cahiers d'Études de Radio-Télévision*, No. 2, 197-227, 1954b.

*————. Die Grundlagen des Musik Genusses. *Gravesaner Blätter*, Nos. 2-3, 1956a.

————. Informationstheorie der Musik. *Nachrichtentechnische Fachberichte*, Bd. 3:*Informationstheorie*, 47-55, 1956b.

*————. Filterversuche über Semantischer und Aestetischer Botschaft. *Gravesaner Blätter*, No. 6, 10-15, 1956c. Nos. 7-8, 85, 1957a (and two records of experiments).

————. *La création scientifique*. Geneva: René Kister, 1957b.

*————. Informationstheorie der Sprache und Musik. *Augenblick*, 2:17-27, 1958.

*————. Les artifices de la perception esthétique. *Revue d'Art International* (Zurich), 3(8):64-76, 1959.

*————. Le combat des signes contre la signification. *Revue d'Art International* (Zurich), 4(8):54-58, 1960a.

————. *Les musique expérimentales*. Zurich: Cercle d'Art Contemporain, 1960b.

*————. Information et message cartographique. *Revue sciences*, 1964.

*Moles, A., and Frances, R. Etude expérimentale sur la perception des structures musicales. *J. Psychologie*, 80-83, 1952.

*Moles, A., and Ussachevsky, V. Emploi du spectrographe acoustique et problème de la partition en musique expérimentale. *Annales des télécommunications*, 9:299-304, 1957.

Nash, L. K. *The nature of the natural sciences*. Boston: Little, Brown & Co., 1963.

Neidhart, P. *Einfuhrung in die Informationstheorie*. Berlin: Verlag Technik, 1957.

Ogden, C. K., and Richards, I. A. *The meaning of meaning*. New York: Harcourt, Brace, 1959.

Olson, H. F., and Belar, H. Electronic music synthesizer. *J. Acoust. Soc. Amer.* 27:595, 1955.

————. Aid to music composition with a random-probability system. *Science*, 133:1368, 1961. (Abstract.)

Osgood, Charles E., Suci, George J., and Tannenbaum, Percy H. *The measurement of meaning*. Urbana: University of Illinois Press, 1957.

Pavlov, I. P. *Selected works*. J. Gibbons, ed. Moscow: Foreign Languages Publishing House, 1955.

Pinkerton, R. C. Information theory and melody. *Sci. Amer.*, 194(2):77, 1956.

Potter, R. K., *et al. Visible speech*. New York: Van Nostrand, 1947.

Prieberg, F. K. *Musika ex Machina*. Berlin: Ullstein, 1960.

Quastler, H., ed. *Information theory in psychology.* New York: Free Press of Glencoe, 1955.

Ruyer, R. *La cybernétique et l'origine de l'information.* Paris: Flammarion, 1954.

Sachs, C. *The history of musical instruments.* New York: Norton, 1940.

Scherchen, H. *Handbook of conducting.* M. D. Calvocoressi, trans. London: Oxford, 1933.

——. *The nature of music.* W. Mann, trans. Chicago: H. Regnery, 1950.

Seashore, C. E. *Psychology of music.* New York: McGraw-Hill, 1938.

Shannon, C. E., and Weaver, W. *The mathematical theory of communication.* Urbana: University of Illinois Press, 1949.

Silbermann, A. *La musique, la radio et l'auditeur.* Paris: Presses Universitaires de France, 1954.

——. *Wovon lebt die Musik?* Regensburg: G. Bosse, 1957.

Souriau, E. *Les deux cent mille situations dramatiques.* Paris: Flammarion, 1950.

Stanislavski, K. S. *An actor prepares.* E. R. Hapgood, trans. New York: Theatre Arts Books, 1948.

Stevens, S. S., et al. *Bibliography on hearing.* Cambridge: Harvard University, 1955.

Stevens, S., and Davis, H. *Hearing.* New York: Wiley, 1938.

Uexküll, J. von. *Streifzüge durch die Umwelten von Tieren und Menschen.* Berlin: Springer, 1934.

Valéry, P. *Collected works.* J. Mathews, ed. New York: Pantheon, 1956.

Walter, W. G. *The living brain.* New York: Norton, 1953.

Wellek, A. *Typologie der Musikbegabung im deutschen Volke.* Munich: Beck, 1939.

Wertheimer, M. *Productive thinking.* New York: Harper, 1959.

Whatmough, J. *Language: a modern synthesis.* New York: St. Martins, 1956.

White, B. W. Recognition of distorted melodies. *Amer. Psychologist,* 13: 384, 1958.

Wiener, N. *The human use of human beings.* Garden City, N.Y.: Doubleday, 1954.

Wieser, W. *Organismen, Strukturen, Maschinen.* Frankfurt am Main: Fischer, 1959.

Winckel, F. *Phänomene des musikalischen Hörens.* Berlin: M. Hesse, 1960.

Woodworth, R. S., and Schlosberg, H. *Experimental psychology.* New York: Holt, 1954.

Wundt, W. M. *Grundriss der Psychologie.* Leipzig: A. Kröner, 1913.

Zipf, G. K. *Human behavior and the principle of least effort.* Cambridge, Mass.: Addison-Wesley, 1949.

Index